# Studies in Economic Theory

Volume 30

**Founded by:** Charalambos D. Aliprantis

More information about this series at http://www.springer.com/series/2584

Suren Basov

# Social Norms, Bounded Rationality and Optimal Contracts

Springer

Suren Basov
Centre for Economics and Financial
Econometrics Research
Deakin University
Burwood, VIC
Australia

ISSN 1431-8849 ISSN 2196-9930 (electronic)
Studies in Economic Theory
ISBN 978-981-10-1039-2 ISBN 978-981-10-1041-5 (eBook)
DOI 10.1007/978-981-10-1041-5

Library of Congress Control Number: 2016938658



Printed on acid-free paper

This Springer imprint is published by Springer Nature
The registered company is Springer Science+Business Media Singapore Pte Ltd.

# Contents

# Abstract

Contracts play an important role in economic life. Therefore, the topic of optimal contract design attracted significant attention from the researchers. Most of the work, however, was done under the assumption that economic agents are fully rational and driven solely by monetary payoffs. However, recent research showed that the assumption of full rationality is untenable, since empirical evidence clearly demonstrates that problem solving leads generally to suboptimal stable solutions. Recently emerged literature uses bounded rationality to provide foundations for incomplete contracts and studies the effect of bounded rationality on the power of incentive provisions, deviations from sufficient statistic theorem, optimal incentive provision in multicultural environments, and incidence of costs of bounded rationality. Another important deviation from the standard paradigm is that the behavior of economic actors relies on social norms. From a mechanism designer's viewpoint, responsiveness of an agent to social norms is both a blessing and a curse. On the one hand, it provides a designer with extra instruments; while on the other it puts restrictions on how these new and more conventional instruments could be used. In this book I investigate this trade-off and study how it shapes different contracts observed in the real world. I also bring into focus all these strands of research, including my own contributions, draw important lessons that can already be learnt from this research, and outline the prospects for future research.

# Chapter 1
# Introduction

Beginning with the work of Allais and Edwards[1] in the early 1950s and continuing through the present, psychologists and economists have uncovered a growing body of evidence that individuals do not necessarily conform to many of the key assumptions or predictions of the subjective expected utility model of choice under uncertainty, and seem to depart from this model in systematic and predictable ways. Subjective expected utility theory provides one with a parsimonious way to map the inputs, such as prices, auction formats, and contract stipulations, into outputs, i.e., demand and supply decisions, bids, and effort exerted. Subjective expected utility theory is based on two pillars. The first pillar is the representation of *preferences* in a simple and analytically tractable form as an expectation of a function defined over the outcomes with respect to some probability measure; the second is the revealed preference doctrine, which states that preferences uniquely determine *choices* via a maximization procedure. In the light of the experimental failure of the expected utility theory one may consider two responses. The first response is to consider alternative models of preferences; the second is to allow for a wedge between preferences and choices. It should be mentioned that these approaches are not mutually exclusive.

Following the first of the outlined routes has led to the development of alternative models of preferences over objectively or subjectively uncertain prospects, which seek to accommodate these systematic departures from the expected utility model while retaining as much of its analytical power as possible.

The models that deviate from the conventional expected utility models as little as possible are the so-called non-expected utility models. Though the agents in these models do not satisfy all of Savage's axioms (Savage 1954) and therefore should be thought of as boundedly rational if one equates rationality with full adherence to Savage axioms, they are still characterized by a well-defined objective, which is defined at the same outcome space as the Bernoulli utility of the Savage model. The most prominent of them are the ones that differentiated between risk and Knightian

[1]See Allais (1953), Edwards (1954).

 
S. Basov, *Social Norms, Bounded Rationality and Optimal Contracts*,
Studies in Economic Theory 30, DOI 10.1007/978-981-10-1041-5_1

uncertainty, going back to Knight (1921), which retain the idea of maximization of a utility functional, but give up the idea of well-defined probabilities and give rise to the idea of ambiguity aversion. I will discuss this class of models in Chap. 2. Another well-known model in this group is the theory of rank dependent utility, developed by Quiggin (1982).

Other groups of models that are usually characterized by a well-defined but nonstandard objective are behavioral models that try to accommodate such phenomena and reference dependence, endowment effect, hyperbolic discounting, and other deviations from predictions of the conventional expected utility theory. In this book I touch on these models only briefly. For a detailed up to date discussion of behavioral economics see, for example, Hochman and Ayal (2013). Models allowing socially based preferences, such as inequity aversion,[2] and psychological costs of breaking social norms,[3] also follow this approach. Models in this group can be seen as conservative in method but radical in their assumptions about the preferences.

The models discussed so far share with the conventional model the main analytical tools: existence of a well-defined objective that captures the economic actors' preferences and the revealed preference doctrine that equates preferences with choices. Following the second approach, on the other hand, led to the development of models that called into question the very utility maximization paradigm and required more drastic deviation from the standard economic model and development of a model of non-maximizing behavior. Such models drive a wedge between preferences and utilities. I will call them *bounded rationality models*. Though such models should be viewed as more radical than models in the first group in tools they exploit, they are more conservative in type of preferences they invoke. Indeed, once one accepts that the preferences do not completely determine choices, experimental evidence that shows that *choices* do not conform to the (expected) utility maximization paradigm can no longer be held as a proof that *preferences* do not. Therefore, in discussing bounded rationality models, I will mostly continue to adhere to the expected utility paradigm as an appropriate model for true preferences and a measure of welfare.

Though nonstandard preferences and bounded rationality can be seen as alternative explanations of experimental evidence that people do not behave according to the prescriptions of the expected utility theory, these alternatives are not mutually exclusive. From an evolutionary point of view bounded rationality and nonstandard preferences may be mutually reinforcing each other. One immediate observation is that most individuals have preferences over intermediate objectives such as food, safety, or sex, rather than for ultimate biological objective of inclusive fitness. As noted by Robson (2001), bounded rationality can help to explain that. Indeed, on the one hand, extreme complexity of computing inclusive fitness leads evolution to

---

[2]See, for example, Fehr and Schmidt (1999).

[3]See for example Basov and Bhatti (2013) and Chap. 7 of this book.

create preferences for intermediate objective. On the other hand, given that the objectives individuals pursue differ from the ultimate evolutionary objective, deviating from rational behavior, engaging in experimentation, and following some simple procedures and rules of thumb can be beneficial, which can explain both boundedly rational behavior and existence of social norms. It can also shed some light on more subtle deviations from the expected utility, such as ambiguity aversion. I will briefly touch on this topic in Chap. 3.

Deviations from rational behavior would not have been of much interest to the economists had they been confined to a laboratory. However, they have been demonstrated to have important economic consequences. Applications considered in this book provide plenty of examples when bounded rationality or nonstandard preferences significantly affects economic outcomes. Especially interesting examples are the ones where infinitesimally small deviation from rational behavior has finite consequences for the economic outcome. For one such example, I will argue that even slightly irrational behavior can lead to a failure of the Revelation Principle, which has important and extensive applications in the theory of optimal taxation, nonlinear pricing, and other areas of mechanism design theory. This failure leads to a profound observation, since as a result even slightly nonrational behavior may significantly affect optimal solutions.

Though importance of being able to take into account non-maximizing behavior is by now widely recognized, difficulty in pursuing this objective lies in the fact that a generally accepted notion of bounded rationality does not exist. Indeed, the only feature that united bounded rationality models is that they drive a wedge between preferences and choices. The term "bounded rationality" was coined by Simon (1957), who argued that bounded rationality was an accurate portrayal of choice and decision when information gathering and processing is costly. An extensive literature on the subject has been developed ever since. Although approaches to the meaning of bounded rationality differ from author to author, existing literature can be broadly divided into two classes, according to the paradigm of bounded rationality used. The first class of bound rationality models, which is closest to the Simon's original idea, was recently revived by Lipman (1991), Vriend (1996) and will be referred to it as the Lipman-Vriend paradigm (LVP), whilst the other class of bounded rationality models, described in Gigerenzer and Selten (2001) will be referred to the Selten-Gigerenzer paradigm (SGP).

According to the models in the first class, human behavior can always be explained in terms of pursuit of self-interest subject to the *perceived* opportunities. The perceived opportunities can, however, differ from the actual ones. An individual is assumed to go through a deliberation procedure, which is similar to the process of the decision-making by a rational agent. However, the deliberation process is subjected to computational, memory, attention, and other types of constraints, which are usually not assumed in conventional models. Simon argues that to overcome such constraints individuals often restore to "rules of thumb." Another way to formalize the concept of perceived opportunities developed in marketing literature and is based on the concept of *consideration sets.*[4] In marketing, the consideration set is made up of the brands that are taken seriously by the consumer in his or her purchase decision. Modern economic papers that formalize the concept in a framework of revealed preference theory are Masatlioglu et al. (2012), Lleras et al. (2010).

The second paradigm of bounded rationality stipulates that decision makers are endowed with a set of simple heuristics, which enable them to make decisions. It diverges from the view of rationality as a coherent domain-general optimization. Instead, heuristics are assumed to be ecologically rational (i.e. they result in the decisions that are good in a typical environment the decision maker faces or has faced in the past) and are presumably hardwired in our brains by the process of Darwinian selection.[5] In practice, this view means that an individual usually follows some rules of thumb, which applied to a situation of repeated choice, translates into a stochastic adjustment process on the set of available alternatives.

Before we go any further in discussing different models of bounded rationality, it will be useful to demonstrate how a well-established experimental phenomenon, known as the endowment effect, is handled by a bounded rationality model versus a model of nonstandard preferences. The effect is first described by Knetsch (1989). In an experiment 76 subjects were given mugs, 87 subjects given chocolate and 55 subjects given nothing. Subjects who owned something could swap their endowment. Subjects with no initial entitlement need to make a choice. Proportion of subjects who preferred not to switch was 89 % among the mug owners and 90 % among the chocolate owners. Among subjects who owned nothing 56 % preferred a mug and 44 % preferred chocolate. Tversky and Kahneman (1991) provide an explanation of the endowment effect by postulating that preferences depend on status quo or reference point. Current endowment is a reasonable choice for a reference point. The utility function has a kink at the reference point, which means that though agents can be risk neutral with respect to lotteries that involve only gains or only losses, they strive to avoid losses more than they strive to achieve gains: the phenomenon known as *loss aversion.* An alternative explanation will postulate that preferences are completely standard, the subjects only care about the final outcome, and endowment does not directly affect preferences. However, rather than making the optimal choice all the time, the subjects are assumed to invoke rule of thumb, for example, "do not trade with a stranger, unless trade provides huge benefits." The rule can be completely rational in many situations. For example, if a stranger asked you to exchange cars of seemingly similar qualities, you may be rationally wary, since her car may turn out to be a lemon. Of course, the lemons story does not directly apply to the case of mugs and chocolate bar, but the important claim of boundedly rational explanation is that it need not to. Rather than

[4]See, for example, Goeree (2008), Hauser and Wernerfelt (1990), Howard and Sheth (1969), Nedungadi (1990), Punj and Brookes (2001), Roberts and Lattin (1991), Roberts and Nedungadi (1995), Wright and Barbour (1977).

[5]Refer to Basov, Blanckenberg and Gangadharan (2007) and Chap. 3 of this book for a detailed discussion of this perspective.

maximizing on the case by case basis, individuals simply select a rule of thumb (heuristic) from a limited menu, which provides higher expected utility than other heuristics on the menu, when facing a random problem in the environment.

Anderson et al. (2004) have produced an interesting example of an application of this approach and argued that it is sometimes justified to skip the modeling of the adjustment, and instead concentrate on the steady state characterized by the distribution of choices. In particular, if individuals follow noisy gradient dynamics the steady state probabilities will be described by the model developed by Luce (1959). Under such an interpretation the probabilistic choice models falls into the second paradigm of bounded rationality.

The two paradigms can be reconciled to some extent if one realized that from an evolutionary perspective Simon's rules of thumb can be crystalized as legal rules and social norms.

There is some well-established literature, which introduces bounded rationality, in the sense of LVP into mechanism design models. Dye (1985) provides an example of explicit complexity costs increasing in the number of contingencies, whilst Green and Laffont (1986, 1987) introduce dimensionality restrictions and data compression techniques in hidden information models. Anderlini and Felli (1994) assume that contracts should be specified in algorithmic terms, and add complexity costs to the model with computability restrictions in Anderlini and Felli (1998). Segal (1999) considers the effects of complexity on the value of the optimal contract, without explicit complexity costs, whilst Battigalli and Maggi (2002) have produced a model relating to the complexity costs associated with a contract. Anderlini and Felli (2004) provide a synthesis of literature in this area.

A more recent paper in a similar stream of literature is that of Renou and Tomala (2012). It characterizes communication networks, for which every incentive compatible function is implementable. The optimal communication network obtained using the revelation principle is, however, too complex as it connects every agent in an organization directly with the top. Complexity costs can be used to explain why so many organizations have developed hierarchical structure instead.

The literature that introduces bounded rationality in the sense of SGP, into mechanism design is, however, much more sparse. Laffont and Martimort (2002) have developed a hidden information model, in which agents can be of two types: efficient and inefficient. The principal offers a menu of contracts; when an agent makes a choice between contracts it is possible that by miscalculation a wrong contract might be chosen. Agents are then ex-ante rational and take the possibility of the mistake into account when making their participation decisions. If the support of mistakes is small, mistakes are made by efficient agents behaving as if they are of the inefficient type. Therefore, the apparent proportion of inefficient agents increases and as a result, the utilities of both the principal and agents of efficient type decrease. Basov and Mirrlees (2009) introduced bounded rationality into Mussa and Rosen (1978) model, assuming that the consumer computes the optimal quality with a mistake.

Basov (2003) developed a hidden action model, in which efficient agents adjust the choice of effort gradually based on recent experiences and observations of the behavior of the other agents. It can, however, be shown that while the average choice converges to the optimum quite quickly, positive variance could persist for a long period of time. As a result, noise adds to technological uncertainty, creating lower-powered incentives, which produce deviations from the sufficient statistics results, and dissipate the social surplus. This model also provides useful insights for the derivation of optimal contracts in multicultural environments, with the cost of the boundedly rational behavior completely born by the principal.

This book is organized in the following way. Chapter 2 discusses models of ambiguity with application to the theory of general equilibrium and foundations of incomplete contracts, and robustness of optimal contracts. Psychological studies suggest that ambiguity aversion can be considered as a form of pessimism concerning unknown probability distributions (see, for example, Pulford 2009). This implies that degree of ambiguity aversion may be an inborn characteristic and mechanism designers may have incentives to screen on it.

Evolutionary approach discussed briefly in Chap. 3, also suggests that ambiguity aversion can be negatively correlated with risk aversion, making relatively risk-loving individuals more ambiguity averse. That can have importance for developing of liquidity supply models in corporate finance. Consider, for example, a quote-driven market of a risky financial asset, where a risk-neutral market maker supplies liquidity to traders. Traditional models assume that the traders are risk-averse, but ambiguity neutral, and that their private information consists just of a signal concerning the value of the risky asset. A more realistic model will assume that they also differ in their degree of risk aversion. Also, if conditional on their signal, they cannot pin down the distribution of returns, their degree of ambiguity aversion may be important. When characterizing the equilibrium of the market for trading based on liquidity demand, it is important to take into account differences in risk and ambiguity attitudes of the traders.

Chapter 2 starts with a brief recap of the Savage's subjective expected utility theory and its modification by Gilboa and Schmeidler to allow for ambiguity aversion. Then it goes on to discuss the theory of general equilibrium with minimax preferences, in particular contributions of He and Yannelis and De Castro and Yannelis. An important result is that area is that in general equilibrium framework ambiguity aversion mitigates the tension between incentive compatibility and efficiency. However, it will be premature to conclude that ambiguity aversion always leads to economically superior outcomes. For example, in the context of the theory of incomplete contracts, Mukerji (1998), Grant et al. (2006) argued that ambiguity aversion diminishes the value of a complete contract and coupled with even small transaction costs, can lead to a null contract been signed, which in turn leads to hold up problems and inhibits relation specific investment. Finally, ambiguity aversion can help to explain simplicity (linearity) of real life contacts and prevalence of fiat money.

Chapter 3 builds a bridge between nonstandard utility models of Chap. 2 and bounded rationality models considered later in the book by discussing a priori reasons for restrictions on allowable preferences or the degree of rationality. In that chapter I also propose some directions for developing a model of coevolution of preferences, social norms, and decision rules. It suggests, for example, gap between utility in fitness, which may be due to bounded rationality or inertia may be counterbalanced by ambiguity aversion, which in turn may make bounded rationality beneficial. Since this book is mainly about the effects of deviations from standard paradigm on the contract design, Chap. 3 is sketchier than other chapters of this book. Its main purpose is to suggest outlines for future research, though it presents some models and techniques.

Chapter 4 discusses issues of complexity and their relevance for the development of optimal contracts. It considers complexity in three guises. The first is direct complexity of writing a contract, were adding each extra clause in some formal language is costly. This line of research was developed by Battigalli and Maggi (2002). Here complexity is equivalent to finite transaction costs, which leads to contracts being optimally incomplete. The second way to model complexity, is as number of possible a priori contracting opportunities, with only one of them ex-post useful. This line is taken by Hart and Moore (1999), Segal (1999). They argue that complexity coupled with impossibility to commit not to renegotiate a contract diminishes the value of complete contract. In that sense, complexity and possibility of renegotiation play the role similar to the ambiguity aversion in Mukerji (1998), Grant et al. (2006) models. Though they do not lead by themselves to contractual incompleteness, even small (asymptotically, infinitesimal) transaction costs will suffice to ensure that a null contract is optimal. Finally, Anderlini and Felli (1994) model complexity as computability constraint on both contracts signed and contract selection procedure. They managed to show that under such constraints the optimal contracts are incomplete without a need to invoke transaction costs, but at a price of assuming an uncountable infinity of states of the world. This model can be viewed as a special case of the model with direct complexity costs, the costs being zero for computable contracts and infinity for non-computable ones.

Chapter 5 discusses mechanism design problem when the choice of the agents is governed by a static probabilistic model. Such models are employed to model bounded rationality starting form Luce (1959). In most applications of such models bounded rationality matters in proportion to its degree: if the agents are nearly rational the standard model of rational behavior provides a good approximation to the boundedly rational models. Particularly interesting applications of this approach arise in screening because in screening models the latter observation does not hold: bounded rationality matters to a greater extent than justified by its degree. Technically, this happens because probabilistic models are characterized by an irrationality parameter with value zero corresponding to the rational choice. The choice correspondence is usually not lower-semi-continuous at the zero value of the irrationality parameter, when set of utility maximizers contains more than one element. This happens because for a finite positive value of the irrationality parameter the probabilistic choice model usually prescribes unique assignment of choice probabilities, while for the fully rational case any probability distribution supported by the set of utility maximizers is allowed. It can potentially lead to violation of the Revelation Principle. As a result, infinitesimally small degree of irrationality can have significant effect on the nature of optimal contracts.

The chapter starts with discussing Laffont and Martimort's (2002) model of monopolistic screening, where consumers may make a mistake when choosing an option from a menu, but a fully aware of this possibility a priori. Under such assumptions, the Revelation Principle still holds and the effect of the mistake is effectively to increase proportion of low types.[6] I also discuss model by Basov (2009), who considers a more drastic deviation from rational model in the context of monopolistic screening with finite types, assuming that consumers' choice probabilities are driven by Luce model. In that case, Revelation Principle no longer holds and the number of the different items on the monopolist's optimal menu will differ from the cardinality of types. In particular, higher quality goods will tend to come in more flavors. Both of these papers discuss a discrete type space. Paper by Basov and Mirrlees (2009), also discussed in Chap. 5, deals with continuous type space, introducing bounded rationality in Mussa and Rosen (1978) model, deriving an integro-differential equation for the optimal tariff and discussing the incidence of cost of boundedly rational behavior. I also discuss in that chapter paper by Basov (2013), which introduces the concept of emotional temperature. A rise in emotional temperature affects utilities, making individuals care stronger about the alternatives, but also clouds rational thinking. As a result, in the context of probabilistic choice Luce model, it is possible to show that there is the optimal emotional temperature that leads to the decisions maximizing expected utility and an associated irreducible probability of error. Two other papers considered in Chap. 5 allow for strategic interaction between players. Paper by Basov and Danilkina (2015) considers a Bertrand oligopoly with boundedly rational consumers and allows the firms to manipulate the degree of rationality at a cost. Note that in this paper the active players, the oligopolists, are fully rational. They are shown to have incentives to obfuscate consumers, but this incentive decreases as the number of the firms increases. This is another beneficial effect of competition. Paper by Anderson et al. (1998) is the only paper in Chap. 5, which discusses a game (all-pay auction) between boundedly rational agents. It shows that predictions of this model are more intuitive and in a better agreement with empirical findings than that of the standard model.

Chapter 6 considers design of optimal contracts in an environment where agents gradually adjust their choices due to learning. The importance of explicit study of learning was stressed by Basov (2005), who argued that steady state probability distributions of generic learning rules fail to satisfy many natural properties such as payoff monotonicity and independence of irrelevant alternatives. It is based on Basov (2003) and considers a hidden action model, where a population of boundedly rational agents adjusts their choices gradually in the light of recent experiences and observations of the other members of the population. The results obtained in the paper allow one to address interesting questions concerning the design of the optimal work place. They also call for modification of the celebrated

[6]Indeed, if mistakes have sufficiently small support, only high type will sometimes behave as a low type, since only one incentive compatibility constraint is binding.

sufficient statistics theorem that states that when several signals of effort are observed, optimal contracts should be based on a sufficient statistic for effort. However, this is not the case when the agents engage in social learning. Intuitively, the reason is that under bounded rationality, effort can be only partly attributed to the incentive scheme. The other part comes from the fact that the choice of effort itself is noisy. Since this noise will affect all the signals equally, one should put more equal weights on different signals than dictated by the sufficient statistics theorem.

Chapter 7 considers interaction of social norms with financial incentives. It starts with a discussion of paper by Basov and Bhatti (2013), where principal can provide an agent with a financial contract and recommend a level of effort. The recommended effort cannot be enforced in a court, but the agent will feel guilt from deviating from it as long as financial incentives are not too powerful. Basov and Bhatti call this a social norm of trust. It is shown that this framework that two distinct cultures emerge: a bureaucratic culture characterized by low power incentives and reliance on social norms and corporate culture characterized by high power incentives with no reliance on social norms. The medium powered incentives largely disappear. It also revisits the idea that contractual incompleteness can be caused by the decrease of the value of the optimal complete contract.[7] The value of the optimal complete contract is eroded by high degree of uncertainty of environment, which can be due to both technological and market uncertainty in translating the unobservable effort into observable output and mistakes made by the agents is selecting the optimal level of effort is response to the contract offered. If the latter plays significant role, the magnitude of mistakes can be considered to be a proxy for the complexity of the environment. In this way the model developed in Chap. 7 is reminiscent of models by Hart and Moore and Segal, discussed in Chap. 4. An important difference, however, is that this model does not invoke transaction costs. Instead it relies on an implicit reciprocal contract, where the principal offers an above-market-fixed wage and the agents reciprocate by exerting positive effort, which increases in wage. The chapter also builds on a model of socioeconomic behavior by Blume and Durlauf to investigate the phenomenon of high performing working systems and presents a model of selecting a manager for a developing country division of a multinational corporation. The idea behind the latter model is similar to Basov and Bhatti's paper discussed above. The firm can either hire a local manager or an international one. The international manager is better qualified, while the local one commands loyalty of the local workers and can use it to mitigate moral hazard. It is shown that relying on the local manager is the preferred choice, when moral hazard is a serious issue, for example, due to highly uncertain environment, creating significant noise when linking the effort to the output. If one hypothesizes

[7]Contract is viewed as incomplete if it does not condition payments on all available information that would have been useful under the assumptions of standard preferences and full rationality. It differs from another definition of incompleteness found in the literature as not specifying actions in some states of the world. See Anderlini and Felli (1994), Hart and Moore (1999) for a defence of such a use of the term.

that development reduces such uncertainty, for example, due to providing a better legal infrastructure, the model will allow to conclude that as countries proceed on the path of development they will switch to the services of international managers. The conclusion can, however, be reversed if further development will improve business education in the country and close the skill gap between the domestic and the foreign manager.

Chapter 8 deals with miscellaneous models that do not easily fall under a particular heading. It starts with a model of monopoly facing viscous demand with customers' turnover. It is shown that the optimal pricing strategy will entail an initial period of either very low price to reach a target market penetration level or of very high price to exploit a fad, followed by a stationary intermediate price. Another model, considered in Chap. 8, considers the effects of bounded rationality on the side of the principal, while assuming the agents are fully rational. Following example set in Basov and Danilkina (2007a), bounded rationality of the principal is manifest in her demand to the agent (expert) to justify his advice, but been unable to understand the formal argument. Due to the quirks of justification technology, mechanisms which otherwise would have been equivalents (e.g. the first price and the second price sealed-bid auctions in the case of independent private values with risk-neutral bidders) lead to different outcomes. The lesson goes far beyond auction theory, which was the initial application considered by Basov and Danilkina and states that one has to take justifiability constraints into account, when devising optimal social institutions. Finally, it discusses the model of boundedly rational addiction. Applying ideas of rational behavior to the theory of addiction, pioneered by Becker and Murphy (1988), is probably the most far-fetched and controversial application of theory of rational behavior. Here I review a paper by Basov and Danilkina (2007b), where individuals initially behave as rational addicts, however, as the level of addiction, measured by addictive capital stock, passes above some threshold value the individuals loose the capacity to make forward looking decisions and simply maximize their instantaneous utility. Individuals in this model are boundedly rational in two different ways: first, they eventually start acting myopically; second, they cannot predict this switch of behavior in advance. The government may try to design policies to minimize incidents of such switches. It can use either taxation or prohibition of achieve this aim. If the government opts for taxation, per unit tax will simply increase the price paid by the consumers for the drug. This will lead to a decrease in the steady state level of consumption and make it less likely that the critical addictive capital level that triggers the switch to irrational behavior if reached. In addition, tax policy can generate considerable tax revenue that can be used for rehabilitation programs. Establishing minimal legal age can also be effective. Prohibition, on the contrary, does not have significant effect on prices of most illegal drugs.[8] It presents the potential consumers with a fixed cost of breaking the law and therefore deters the consumers whose life-time utility from the drug consumption is low. But, these are exactly the consumers who remain

[8]For a discussion of empirical evidence, see Basov et al. (2001).

rational addicts though their lives. Therefore, prohibition leads to the loss of utility from consumption to the rational users without significant deterrence of run-away consumption, and is also associated with high costs of enforcement, criminalization of the society, and the loss of the tax revenues.

Chapter 9 concludes with a summary of achievements of these approaches and discusses challenges ahead and some practical applications of the findings. It comes back to the issues raised in the Introduction and discusses what light the content of the book has shed on them. It also suggests that some particular interesting applications of the results can be found in fast growing industry of Islamic finance and refers the reader to a forthcoming monograph by Basov and Bhatti (2016) that provides the reader with the understanding of the basic legal tenets of Islamic finance industry and studies the real economic effects of those tenets using the tools of the modern mechanism design theory. I also suggest directions for future research, in particular concentrated on coevolutionary models similar to those described in Chap. 3.

## References


Allais, M. (1953). Le comportement de l'homme rationnel devant le risque: critique des postulats et axiomes de l'école Américaine". *Econometrica, 21*, 503–546.

Anderlini, L., & Felli, L. (1994). Incomplete written contracts: Undescribable States of nature. *Quarterly Journal of Economics, 109*, 1085–1124.

Anderlini, L., & Felli, L. (1998). Describability and agency problems. *European Economic Review, 42*, 35–59.

Anderlini, L., & Felli, L. (2004). Bounded rationality and incomplete contracts. *Research in Economics, 58*, 3–30.

Anderson, S. P., Goeree, J. K., & Holt, C. A. (1998). Rent seeking with bounded rationality: An analysis of ALL-PAY AUCTION. *Journal of Political Economy, 106*, 828–853.

Anderson, S. P., Goeree, J. K., & Holt, C. A. (2004). Noisy directional learning and the logit equilibrium. *The Scandinavian Journal of Economics, 106*, 581–602.

Basov, S. (2003). Incentives for boundedly rational agents, 2003. *The BE Journal in Theoretical Economics (Topics), 3*, 1–14.

Basov, S. (2005). Bounded rationality: Static versus dynamic approach. *Economic Theory, 25*, 871–885.

Basov, S. (2009). Monopolistic screening with boundedly rational consumers. *The Economic Record, 85*, S29–S33.

Basov, S. (2013). Emotional temperature, probabilistic choice, and the optimal power of incentives. *The Economic Record, 89*(s), 84–94.

Basov, S., & Bhatti, M. I. (2013). Optimal contracting model in a social environment and trust-related psychological costs. *The BE Journal in Theoretical Economics (Contributions), 13*, 1–14.

Basov, S., & Bhatti, M. I. (2016). Islamic finance in light of modern economic theory. Palgrave-Macmillan: Basingstoke, UK.

Basov, S., & Danilkina, S. (2007a). Auctions with opportunistic experts. *The BE Journal in Theoretical Economics (Topics), 7*, 1–11.

Basov, S., & Danilkina, S. (2007b). Bounded rationality, taxation, and prohibition. IN Proceedings of the Econometric Society Australasian Meeting. https://editorialexpress.com/cgi-bin/conference/download.cgi?db_name=ESAM07&paper_id=159.

Basov, S., & Danilkina, S. (2015). Bertrand oligopoly with boundedly rational consumers. *The BE Journal for Theoretical Economics (Topics), 15*, 107–123.

Basov, S., & Mirrlees, J. A. (2009). Nonlinear pricing under bounded rationality. *SSRN Electronic Journal*. http://papers.ssrn.com/sol3/papers.cfm?abstract_id=1399924.

Basov, S., Jacobson, M., & Miron, J. (2001). Prohibition and the market for illegal drugs. *World Economics, 2*, 133–158.

Basov, S., Blanckenberg, L., & Gangadharan, L. (2007). Behavioral anomalies, bounded rationality and simple heuristics. Department of Economics, Working Papers Series 1012, The University of Melbourne.

Battigalli, P., & Maggi, G. (2002). Rigidity, discretion, and the costs of writing contracts. *American Economic Review, 92*, 798–817.

Becker, G., & Murphy, K. (1988). A theory of rational addiction. *Journal of Political Economy, 96*, 675–700.

Dye, R. A. (1985). Costly contract contingencies. *International Economic Review, 26*, 233–250.

Edwards, W. (1954). The theory of decision making. *Psychological Bulletin, 51*, 380–417.

Fehr, E., & Schmidt, K. (1999). A theory of fairness, incentives, and contractual choices. *Quarterly Journal of Economics, 114*, 817–868.

Gigerenzer, G., & Selten, R. (2001). *Bounded rationality: adaptive toolbox*. Cambridge, MA, USA: The MIT Press.

Goeree, M. S. (2008). Limited information and advertising in the U.S. *Personal Computer Industry, Econometrica, 76*, 1017–1074.

Grant, S., Kline, J., & Quiggin, J. (2006). Lost in translation. Business Papers, Bond University.

Green, J. R., & Laffont, J. J. (1986). Incentive theory with data compression, in Essays in honor of Kenneth J. Arrow, v. 3: Uncertainty, information, and communication, Cambridge University Press: Cambridge, UK.

Green, J. R., & Laffont, J. J. (1987). *Limited communication and incentive compatibility, in Information, incentives, and economic mechanisms: Essays in honor of Leonid Hurwicz*. Oxford, UK: Blackwell.

Hart, O., & Moore, J. (1999). Foundations of incomplete contracts. *Review of Economic Studies, 66*, 115–139.

Hauser, J. R., & Wernerfelt, B. (1990). An evaluation cost model of consideration sets. *The Journal of Consumer Research, 16*, 393–408.

Hochman, G., & Ayal, S. (2013). *Behavioral economics*. Oxford, UK: Oxford University Press.

Howard, J. A., & Sheth, N. (1969). *The theory of buyer behavior*. New York, NY, USA: Wiley.

Knetsch, J. L. (1989). The endowment effect and evidence of nonreversible indifference curves. *American Economic Review, 79*, 1277–1284.

Knight, F. H. (1921). *Risk, uncertainty, and profits*. Boston, MA: Hart, Schaffner & Marx; Houghton Mifflin Co.

Laffont, J. J., & Martimort, D. (2002). *The theory of incentives*. Princeton, NJ, USA: Princeton University Press.

Lipman, B. (1991). How to decide how to decide how to…modeling limited rationality. *Econometrica, 59*, 1105–1125.

Lleras, J., Masatlioglu, Y., Nakajima, D., & Ozbay, E. (2010). When more is less: limited consideration. University of Michigan Working Paper. http://econweb.umd.edu/~ozbay/clc.pdf.

Luce, R. D. (1959). *Individual choice behavior*. New York, NY, USA: Wiley.

Masatlioglu, Y., Nakajima, D., & Ozbay, E. (2012). Revealed attention. *The American Economic Review, 102*, 2183–2205.

Mukerji, S. (1998). Ambiguity aversion and incompleteness of contractual form. *American Economic Review, 88*, 1207–1231.

Mussa, M., & Rosen, S. (1978). Monopoly and product quality. *Journal of Economic Theory, 18*, 301–317.

Nedungadi, P. (1990). Recall and consumer consideration sets: influencing choice without altering brand evaluations. *Journal of Consumer Research, 17*, 263–276.

Pulford, B. D. (2009). Is luck on my side: Optimism, pessimism, and ambiguity aversion. *Quarterly Journal of Experimental Psychology, 62*, 1079–1087.

Punj, G., & Brookes, R. (2001). Decision constraints and consideration-set formation in consumer durables. *Psychology and Marketing, 18*, 843–863.

Quiggin, J. (1982). A theory of anticipated utility'. *Journal of Economic Behavior & Organization, 3*, 323–343.

Renou, L., & Tomala, T. (2012). Mechanism design and communication networks, department of economics, University of Leicester. *Theoretical Economics, 7*, 489–533.

Roberts, J. H., & Lattin, J. M. (1991). Development and testing of a model of consideration set composition. *Journal of Marketing Research, 28*, 429–444.

Roberts, J. H., & Nedungadi, P. (1995). Studying consideration in the consumer decision process: progress and challenges. *International Journal of Research in Marketing, 12*, 3–7.

Robson, A. (2001). Why would nature give individuals utility functions? *Journal of Political Economy, 109*, 900–914.

Savage, L. J. (1954). *Foundations of statistics*. New York, NY, USA: Wiley.

Segal, I. (1999). Complexity and renegotiation: A foundation for incomplete contracts. *Review of Economic Studies, 66*, 57–82.

Simon, H. A. (1957). *Models of man: social and rational*. New York, NY, USA: John Wiley and Sons.

Tversky, A., & Kahneman, D. (1991). Loss aversion and riskless choice: a reference dependent model. *Quarterly Journal of Economics, 106*, 1039–1061.

Vriend, N. J. (1996). Rational behavior and economic theory. *Journal of Economic Behavior & Organization, 29*, 263–285.

Wright, P. R., & Barbour, P. (1977). Phased decision strategies: sequels to initial screening. In M. K. Starr, & M. Zeleny, (Eds.), North Holland TIMS Studies in the Management Science: Multiple Criteria Decision Making. Amsterdam, North Holland.

# Chapter 2
# Ambiguity, Robustness, and Contract Design

Economic actors are often forced to make choices without full knowledge of the consequences. Consider, for example, the decision whether to take an umbrella with you today. The decision would be easy if you knew whether it will rain. But what should your choice be if you are not sure? Your choice would still be easy if you knew the objective probability that it will rain today. But what if even the probability is not known?

Knight (1921) suggested that individuals behave differently when faced with risk (which entails knowledge of objective probabilities of future outcomes, as in the case of coin toss) and uncertainty, when such probabilities are not known. Later, Savage (1954) argued that there is no difference between the two situations. In the case of uncertainty one should simply form subjective believes about possible outcomes and use them to evaluate the expected utility of different choices. However, future experimental work, in particular by Ellsberg (1961) demonstrated that sometimes an individual's choices cannot be rationalized as a result of maximizing a subjective expected utility functional.

In response to the experimental difficulties of subjective expected utility theory researchers have revived the Knightian concept of uncertainty and developed theories about how people react to it. One of the main insights of these theories is that individuals prefer situation of risk to those of uncertainty, the phenomenon known as *ambiguity aversion.*

Concept of ambiguity aversion was formalized by Gilboa and Schmeidler (1989). An ambiguity-averse individual will react by taking into account the worst possible state that can occur, i.e., what will happen if she goes out without an umbrella.

In economics and finance a key issue is how ambiguity aversion will affect contracts the individuals write. In particular, does ambiguity prevent individuals from writing complete contracts and can it sometimes be beneficial by preventing an individual from being cheated in a contract? Will it make decision-makers adopt riskier policies lead to bankruptcies and crises or make them hedge against the



S. Basov, *Social Norms, Bounded Rationality and Optimal Contracts*,
Studies in Economic Theory 30, DOI 10.1007/978-981-10-1041-5_2

worst possible state and stabilize the economy? More generally, how will it affect equilibria of the economy and the very concept of equilibrium?

Related to such questions, there is a new stream of thought in asymmetric information economies based on non-expected utility theory (ambiguity/robustness). When we deal with uncertainty, the choice of expected utility (EU) plays an important role. Even with the same primitives in an economy, if one computes a certain equilibrium concept with different expected utilities (which means a different functional form, as different expected utilities provide alternative functional forms) one will get different results. But then, which formulation of EU is better? Can one compare expected utilities, and on what criteria?

In this chapter I consider the effects ambiguity has on the equivalence of Walrasian equilibria and core allocations to an ambiguous asymmetric information economy; efficiency of the monetary; robustness of the linear contracts in a moral hazard problem; modified Bayesian updating rule for ambiguous beliefs; and the role of ambiguity on the contract incompleteness.

Before describing models built around the concept of ambiguity aversion, let us address a philosophical issue: how ambiguity aversion fits with the subject matter of this book: social norms and bounded rationality?

Suppose an actor has to choose an act $a \in F$ which, together with a state of the world, $s \in S$ will determine a consequence $c = a(s) \in C$.[1] The decision-maker does not know the state if the world and is characterized by some preferences over $C$. Savage (1954) postulated certain axioms that allow to evaluate acts according a numerical criterion:

$$U(a) = \int u(a(s))\mathrm{d}\mu(s), \tag{2.1}$$

where $u(c)$ is interpreted as utility of the consequence $c$, and is unique up to a positive affine transformation and $\mu$ is a uniquely determined[2] probability measure that captures the decision-maker's beliefs about possible states of the world.

To arrive at representation (2.1) Savage makes the following assumptions (postulates):

P.1: *A preference relation is a transitive and complete binary relation on F.* This postulate ensures that all the acts are comparable. The second axiom, also known as the sure thing principle, requires that the preference between acts depends only on the consequences in states where the payoffs of the two acts being compared are different. This is the key postulate that drives additive separability across the events.

---

[1]Space $S$ is assumed to be a measure space and acts are assumed to be measurable functions from $S$ into $C$.

[2]The uniqueness of the probability in Savage's theory is predicated on the convention that the utility function is state independent. Savage axioms guarantee state independence of preferences, but not of the utility and beliefs separately.

P.2: *For all acts, f, f', that agree on some event E, preferences among them will not change if they are simultaneously altered on E, while still agreeing with each other.*

The third postulate asserts that the decision-maker cares only about the consequences of her actions, not the actions or states of the world per se.

P.3: *The ordinal ranking of consequences is independent of the event and the act that yield them.*

The fourth postulate requires that the betting preferences are independent of the way the bets are made.

P.4: *For all events E and E' and constant acts x, y, x', and y' such that x is preferred to y and x' is preferred to y' act that results in x on E and y on its complement is preferred to the act that results in x on E' and y on its complement if and only if act that results in x' on E and y' on its complement is preferred to the act that results in x' on E' and y' on its complement.*

Intuitively, both preferences reflect the idea that event $E$ is more likely than $E'$. Postulate five rules out trivial preferences. It is crucial in establishing uniqueness of the probability measure in (2.1).

P.5: *There are some constant acts x and y, such that x is strictly preferred to y.*

The sixth asserts that no consequence is either so bad that the decision-maker will not tolerate any act that exposes it even to slightest chance of it happening, no matter how beneficial its other consequences may be, or so good that the decision-maker will not take an act that slightly reduces its probability, even if this act may help to prevent a disaster.

P.6: *For all acts f, g, and h such that f is strictly preferred to g, there is a finite partition*

$$\{E_i \subset S : \bigcup_{i=1}^{n} E_i = S, E_i \cap E_j = \emptyset \text{ for } i \neq j\}$$

*of the set of states such that, for all i, f is strictly preferred to act that coincides with h on $E_i$ and with g on its complement and act that coincides with h on $E_i$ and f on its complement is strictly preferred to g.*

This postulate implies that there are infinitely many states of the world and that, if there exists a probability measure representing the decision-maker's beliefs, it must be nonatomic.

Finally, the last postulate states

P.7: *If the decision strictly prefers an act to each of the payoffs of another act on a given event, then the former act is strictly preferred to the latter conditionally on the event.*[3]

[3]Technically, one should speak about the non-null events, but this is not important for the current discussion.

Savage's theorem stipulates that the preference relation satisfies P.1–P.7 if and only if it can be represented by functional (2.1). Probability measure $\mu$ in (2.1) summarizes the decision-maker beliefs and erases any distinction between risk and uncertainty.

Savage presented his seven postulates as defining the concept of rational individual. From such point of view any deviation from subjective expected utility theory, in particular behavior that exhibits ambiguity aversion, is a form of bounded rationality.

However, almost from the moment of it inception, the descriptive validity of Savage's model has been criticized. In particular, the sure thing principle, responsible for additive separability of the functional represented preferences across events got under the fire. Ellsberg[4] (1961) demonstrated using simple experiments that individuals display choice patterns that are inconsistent with the existence of beliefs representable by a probability measure. This work leads to creation on non-expected utility models, which often are also built on axiomatic foundations, and require the decision-maker to maximize a certain functional, though a different one from the SEU functional of Savage's theory. If one sees maximizing behavior as a hallmark of rationality, then these theories will still classify as models of rational choice. Therefore, non-expected utility theories, in particular theory of choice by ambiguity-averse decision-makers can be seen as transitional models between models of Savage rationality and models of bounded rationality that completely dispense with maximizing behavior. It is only logical to start this book from considering the consequences of these models.

## 2.1 A Model of Ambiguity Aversion

Model of ambiguity employed in this book is due to Gilboa and Schmeidler (1989). To understand the motivation behind the model and the way it differs from the SEU framework, consider the following choice problem, known as the *Ellsberg Paradox* (see, Ellsberg 1961). An urn contains thirty red balls, and sixty green and blue balls, in unspecified proportions; subjects are asked to compare (i) a bet on a red draw versus a bet on a green draw, and (ii) a bet on a red or blue draw versus a bet on a green or blue draw. If the subject wins a bet, she receives ten dollars; otherwise, she receives nothing.

The modal preferences in this example are to prefer betting on red to betting in green in (i), but to prefer betting on green or blue to betting red or blue in (ii). One may try to rationalize it follows: betting on red is "safer" than betting on green, because the urn may actually contain zero green balls; on the other hand, betting on green or blue is "safer" than betting on red or blue, because the urn may contain

[4]I describe briefly Ellsberg's experiments in the next section.

zero blue balls, making total number of red or blue balls only thirty, as compared with sixty green or blue balls.

These choices are, however, inconsistent with the SEU framework. Indeed, according to Savage the decision-maker should assign probabilities to a ball been green, blue, or red, i.e., choose three nonnegative numbers,[5] $p_g, p_b$, and $p_r$ such that

$$p_g + p_b + p_r = 1.$$

Choice in scenario (i) reveals that the decision-maker believes $p_g < p_r$, but then $p_g + p_b < p_r + p_b$, therefore, the decision-maker should prefer betting on red or blue in (ii), contrary to the observed choice. To make sense of this choice assume that rather than having a single belief system the decision-maker allows for multiple beliefs and then computes the most pessimistic expectation with respect to these beliefs. Assume that the allowable beliefs assign probability 1/3 to the drawn ball being green and allow for any pair of nonnegative $p_b$ and $p_r$ as long as the following condition holds

$$p_b + p_r = \frac{2}{3}.$$

Then, when evaluating choices in (i) and considering betting on green one will compute expected value as if $p_g = 0$, while when evaluating choices in (ii) one will compute expected value as if $p_b = 0$. Note that one does not to entertain a view that $p_g = p_b = 0$ simultaneously. One has simply to evaluate expected utility under the worst possible scenario.

This is the essence of the model of ambiguity aversion proposed by Gilboa and Schmeidler (1989). In their model agent distinguishes between situations where probabilities of unknown prospects are known (risk) and situations where they are unknown (uncertainty). The former are characterized by a single probability distribution, while under the second the decision-maker entertains multiple possible subjective beliefs. In Savages theory such a decision-maker will simply have second order probabilistic beliefs about first order probabilistic beliefs and use formula for full probability to collapse them into beliefs about the outcomes. In Gilboa and Schmeidler, on the other hand, the decision-maker will take expectations with respect to the objective beliefs but use min–max criterion with respect to the subjective ones.

Gilboa and Schmeidler provide axiomatic characterization of their criterion. Most axioms are similar to those of Savage. However, they introduce a new axiom that ensures that risk and preferred to uncertainty. To understand it, suppose that we have two urns, each contains 90 balls, and there are 30 red balls in each urn. There are 60 green and 60 blue balls in total, but the decision-maker does not know how they are distributed among urns. We already know that faced with a choice to bid

[5] In the decision-makers beliefs respect objective information then probability of drawing out green ball should be 1/3. The latter is, however, immaterial for our argument.

on red on green ball being drawn from a particular urn a decision-maker will choose to bid on red. No, suppose that urn itself is chosen as a result of a fair coin toss. So, effectively the decision-maker bets either on red or green among one hundred and eighty balls of which 60 are red and 60 are green. Therefore, we eliminated subjective uncertainty and ended up with a situation of pure risk. It is reasonable to assume that now she will be indifferent between betting on red or green and strictly prefer this to bidding on green drawn from any one of the urns. If the coin in the question had not been fair subjective uncertainty would not have been eliminated but would have been reduced. This is the essence of postulate in Gilboa and Schmeidler.

The pessimism of ambiguity-averse decision-makers might under certain circumstances turn out to be quite useful. For example, it can help to mitigate, and sometimes completely resolve, tensions between efficiency and incentive compatibility, both in the framework of Walrasian equilibria and under bilateral bargaining under private information. We will analyze scenarios where it happens below. However, it can also prevent decision-maker pursuing uncertain but ultimately beneficial courses of action, for example, investing in fundamental research. Therefore, ambiguity aversion shares with other forms of deviations from behavior based on Savage style rationality and individualistic preferences, such as bounded rationality and sensitivity to social norms, the distinction of been both a blessing and a curse. They are blessings since, if properly used, they can mitigate some traditional trade-offs, but a curse since they come with costs of their own. I will return to this topic in Chap. 6, where I discuss interaction of social norms with optimal incentives provision.

## 2.2 Equilibrium Theory and Ambiguity

This section is based on the work of He and Yannelis (2015) and considers how concepts of core, Walrasian equilibrium, and relation between them can be generalized to an ambiguous asymmetric information economy.

They start by remarking that the standard Arrow-Debreu state contingent model allows the state of nature of the world to be involved in the initial endowments and payoff of the agents, who make contacts ex-ante, i.e., before the state of nature is realized and once the state is realized the contract is executed and consumption takes place. Radner (1968, 1982) extended the analysis of Arrow and Debreu by introducing asymmetric private information. The private information is modeled as a partition of a finite state space, with the requirement that the initial endowments of each agent measurable with respect to sigma-algebra generated by her partition. The issue of incentive compatibility does not arise in this model, as all the contracts signed ex-ante are assumed to be binging. However, for this to make sense one must assume that there is an exogenous court or government that enforces the contract ex-post, otherwise agents may find it beneficial to renege.

Holmström and Myerson (1983) argued that if one assumes that the agents are Bayesian expected utility maximizers, it is not possible to have allocations which are both first best efficient and also ex-post incentive compatible. He and Yannelis asked whether one can find another decision theoretic framework that will allow defining concepts of Walrasian equilibrium and core in the symmetric information economy in such a way that both core and Walrasian equilibria exist, and are both incentive compatible and first best efficient. Their main finding is that such a framework is provided by maximin expected utility, i.e., by exactly the kind of preferences used by Gilboa and Schmeidler to model ambiguity aversion.

To give the reader the main idea of the argument, let us consider the following example, found in He and Yannelis. Consider an economy with one commodity, two agents, indexed 1 and 2 and three states of the world, indexed *a, b,* and *c*. The initial endowments of the agents are

$$e_1 = (5, 5, 0); e_2 = (5, 0, 5).$$

Their information partitions of are given by[6]

$$\Pi_1 = \{\{a, b\}, c\}; \Pi_2 = \{\{a, c\}, b\},$$

i.e., each agent can be either poor or rich. If the agent is poor she knows that the other agent is rich, but the rich agent does not know whether the other agent is rich or poor.

Recall, that Yannelis and He define a tuple consisting of an allocation vector and a vector of prices to be a Walrasian expectations equilibrium (WEE) for the economy, if each agent's allocation is measurable with respect to her information partition and maximizes her expected utility given prices and her beliefs; and the price vector is such the markets clear. Measurability requirement is crucial in this definition. In the example above it can be interpreted in the following way: each agent has to pay a tax/receive a subsidy depending on whether she is rich or poor, but independent on the wealth of the other agent. Now friction between ex-post incentive compatibility and efficiency can be understood and an incentive to lie about once wealth.

Maximin expectation equilibrium (MEE) differs from WEE by assuming that the agents maximize the expected utility under most pessimistic expectations consistent with their signal and the measurability requirement is not imposed. We will see when discussing the example why dropping measurability requirement is reasonable in the case of MEE.

To continue with the example, let us assume that both agents have identical Bernoulli utility function

$$u(x) = \sqrt{x}$$

[6]Note that the endowments are measurable with respect to their partitions.

and the prior beliefs of both agents are the same

$$\mu(\omega) = \frac{1}{3} \text{for } \omega \in \{a, b, c\}.$$

Suppose that agents are both Bayesian expected utility maximizers. It can be easily checked that there is no nonfree disposal Walrasian expectation equilibria with positive prices.

If we allow for free disposal, then

$$x_1 = (4,\ 4,\ 1) \text{ and } x_2 = (4,\ 1,\ 4)$$

is a (free disposal) WEE allocation with the equilibrium price $p(a) = 0$ and $p(b) = p(c) = \frac{1}{2}$. However, this allocation is not incentive compatible.

On the other hand, if the agents are maximin expected utility maximizers, then there exists maximin expectations equilibrium $(y, p)$, where

$$y_1 = (5,\ 4,\ 1), y_2 = (5,\ 1,\ 4)$$

and price is given by $p(a) = 0, p(b) = p(c) = \frac{1}{2}$. If state $b$ or $c$ is realized, the ex-post utility of agent one will be the same in both Bayesian preference setting and maximin preference setting, since $x_1(b) = y_1(b)$ and $x_1(c) = y_1(c)$. But if state $a$ occurs, the ex-post utility of agent one with maximin preference will be strictly higher than that in the Bayesian preference setting, since

$$x_1(a) = 4 < 5 = y_1(a).$$

Therefore, the maximin preference allows agents to reach higher efficiency.

To understand the difference between Bayesian and maximin preferences it will be desirable to recast the above example as a social choice problem. There are three states of the world, in one both agents are rich and in the other two one agent is rich and the other is power. A priori the agents will find it beneficial to agree to tax the rich agent and subsidize the poor one. Suppose once endowments are realized the agents must declare whether they are rich or poor. If an agent declares to be rich she has to pay \$1 and then the tax revenue is distributed in the following way: first the agent who declared herself poor receives \$1, and if there are more tax proceeds collected the rich agents also receive \$1. The announcement triggers an audit if and only if the reported state is inconsistent with prior information, i.e., both agents claim to be poor. In this case the social planner finds the truth, and she either taxes the rich agent and pays the poor one or does nothing if both turn to be rich. I would like to argue that truth telling is not Bayes-Nash equilibrium (BNE) under Bayesian preferences, but it is a BNE under the maximin preferences.

Note that the poor agent never has incentive to lie, so she will always announce to be poor. Let us consider incentives of the rich agent. If she claims to be rich, her payoff will be \$5 if the other agent claims to be rich and \$4 if the other agent claims to be poor. If, on the other hand, she claims to be poor, her payoff will be \$4 if the other agent claims to be poor and is found to be poor, \$5 if the other agent claims to be poor, but is found to be rich, and \$6 if the other agent claims to be rich. Since there is positive probability (50 %) that the other agent is in fact reach, a rich agent with Bayesian preferences will strictly prefer to say she is poor. For the agent with maximin preferences, on the other hand, the only contingency that matters is the one when the other agent is poor, therefore, she will be indifferent between telling the truth and lying.

Note, however, that since the lottery generated by lying first order stochastically dominates the one generated by telling the truth, truth telling remains a weakly dominated strategy. One can avoid it by imposing fine if one is audited and caught lying. Then the result can be interpreted as stating that with maximin preferences even a small fine will induce truth telling, since as long as it is possible to be caught such agents will act as if they are certain to be caught. This is the key insight that explains why ambiguity-averse preferences mitigate tension between efficiency and incentive compatibility. It turns out, as I will explain later in this book, that the maximin preferences are the only preferences that eliminate the trade-off completely. However, if preferences are convex combination of maximin and Bayesian, the information rents necessary for truthful revelation will be smaller than for purely Bayesian preferences. He and Yannelis proceed to argue that under the maximin preferences the MEE coincide with private core[7] for large economies.

In conclusion, He and Yannelis developed a new asymmetric information economy framework, which allows for ambiguity-averse preferences. They derived new existence and equivalence results for MEE and private core. The most important insight of this work is that ambiguity aversion eases tensions between efficiency and incentive compatibility. We will see other instances of this insight later in this chapter.

## 2.3 Ambiguity Aversion and the Myerson-Satterthwaite Theorem

This section is based on De Castro and Yannelis (2011) and discusses the way ambiguity aversion allows one to avoid conclusions of Myerson-Satterthwaite theorem. The conflict between efficiency and incentive compatibility arises in many areas of economics. In particular, it features in auction theory, bargaining theory, and the theory of general equilibrium with asymmetric information, among other cases. One of the key insights we got in the last section is that, at least in the case of general equilibrium models, this conflict can be mitigated if the agents are ambiguity-averse. Moreover, when individuals have maximin expected utility

[7]Definition of private core is similar to that of core, but with crucial requirement that allocations are measurable with respect to private information partitions.

(MEU) preferences, then the conflict can be resolved completely, any efficient allocation is incentive compatible. Conversely, only MEU preferences have this property, though tension is substantially mitigated for much broader class of preferences.

To fix ideas let us start with the following example from De Castro and Yannelis (2011). Consider a seller and a buyer, who both have private valuations of an object. The seller's valuation is $v \in [0; 1]$ and the buyer's valuation is $t \in [0; 1]$. Trade will result in an efficient allocation if it happens if and only if $t > v$. Assuming both the buyer and the seller are expected utility maximizer's, Myerson and Satterthwaite (1983) have proved that there is no incentive compatible, individual rational, budget balanced mechanism that would achieve ex-post efficiency in this situation.

Let us consider the following mechanism, known as the double auction. The seller places an asking price $a$ and the buyer submits a bid $b$. If the bid is above the ask, they trade at price

$$p = \frac{a+b}{2}.$$

If the bid is below the asking price, there is no trade. Therefore, if they if the trade occurred at price $p$, the (ex-post) profit for the seller will be $p - v$, and $t - p$ for the buyer; otherwise both get zero. Since the announcement of the agent affects price at which trade occurs the buyer will have incentives to shed her value and the seller an incentive to exaggerate the cost. The logic behind this result is the same as behind shedding the value in the first price sealed-bid auctions.[8] This means that if the value of the buyer is only slightly above that of the seller the trade will not occur, despite the efficiency gains it will bestow. Myerson and Satterthwaite (1983) argued that under the Bayesian paradigm this efficiency cannot be avoided by using a more sophisticate mechanism as long as it is required to be incentive compatible, individual rational, budget balanced.

One can avoid this conclusion if one dispenses with the assumption of probabilistic sophistication that requires that each agent forms a single prior about the distribution of the other agents' values and allow her to entertain a variety of possible beliefs. This implies that both the buyer and the seller have to make choice in a situation of Knightian uncertainty. Following Gilboa and Schmeidler, we will model it using the maximin criterion.[9]

The maximin criterion implies that each individual considers the worst-case scenario for each action, and chooses the action that leads to the best worst-case outcome. Let us argue that true revelation is incentive compatible under this criterion. Indeed, truthful announcements of $a = v$ by the seller and $b = t$ by the buyer are incentive compatible if buyer and seller do not have any incentive to choose a

[8]This logic assumes that both agents are expected utility maximizers.

[9]Use of the maximin criterion in classical statistics dates back to Wald (1950), but the behaviorial foundations where first provided by Gilboa and Schmeidler (1982).

different action. If the buyer chooses $b = t$, the worst-case scenario is to end up with zero (either by buying by $p = t$ or by not trading). If she chooses $b > t$, the worst-case scenario is to buy by $p > t$, which leads to a (strict) loss. If she considers $b < t$, the worst-case scenario is to get zero (it always possible that there is no trade). Therefore, neither $b < t$ nor $b > t$ is better (by the maximin criterion) than $b = t$ and she has no incentive to deviate. The argument for the seller is analogous.

Note, however, that truthful announcement is as good as any announcement below true value for the buyer and above the cost for the seller. One may argue that telling lies may require more cognitive resources that telling the truth. This will make truth telling strictly dominant under the maximin criterion. Therefore, combination of ambiguity aversion with bounded rationality can more convincingly resolve friction between efficiency and incentive compatibility, then any of them can achieve of their own.

De Castro and Yannelis (2011) also note that another interesting property of these preferences is that the set of efficient allocations is not small. At least in the case of one-good economies, the set of efficient allocations under maximin preferences includes all allocations that are incentive compatible and efficient for the expected utility maximizers. They also argued that under some reasonable conditions imposed on preferences[10] maximin preferences are the only preferences that resolve the conflict between efficiency and incentive compatibility. However, if one settles for mitigation rather than the complete resolution of the conflict, more general ambiguity-averse preferences can help.

Note that ambiguity does not always improve social welfare. Mukerji (1998), for example, argued that in hidden action models[11] it may decrease efficiency, by limiting trading opportunities. We will review that paper in the next section. It may also lead to contractual incompleteness, as noted by Mukerji (1998) and Grant et al. It is also important to mention that the maximin preferences are the only ones that allow to completely resolving the conflict between incentive compatibility and efficiency, though any ambiguity-averse preferences mitigate this conflict.

Other ways to get around the problem of conflict between incentive compatibility and efficiency were proposed in the literature. Yannelis (1991), for example, imposes the private information measurability condition and argues in a series of papers[12] that it forces incentive compatibility of any Pareto optimal allocation. Indeed, if an agent trades a nonmeasurable contract, she effectively makes promises depending on conditions that she cannot verify. Therefore, other agents may have an incentive to cheat her, which leads to the failure of incentive compatibility. Insistence on only measurable contracts preserves incentive compatibility; however

[10]The conditions are rationality, monotonicity, and continuity.

[11]As we will see later, hidden action and hidden information models often respond in different ways to deviations from Bayesian rationality. For example, the costs of boundedly rational behavior are usually borne by the principal in hidden action models, but can be borne by either the principal, or the agent, or both in hidden information models.

[12]See papers by Krasa and Yannelis (1994), Koutsougeras and Yannelis (1993), Hahn and Yannelis (1997).

it restricts trade and may lead even lead to no trade. In financial markets this requirement will mean that the traders cannot use the price of the assets to deduce information possessed by other traders, i.e., it will exclude the procedure which underlies the rational expectation equilibria and leads to the efficient market hypothesis.

Gul and Postlewaite (1992), McLean and Postlewaite (2002) proposed yet different solutions to the conflict. They assumed that the agents are "informationally small" and showed the existence of incentive compatible and approximately Pareto optimal in a replica economy.

The above approaches, however, preserve Bayesian rationality paradigm. Given growing empirical and experimental evidence that calls this paradigm into question, it is important to ask how common and how severe the conflict is. The answer that emerges from this research is: quite common, but probably not as severe as we originally thought.

Finally, it would be interesting to study an evolutionary model of populations of agents with different attitudes to ambiguity. Such a model forms into a more general class of the models of evolution of preferences. Robson provided a comprehensive review of such models. Bounded rationality plays important role in this approach, since fully rational agents will simply have their utility equal to their expected inclusive fitness. Therefore, one should attempt to build a model, where preferences and decision-making rules coevolve. In the next chapter I will make some remarks about how such models can be built.

## 2.4 Ambiguity Aversion, Moral Hazard, and Contractual Incompleteness

In the previous section we saw examples of situations where ambiguity aversion allows improving efficiency by mitigating tensions between incentive compatibility and efficiency in Walrasian and Myerson-Satterthwaite settings. The common feature of examples considered so far was that economic agents possessed hidden information but did not have to undertake hidden actions. In this section we will consider the situation, when the agents have to undertake such an action, in particular, a relation-specific investment, which will affect the value of a widget for both parties. Building on the ideas developed by Mukerji (1998), Grant et al. (2006), I will argue that in this case ambiguity-averse preferences will lead to incomplete contracts and therefore, loss of efficiency.

Let us start with an example that appears in Mukerji (1998). Consider two vertically related risk-neutral firms, $B$ and $S$. Assume that the set of possible states of the world, $\Omega$, contains three elements, i.e.,

$$\Omega = \{\omega_0, \omega_b, \omega_s\}.$$

At date zero each firm decides on the level of relation-specific investment, which can be either high or low. Let $\beta_L(\sigma_L)$ and $\beta_H(\sigma_H)$ denote low and high levels of investment for firm $B(S)$, respectively. The social surplus in the states of the world is given by

$$s(\omega_0) = 0, s(\omega_b) = s(\omega_s) = 200$$

and the costs of investment are

$$h_B(\beta_L) = h_S(\sigma_L) = 10, h_B(\beta_H) = h_S(\sigma_H) = 85.$$

As before, we assume that agents maximize minimal expected utility with respect to a set of beliefs. To formalize the idea of allowable beliefs Mukerji makes use of idea on nonadditive measure (capacity), which is defined in the following way.

**Definition** Let $\Omega$ be a finite set. A function $\pi : 2^\Omega \to [0, 1]$ is called a nonadditive measure (capacity) if it has the following properties: (i) $\pi(\emptyset) = 0$, (ii) $\pi(\Omega) = 1$, (iii) for any $A, B \in 2^\Omega$, $(A \subset B) \Rightarrow (\pi(A) \leq \pi(B))$. Capacity $\pi(\cdot)$ is called convex if for all $A, B \in 2^\Omega$

$$\pi(A \cup B) \geq \pi(A) + \pi(B) + \pi(A \cap B).$$

One can interpret capacity of a set as the minimal possible probability the decision-maker assigns to the set. Given a convex capacity, the set of possible probabilistic beliefs a decision-maker entertains is given by its core

$$\Pi(\pi) = \{\pi_j \in \Delta(\Omega) | \pi_j(X) \geq \pi(X) \text{ for all } X \in 2^\Omega\}.$$

As in the previous two sections, the decision-maker makes her choices on the basis of the maximin expected utility, however, the beliefs are restricted to belong to a core of a given capacity, rather than being arbitrary.

Let us, following Mukerji, assume that

$$\pi(\beta_L, \sigma_L) = (0.78, 0.01, 0.01),$$

i.e., if both buyer and seller choose low levels of investment, state $\omega_0$ will realize with at least 78 % chance, while states $\omega_b, \omega_s$ will realize with at least 1 % probability each. Similarly,

$$\pi(\beta_H, \sigma_H) = (0.02, 0.39, 0.39)$$
$$\pi(\beta_H, \sigma_L) = (0.42, 0.365, 0.015)$$
$$\pi(\beta_L, \sigma_H) = (0.42, 0.015, 0.365).$$

Therefore, the buyer's effort shifts likelihood from the low surplus state predominately to the state favored by the buyer, while the seller's effort shifts it predominately to the state favored by the seller. Let us further assume that

$$\pi(\{\omega_b, \omega_s\}|\beta, \sigma) - \pi(\{\omega_b\}|\beta, \sigma) - \pi(\{\omega_s\}|\beta, \sigma) = 0.1$$
$$\pi(\{\omega_0, \omega_s\}|\beta, \sigma) - \pi(\{\omega_0\}|\beta, \sigma) - \pi(\{\omega_s\}|\beta, \sigma) = 0$$
$$\pi(\{\omega_b, \omega_0\}|\beta, \sigma) - \pi(\{\omega_b\}|\beta, \sigma) - \pi(\{\omega_0\}|\beta, \sigma) = 0.$$

Also each agent assigns higher minimal probability that a good state will occur than the sum of minimal probabilities that the buyer's and the seller's preferred states will occur. Intuitively, this implies that though each agent is optimistic about the possibility of her investment to result in a high surplus state, both agents are worried that the other guy will benefit.

One can verify by a direct calculation using maximin expected utility criterion that $(\beta_H, \sigma_H)$ is the first best, and $(\beta_L, \sigma_L)$ is the second-best action profile. Given that each agent's effort mainly increases the likelihood of her preferred high surplus state, it would be natural to guess that the first best can be by allocating the entire surplus at $\omega_b$ to the buyer and at $\omega_s$ to the seller. Such a contract will, indeed, be incentive compatible. However, no ex-ante transfers may be arranged to make it individually rational. Also, since the incentive constraints bind, any contract which attempts to smoothed the ex-post payoffs would break at least one of the incentive constraints. Therefore, the first best cannot be implemented.

Let us assume that in the case of lack of a contract, the social surplus in the resulting state is split equally. Then it is straightforward to verify that the null contract implements the second-best investment profile. One can see the null contract as a complete contract that instructs that no trade should occur in every contingency, but allows for ex-post renegotiation. Obviously, it is as good as leaving the contingencies unmentioned, i.e., an ultimate incomplete contract. One needs to assume transaction costs (which could be infinitesimally small), to make the incomplete contract strictly optimal.

Another way in which ambiguity aversion could interact with bounded rationality to lead to contractual incompleteness was explored by Grant et al. (2006). Their central idea is that boundedly rational individuals do not have access to a language sufficiently rich to describe all possible states of nature, which leads to ambiguity of a contract. As a result, risk-averse agents may forgo potential gains from risk sharing and choose incomplete contracts instead. It can be illustrated by a simple example.

Suppose two farmers Robin and Clarke are considering a possibility of entering a risk sharing contract. They grow different crops and know that if the weather is rainy then Robin will have a good harvest, and Clarke will get none, and if there it is sunny their fortunes will be reversed. However, each observes only weather on their own farm and is unaware of the possibility that weather may differ at different locations. Been risk averse, they would prefer a priori to share harvest equally, however, being boundedly rational they can only think of a contract of a form: *if it is rainy Robin delivers half of her harvest to Clarke, and if it is sunny Clarke delivers half of her harvest to Robin.*

In the formal framework developed below, if such a contract were signed, the presumption is that each party translates the contingencies on which the transfer function depends into her or his own experience. Therefore, if it is rainy at Robin's farm and sunny at Clarke's or vice versa, the terms of contract will lead to disagreement. The first scenario is less problematic, since both parties are expected to deliver, and therefore dispute can be easily resolved by exchange. In the second case, however, this can lead to a serious dispute. The authors assume that there are costs to dispute resolution.

This example demonstrates that boundedly rational players may be unable to formulate a sufficiently refined description of the states of the world to avoid dispute. However, as argued by Grant et al. (2006), they may be aware that disputes are possible. This may lead them to choose a null contract.

This corresponds closely to the distinction between risk and uncertainty I discussed above. The larger is the gray area giving rise to dispute, the less will parties benefit from a complete contract. On the other hand, they will benefit more from such a contract the more risk-averse. Thus risk and ambiguity work in opposite directions.

In both Mukerji and Grant et al. approaches some transaction costs are necessary to justify contractual incompleteness. However, though transaction costs (which are ultimately a form of bounded rationality) are ultimately necessary to justify contractual incompleteness, ambiguity aversion significantly reduces marginal gains from including more details in the contract and allows one to get away with small (sometimes even infinitesimal) transaction costs. Segal (1999), Hart and Moore (1999) have shown that complexity of the environment can have similar effects. I will discuss that paper in Chap. 4.

## 2.5 Some Other Economic Effects of Pessimism

Ambiguity aversion can be considered as a form of pessimism concerning unknown probability distributions. This view of ambiguity aversion is supported by psychological studies. Pulford (2009), for example, studied the influences of optimism and pessimism on ambiguity aversion in a standard Ellsberg urn experiment and found that highly optimistic people showed significantly less ambiguity aversion than their pessimistic counterparts, when information was given that the number of balls was randomly determined. When ambiguity is clear, and trust issues are removed, subjects' optimistic outlook influences their degree of ambiguity aversion and thus their decisions. This pattern was present but less pronounced in the condition when the composition of the ambiguous urn could be interpreted as being influenced (rigged) by the experimenter. Pulford has also observed that the perception of the situation, especially the degree of trust in the experimenter, was significantly influenced by the participants optimism. This observation potentially opens the door for modeling of coevolution of the social norms, such as trust, attitudes to ambiguity. I will briefly touch on building of coevolutionary models of preferences, decision rules, and social norms in Chap. 3.

Ambiguity aversion can be considered as a form of pessimism concerning unknown probability distributions. We have seen that consequences of this can be both: positive, for example, allowing for mitigation of the trade-off between incentive compatibility and efficiency, and negative, for example, leading to the contractual incompleteness. Here I will briefly describe some other economic phenomena, which are governed by some form of pessimism of economic actors, though not necessarily by ambiguity aversion.

### 2.5.1 Robustness and Linear Contracts: Uncertainty Over Agent's Actions

Linear contract are prevalent in economic life. They also are used widely in contract theory and will make use of them later in this book. But what is the ultimate rationale for linearity? Carroll (2015) tackles this question and argues that it may be the principal's uncertainty concerning the set of actions the agent can take. The framework is the following.

A principal hires an agent to perform a costly action on her behalf. Both the principal and the agent are risk neutral. Action is not observable, but gives rise via a stochastic technology to an observable output; $y \in Y$. It is assumed that the set of possible outputs, $Y$, is a compact subset of the real line with the minimal element normalized to be zero. The agent's action is a pair $(F, c) \in \Im \subset \Delta(Y) \times R_{+}$, i.e., the agent selects a distribution of outputs at some nonnegative cost, where the set of allowable pairs are given by technology $\Im$, where $\Im$ is assumed to be compact. When choosing an action, the agent optimally responds to the incentive scheme, provided by the principal, where the scheme specifies payment $w(y)$ for the output value $y$, where $w(\cdot)$ is assumed to be continuous and nonnegative.[13] Let $A^{*} \subset \Im$ be the set of agent's optimal choices, which is guaranteed to be nonempty.

[13]The latter is the limited liability constraint, which prevents the principal from selling the enterprise to the agent.

If the principal knows the technology then this is a standard principal agent problem. Carroll, however, assumes that the principal does not know the technology and maximizes her minimal payoff, where minimum is taken over all technologies which allow agent to exert no effort and produce no output. Under these assumptions Carroll shows that the optimal contract is the linear one.

Intuition for Carroll's result is easy to understand. Suppose optimal contract (whatever form it might take) achieves expected payoff $\pi_P$ for the principal and $\pi_A$ for the agent. This means that the total expected output is given by

$$y = \pi_P + \pi_A.$$

Note that principal can achieve the same outcome by offering the agent linear contract

$$w(y) = \frac{\pi_A}{\pi_P + \pi_A} y.$$

Indeed, since agent had chosen before action that resulted in expected payoff $\pi_A$, she will know choose action that results in at least the same expected payoff, and since under the linear scheme payoffs of the principal and the agent are proportional, the principal will end up earning at least $\pi_P$. The rigorous argument has to deal with some technical subtleties; interested reader is referred to Carroll (2015) for the details.

Carroll also points out that to explain prevalence of linear contracts in practice via this model one need not interpret it literally. Instead, one may assume that decision-makers are just looking for the simplest contact that guarantees to perform reasonably, akin to Simon's (1956) notion of satisfying, providing further link between models build around the concept of pessimism and models of boundedly rational decision-making. Finally, Carroll notes that this model cannot be used to justify the common practice in applied theory to assume full knowledge of the environment, but assume linearity for tractability, since the optimal linear contract in that case is different from the maximin optimal contract.

### 2.5.2 *Monetary Equilibria with Wary Agents*

Yet another form pessimism can take is wariness about the future. Araujo et al. (2014) assumed that when choosing their life-time consumption profiles agents neglect gains at distant dates, but take into account losses. They argued that to implement the efficient allocation among wary agents one will require a nonvanishing supply of money.

To model wariness, Araujo et al. assume that utility of an agent is given by

$$U(x) = \sum_{t=1}^{+\infty} \delta^t u(x_t) + \beta \inf_{t\geq 1} u(x_t).$$

Here $\{x_t\}_{t=1}^{\infty}$ is a bounded consumption profile that is financed by the period endowment and fiat money holdings net of tax obligations. Fiat money is injected into the economy at time zero. At the later dates money supply evolves endogenously, with aggregate money supply at a particular date equal to the aggregate money supply at the previous date net of tax payments. Walrasian equilibrium of the economy is defined in the usual fashion.

It is the last term in the utility function, which depends on the potential unfavorable shock in the future that makes fiat money holding attractable. Note that if $\beta = 0$ the agents are conventional discounted expected utility maximizers, and fiat money will not have any value at equilibrium. Intuitively, if one assumes that $\beta > 0$ fiat money holding will allow the consumers the marginal benefit of raising infimum of consumption, provided it is never reached in finite time (the worst is always yet to come). If this cost outweighs the opportunity cost of carrying fiat money, positive money holding become optimal.

## 2.6 Concluding Remarks

In this chapter I discussed effects of ambiguity aversion and other forms of pessimistic biases on economic decision-making. Discussion in this chapter shows that such behavior can help to mitigate some important trade-offs, such as the trade-off between implementability and Pareto optimality and as a result improve economic outcomes. It can, however, also lead to contractual incompleteness, which in turn leads to hold-up problems and decreases relation-specific investments below the efficient levels. This kind of behavior can also help to explain some common economic phenomena such as simplicity of real life contracts in comparison with the ones suggested by the optimal contract literature and the prevalence of the fiat money.

In the later chapters I will discuss other, more drastic, forms of deviations from the Savage's paradigm and study how they modify the nature of the optimal contracts. In particular, I will note some similarities between the ways complexity and ambiguity aversion affect the structure of the optimal contracts.

Before discussing in depth effects of bounded rationality and social forces on the optimal contracts, I will pause and ask is there a common threat that unites different deviations from the Savage's paradigm. I will investigate this question from the evolutionary point of view and suggest a possible way to model coevolution of bounded rationality and ambiguity aversion.

## References


Araujo, R., Gama-Torres, J. P., Novinski, R., Pascoa, M. R. (2014). *On efficiency of monetary equilibria when agents are wary*. http://www.laef.ucsb.edu/pages/conferences/are15/papers/araujo.pdf

Carroll, G. (2015). Robustness and linear contracts. *American Economic Review, 105*, 536–563.

De Castro, L. I., & Yannelis, N. C. (2011). *Ambiguity aversion solves the conflict between efficiency and incentive compatibility*. University of Manchester Economic Discussion Papers Series, EDP-1106.

Ellsberg, D. (1961). Risk, ambiguity, and the savage axioms. *Quarterly Journal of Economics, 75*, 643–669.

Gilboa, I., & Schmeidler, I. D. (1989). Maximin expected utility with non-unique prior. *Journal of Mathematical Economics, 18*, 141–153.

Grant, S. H., Kline, J. J., & Quiggin, J. (2006). *Lost in translation: honest misunderstandings and expost disputes*. Bond Business School Publications, Paper 3. http://epublications.bond.edu.au/business_pubs/3

Gul, F., & Postlewaite, A. (1992). Asymptotic efficiency in large exchange economies with asymmetric information. *Econometrica, 60*, 1273–1292.

Hahn, G., & Yannelis, N. C. (1997). Efficiency and incentive compatibility in differential information economies. *Economic Theory, 10*, 383–411.

Hart, O., & Moore, J. (1999). Foundations of incomplete contracts. *Review of Economic Studies, 66*, 115–139.

He, W., & Yannelis, N. C. (2015). Equilibrium theory under ambiguity. *Journal of Mathematical Economics, 61*, 86–95.

Holmström, B., & Myerson, R. B. (1983). Efficient and durable decision rules with incomplete information. *Econometrica, 51*, 1799–1819.

Knight, F. H. (1921). *Risk, uncertainty, and profits*. Boston, MA: Hart, Schaffner & Marx; Houghton Mifflin Co.

Koutsougeras, L., & Yannelis, N. C. (1993). Incentive compatibility and information superiority of the core of an economy with differential information. *Economic Theory, 3*, 195–216.

Krasa, S., & Yannelis, N. C. (1994). The value allocation of an economy with differential information. *Econometrica, 62*, 881–900.

McLean, R., & Postlewaite, A. (2002). Informational size and incentive compatibility. *Econometrica, 70*, 2421–2454.

Mukerji, S. (1998). Ambiguity aversion and incompleteness of contractual form. *American Economic Review, 88*, 1207–1231.

Pulford, B. D. (2009). Is luck on my side: Optimism, pessimism, and ambiguity aversion. *Quarterly Journal of Experimental Psychology, 62*, 1079–1087.

Radner, R. (1968). Competitive equilibrium under uncertainty. *Econometrica, 36*, 31–58.

Radner, R. (1982). Equilibrium under uncertainty. In K. J. Arrow & M. D. Intriligator (Eds.), *Handbook of mathematical economics, vol. II*. Amsterdam: North Holland.

Savage, L. J. (1954). *Foundations of statistics*. New York, NY, USA: Wiley.

Segal, I. (1999). Complexity and renegotiation: A foundation for incomplete contracts. *Review of Economic Studies, 66*, 57–82.

Simon, H. A. (1956). *Reply: Surrogates for uncertain decision problems*. Office of Naval Research.

Wald, A. (1950). *Statistical decision functions*. New York, NY, USA: John Wiley & Sons.

Yannelis, N. C. (1991). The core of an economy with differential information. *Economic Theory, 1*, 183–197.

# Chapter 3
# Evolution of Preferences, Social Norms, and Decision Rules

By now it is commonly accepted that ambiguity aversion, bounded rationality, social norms, and other deviations from SEU play important role in determining economic outcomes. However, a critic may complain that such explanations lack discipline, since by invoking a suitable model of boundedly rational behavior or a particular social norm one can explain everything, virtually explaining nothing. This concern is certainly justified and deserves to be answered. The answer can proceed along two different lines: theoretical and empirical. On empirical side one may study in a laboratory or in the field the actual ways people make decisions and document decision procedures, preferences, customs, and social norms. A lot of such work was indeed done during the previous three decades and it is still an active field of research. I will not endeavor to describe this work here. Instead, I will suggest that a theorist can approach this challenge from an evolutionary perspective and ask how preferences, decision rules, and social norms coevolved. Research in this area deserves a separate monograph. Here I will only provide some general guidelines along which such research might proceed.

I will start with discussing the evolution of preferences, followed by discussion of evolution decision rules, social norms, and finally sharing some thoughts about their coevolution.

## 3.1 Evolution of Preferences

Informally the idea that preferences evolve was part of economic thinking for a long time. More recently the area received some attention from economic theorists, leading to creation of formal theories. For a comprehensive review of this literature, see Robson and Samuelson (2011). To understand some issues tackled in this literature, recall that it is a standard assumption in economics that individuals make choices to maximize their utilities. In the standard analysis the utilities are taken to be fundamentals. However, from a broader evolutionary perspective the utilities



S. Basov, *Social Norms, Bounded Rationality and Optimal Contracts*,
Studies in Economic Theory 30, DOI 10.1007/978-981-10-1041-5_3

guide an individual's choices to maximize her inclusive fitness.[1] Formally, the problem of evolution of preferences can be summarized as

$$\max_{u(\cdot)} f(x) \tag{3.1}$$

$$s.t. x \in \arg\max_{x \in \Omega} u(x), u(\cdot) \in U_{ad}.$$

In Eq. (3.1), $f(\cdot)$ is the expected inclusive fitness associated with choice $x$, $u(\cdot)$ is the individual's utility function, $\Omega$ is the set of admissible choices, and $U_{ad}$ is the set of admissible preferences. It is straightforward to observe that if $f(\cdot) \in U_{ad}$ then

$$u = f \tag{3.2}$$

solves problem (3.1). If set $\Omega$ is fixed then solution, in general, is not unique. Indeed, any admissible utility $u(\cdot)$ such that

$$\arg\max_{x \in \Omega} u(x) = \arg\max_{x \in \Omega} f(x) \tag{3.3}$$

will solve (3.1).

One might argue that to save on the computational costs, evolution could have programmed the optimal choice rather than the utility function into the individual's genetic make. Robson (2001) deals with this objection and argues that endowing an individual with a utility function allows for a better response to a changing environment. On the other hand, note that on flexibility ground one should have chosen solution (3.2) is the only solution that works for all sets $\Omega$.

We have seen that to save on computational costs one should have behavior directly programmed into the individual's genes, while to give individuals more flexibility to meet new challenges, they should have identical preferences that coincide with their expected inclusive fitness. Both of these observations clash with causal empiricism that suggests that in real life individuals have diverse preferences, which are only loosely related with their fitness. To explain the diversity of preference one has to assume that either the individuals are not utility maximizers, i.e., they are boundedly rational, or expected fitness does not belong to the set of admissible preferences. Note that one reason for expected fitness to be inadmissible as a utility function is complexity. Presumably, preferences have to be coded by some neural mechanism, which limits their admissible complexity. Therefore, excluding expected fitness from the set of admissible preferences also implies a form of bounded rationality.

[1] Inclusive fitness is the number of direct and indirect progeny weighted by a degree of relatedness.

### 3.1.1 Evolution of Optimal Preferences Under Bounded Rationality

In this Section I am going to give an example of evolutionary optimal preferences under boundedly rational behavior. I will argue that the utility assigned to the good choices exceeds their fitness, while the utility assignment to the bad choices is below their fitness value. Moreover, the deviation of utility from fitness can be quite substantial. Assuming the process of evolution of preferences is continuous, the latter observation may help to explain why, when the environment changes, sub-optimal choices persist for a long time.

Assume that an individual faces a choice from a finite set of alternatives $\Omega = \{1, \ldots, n\}$ with fitness values $f_1, \ldots, f_n$ and utilities $u_1, \ldots, u_n$. Also assume that $U_{ad} = [0, 1]$. The latter assumption essentially is that the set of admissible utilities is bounded. Such an assumption seems natural, since feeling of pleasure and pain associated with different choices are mediated through the release or particular chemicals, which can be released only in finite quantities. I will also assume that fitness values lie inside admissible utility range, i.e., having preferences that coincide with fitness is feasible.

Without loss of generality, assume $f_1 \geq f_2 \cdots \geq f_n$. To capture bounded rationality of a decision maker, I assume that their choice is probabilistic, i.e., the utilities associated with different choices determine the probabilities with which these choices are made. The first probabilistic choice model in economics was proposed by Luce (1959). He showed that if one requires the choice probabilities to be independent of a sequence in which choices are made, then they must be represented by

$$q_i = \frac{\exp(\frac{u_i}{\lambda})}{\sum_{j=1}^{n} \exp(\frac{u_j}{\lambda})}, \tag{3.4}$$

where $n$ is the number of alternatives, $q_i$ is the probability that alternative $i$ is chosen, and $u_i$ is the utility associated with alternative $i$. Note that according to this model any two alternatives that have the same utility are selected with the same probabilities. Parameter $\lambda$, which can take values from zero to infinity, can be usefully thought of as representing the degree of the consumer's irrationality. If $\lambda = 0$ then

$$q_i = \begin{cases} \frac{1}{k}, & \text{if } u_i \in \{u_1, \ldots, u_n\} \\ 0, & \text{otherwise} \end{cases}$$

Here integer $k$ is the cardinality of the set of the utility maximizers, which is consistent with rational behavior. At the other extreme, as $\lambda \to \infty$ the choice probabilities converge to $1/n$, i.e., the choice becomes totally random, independent of the utility level. This is the case of fully irrational consumer.

I would like to argue that even small degree of irrationality results in drastic deviation of utilities from the fitness levels. To see this, notice that given the choice set $\Omega$ and the fitness levels, the evolution will select for utilities to maximize the expected fitness:

$$\mathrm{EF} = \sum_{i=1}^{n} q_i f_i$$

subject to (3.4). Let us consider first the case $n = 2$. One can evaluate derivatives of the expected fitness with respect to utility levels to be:

$$\frac{\partial(\mathrm{EF})}{\partial u_k} = \frac{\lambda(f_k - f_i)\exp\left(\frac{u_1+u_2}{\lambda}\right)}{\left(\exp\left(\frac{u_1}{\lambda}\right) + \exp\left(\frac{u_1}{\lambda}\right)\right)^2}$$

From this expression one can immediately see that evolutionary fitness is maximized when $u_1 = 1$ and $u_2 = 0$, that is the choice that conveys higher fitness is assigned the highest possible utility, while the choice that conveys lower fitness is assigned the highest possible utility.

Note that an important feature of this example is that difference in utilities among different choices is significantly greater than difference in their fitness. This result can be generalized to more than two choices. Robson and Samuelson (2011) come to similar conclusions in a slightly different framework.

## 3.2 Evolution of Decision Rules

In the previous Section I discussed briefly a model of evolution of presences under bounded rationality, taking the boundedly rational decision rule as given. In this section, I will discuss a model of evolution of boundedly rational decision rules themselves. For this purpose, I will model boundedly rational decision-making invoking the notion of a heuristics. This approach to decision-making is appealing due to its intuitive foundations. It is difficult to validate the conviction that individuals possess the analytical skills to construct a model, assess the relevant probabilities and finally maximize their expected utility on a routine basis. A far more realistic scenario is the one where an individual, faced with an unfamiliar and uncertain decision, instinctively invokes a simple rule of thumb or heuristic. Heuristics-based approaches to decision-making was pioneered by Simon (1955, 1956). Heuristics have applications and relevance in a wide range of disciplines including fields within economics, cognitive psychology and computer science. To relate this view of bounded rationality to a probabilistic choice model, considered above, note that a dynamic heuristic can be viewed as a way to adjust choice in the light of new experiences, in which case it will give rise to a Markov process on the set of relevant choices, in which case the probabilistic choice model will emerge as the steady state of the Markov chain. Alternatively, the static heuristic will make a choice, using clues from the environment, and it is the random nature of these clues that is behind the probabilistic choice.

In the psychology literature, heuristics generally represent simple, efficient decision-making rules which are learnt or developed to solve complex problems (see, Gigerenzer and Selten 2001). Often, these heuristics work well under many circumstances. However, because they are necessarily incomplete (or approximate) decision-making tools, they can lead to systematic decision-making errors or cognitive biases.

In the computer science literature, heuristics are defined more literally as logical algorithms used to find acceptable solutions to complex problems. Like in the psychology literature, heuristics in computer science are algorithms that approximate, rather than exactly solve, complex problems—their value being an ability to approximate the solution to problems for which no closed-form solution exists; or where time, memory or processing constraints necessitates a suitable approximation (rather than exact evaluation) of a problem. In this context, a heuristic's complexity is generally a function of its computational intensity, such as the number of lines of code or sequential operations it requires.

An example of simple heuristic is satisfying, which was suggested in the pioneering work of Simon (1955, 1956). A recent paper by Bendor et al. (2009) determines a class of problems for which the satisfying heuristics performs reasonably well in a sense that it eventually leads to the optimal choice. Basov et al. (2007) defined a heuristic in a way that combines elements from both psychology and computer science literature, as a simple decision rule, which an agent may invoke when faced with a decision to make. Agents select a given heuristic from their repertoire by embedding the decision they currently face into a class of similar decisions they have faced in the past and solved with that particular heuristic. As in the computer science literature, we further refine our definition of a heuristic by reference to its complexity. Basic heuristics are heuristics which are computationally simple or which require minimal cognitive resources. Complex heuristics are more computationally complex, cognitively demanding decision rules, which are formed by partitioning a problem and relying on more than one basic heuristic in much the same way that elementary programming operators can be combined to generate more complex algorithms.

A heuristic decision-making process, rather than a normative expected utility maximization framework, is appealing in the face of numerous well documented behavioral anomalies. For a broad collection and discussion of such anomalies, see Thaler (1991). While much of the behavior elicited and observed in behavioral experiments runs contrary to the outcomes expected from a EUT-maximizing decision-making framework, most anomalous experimental outcomes are consistent with a heuristic decision-making process. We briefly consider two such examples below.

Define the *caution heuristic* as a simple rule which states "when faced with a risky decision involving a choice between the status quo and an alternative outcome, always choose the status quo." Such a heuristic embodies the maxim "best to stick with what you know." Consider an environment involving such a choice, where a finite population of individuals is faced with a family of problems, $P$. Each problem $p \in P$ can be represented as a choice between two actions: safe and risky. The safe choice results in a certain payoff, $\pi_H(p)$, while the risky choice is represented as a binary lottery:

$$\pi^l(p) \text{ with probability } \gamma(p)$$
$$\pi^h(p) \text{ with probability } 1 - \gamma(p)$$

where $0 \leq \gamma(p) \leq 1$ and $\pi^l(p) \neq \pi^h(p)$. Payoffs and probabilities vary from problem to problem, and we assume that there are problems $p_1, p_2 \in P$ such that

$$\gamma(p_1)\pi^l(p_1) + (1 - \gamma(p_1))\pi^h(p)(p_1) > \pi_H(p_1)$$
$$\gamma(p_2)\pi^l(p_2) + (1 - \gamma(p_2))\pi^h(p_2) > \pi_H(p_2),$$

i.e., for some problems the safe option is the optimal choice and for the others the risk is worth taking. If an individual is cognitively unable to optimize for all problems in $P$, but has instead to choose either always safe option or always risky option, i.e., to choose between *Caution Heuristic* and *Gambling Heuristic* than *Caution Heuristic* is optimal if the safe option is optimal for sufficiently many problems in $P$.

This environment can be used to justify the commonly-observed endowment effect. We define the endowment effect as the tendency for individuals to value a commodity they own more than an identical one they could obtain through a market transaction. In a typical experiment to demonstrate the endowment effect, mugs bought at a university shop are distributed randomly among participants. Those who received a mug are asked about the minimal price at which they would be willing to part with the mug (WTA), while those who did not receive a mug are asked about the maximal price at which they would be willing to buy the mug (WTP). A consistent experimental finding is that WTA > WTP. To explain this result under assumptions of perfect rationality one must either assume unreasonably large income effects or postulate a direct preference for the endowment.

We argue, however, that neither is necessary if one gives up the idea that choices should be rationalized on a case-by-case basis. Instead, if one accepts the existence of a risk-averse heuristic such as the Caution Heuristic, which is instinctively invoked in environments involving a choice between the status quo and some alternate state-of-the-world, this pattern of behavior is justifiable and expected.

An important question to ask when considering such a model is: what determines the repertoire of heuristics available to a given agent? Our answer: evolution. To formalize this idea, one has to give up the assumption that individuals maximize utility on a case-by-case basis and specify instead a set of problems $P$ an agent faces and assume that there is a finite set of basic heuristics, $H$, available to that agent. The agent selects heuristic $h_j \in H$ and applies it to all problems in $P$. This generates a payoff $\pi(h_j, x)$ where $x = (x_1, \ldots, x_H)^2$ and $x_i$ is the fraction of the population that uses heuristics $h_i$. Then one has to specify the rule that governs the evolution of $x_i$. For example, Basov et al. (2007) assumed that it is described by the replicator dynamics and that the distribution of heuristics in a population correspond to asymptotically stable steady states of these dynamics.

## 3.3 Evolution of Social Norms

Recent research in a variety of social sciences suggests that social norms are important in governing incentives of workers within firms, managers, and independent agents. They were introduced into economic analysis by Akerlof (1976, 1982). Subsequently, Fehr (2000) demonstrated importance of reciprocal behavior in a series of controlled experiments, and Fehr and Gächter (2000) discussed the role of reciprocity in the general incomplete contracting framework. Some other types of social norms were studied in the literature. For example, Bernheim (1994), explicitly introduced the norm of conformity; Bohnet et al. (2001), studied the importance of trust; and Fehr and Schmidt (1999, 2000), studied the effects of norms of fairness on optimal incentives.

Relatively little is known, however, where social norms come from. One exception to this rule is a particular class of social norms, known as *conventions*, which are often modeled as pure strategy Nash equilibria in coordination games. Particularly large literature exists for $2 \times 2$ coordination games. Here I will discuss main techniques and findings in this area with the eye to applying them to the study of evolution of more general social norms.

The pioneering papers in the area, that of Foster and Young (1990), Kandori et al. (1993), and Young (1993), used evolutionary models with a persistent randomness to study the evolution of conventions. They focused on the models where agents from a homogeneous population interact over time. In these models in the medium-run a single convention prevails (though which one depends on the initial conditions), while in the long-run the risk-dominant outcome is selected as the unique stochastically stable solution. This means that, as time goes to infinity, the fraction of time the society will find itself playing the risk-dominant equilibrium goes to one. However, the society will return to the vicinity of the other equilibrium infinitely often. The main finding of these paper that in the long-run the society finds itself coordinating on the risk-dominant equilibrium for almost all time.

Evolution in these models takes place only in time and the spatial dimension is completely ignored. If one to take evolutionary models seriously as describing the life of our hunter-gathering ancestors, it is important to introduce spatial dimension

[2]With the standard abuse of notation we use $H$ for both the set of heuristics and its cardinality.

to study how customs, ways of behavior, and conventions spread from one group to another and how they are affected by physical factors.

In the context of the study of evolution of conventions, the papers that first introduced some spatial relationship between the players were Anderlini and Ianni (1996), Blume (1993, 1995), Ellison (1993), and Young (1999). In these papers the locations of different players are fixed, the players are connected by some network, and the behavior adopted by an individual depends on its intrinsic payoff and the behavior of her neighbors. This literature confirms the equilibrium selection results described above and shows that the speed of evolution is facilitated by the local nature of the interactions. Oechssler (1999), Ely (2002), Mailath et al. (2001), Dieckmann (1998), Bhaskar and Vega-Redondo (2004), Anwar (2002), and Blume and Temzelides (2003) allowed individuals to change their location. In all these models the location space is represented by a finite set of "cities." Over time the players may adjust both their strategy and their location.

In Oechssler's model there are no frictions to the adjustment process. He shows that the efficient convention will eventually prevail provided it was adopted from the start by at least one city. Ely's model is similar to that of Oechssler. He is able to drop the assumption that the efficient convention is initially present by allowing for mutations. In both models different conventions cannot coexist even in the medium-run, since individuals from the location where the inefficient equilibrium is played will migrate to the location where the efficient one is played at the first opportunity. Dieckmann's paper shows that the results are robust to the introduction of imperfect information. In all these models an opportunity to revise a strategy arrives at the same moment as an opportunity to migrate.

The paper by Mailath, Samuelson and Shaked allows for endogenous interactions, i.e. the players can avoid an undesired match. In addition, in their model time is continuous. They show that the long-run outcome in this case should be efficient.

New consensus seemed to arise from this literature. It holds that, in the presence of migration opportunities, Pareto efficient rather than risk-dominant outcome is going to be selected in the long-run.

Bhaskar and Vega-Redondo challenge the emerging consensus. Contrary to the rest of the recent literature, they assume that opportunities to revise strategy and to migrate never arise simultaneously. They show that the coexistence of the conventions in the medium-run is possible in the pure coordination games. They also show that an inefficient equilibrium can be selected in the long-run. Their equilibrium selection result, however, has nothing to do with the risk-dominance.

Anwar looks at the consequences of player movement between locations when there are constraints which limit the number of agents who can reside at each location. He concludes that if the constraints are sufficiently tight then the risk-dominance result continues to hold. However, when sufficient movement is possible, different conventions can coexist in the long-run. Moreover, the location with the tighter constraint coordinates on the payoff-dominant strategy.

Blume and Temzelides allow only to some agents to change their location. Both the strategy choice and the location is a myopic best response to the current strategy profile. The strategy choice is subject to noise, while the choice of the location is not. The authors conclude that if mobility of the mobile agents is restricted, the risk-dominant equilibrium is selected at every location. However, if there are enough mobile players to ensure efficient play at some location, then all mobile agents will move to that location. The utility of immobile agents depends on the mobility in a nonmonotone way. It increases at the low levels of mobility and decreases otherwise. Note, that migration in this model is strategic, though myopic. The equilibrium selection result crucially depends on the level of mobility within the country.

Despite all the differences in modeling assumptions in the papers cited above, the technical tools used by the authors are rather similar. In these sense they are all standard evolutionary game models as described in paragraph two of this Introduction.

A paper that stands apart from the most literature is Hofbauer et al. (henceforth, HHV) (1997). They model the deterministic dynamics by a differential equation for the share of players who play a particular strategy (e.g. the replicator dynamics) and add local non-strategic migration as a diffusion term. Therefore, they obtain a nonlinear partial differential equation (henceforth, PDE) for the share of population playing a particular strategy at a particular location. In this approach the medium-run outcomes correspond to the asymptotically stable steady states of the master PDE, which is similar to the notion of the medium-run outcome in a standard evolutionary game model. The notion of a long-run outcome is, however, somewhat different. In the HHV model the long-run outcome corresponds to the so-called spatial equilibrium. Intuitively, assume that a population is playing a medium-run outcome and a new strategy profile (not necessarily close to the initial one) spontaneously arises in a neighborhood of a particular location. The new strategy profile corresponds to a spatial equilibrium if the bubble of these new strategists will eventually cover the entire population. HHV (1997) proved that thus defined spatial equilibrium coincides with the risk-dominant equilibrium in $2 \times 2$ symmetric coordination games. I believe that this particular approach is best adapted to study evolution of general social norms in a real hunter-gathering society and will describe it and some of its generalizations in more details below.

Finally, it would be fair to mention the paper of Hansen and Kaarbøe (2002), which looked at the problem of equilibrium selection from a completely different point of view. In a recent paper they argued that if the interaction between players is conducted jointly at a population-wide level and does not lend itself to modeling with pairwise interaction any strict Nash equilibrium may be selected.

### *3.3.1 Evolution of Conventions with Mobile Players and Spatially Homogeneous Payoffs*

Let us start with the model evolution with migration and briefly summarize the results for the case of spatially homogenous payoffs. The model was first introduced by HHV (1997). It turns out that HHV's dynamics emerges from a spatial modification of Samuelson's (1997) aspiration and imitation model, provided that migration occurs much more often than the strategy revision. I will start by describing the HHV's concept of spatial equilibrium as the long-run outcome of the model, and extend the analysis to study some properties of the medium run outcome.

Consider a population of players who dwell in a measurable region $\Omega$ of the Euclidean space and are matched to play a symmetric $2 \times 2$ game. The strategy space of player $\alpha$ is $S_\alpha = \{X, Y\}$. Assume that payoffs are independent of the location and the underlying game is a coordination game. Hence, it has two Pareto ranked pure strategy equilibria $(X, X)$ and $(Y, Y)$, and a mixed strategy equilibrium.

Let $u(x, t)$ be the fraction of the individuals who are located at x at time $t$ and play strategy $X$. I will assume that $x \in R^n$. In applications $n = 1$ (community leaving along a river) or $n = 2$ (community populating a savannah) but I develop the theory for the general case in the anticipation of the space travel.

Let $\varphi(u)$ be the difference in the expected payoffs to strategies $X$ and $Y$ respectively, which depends on the fraction of the individuals playing strategy $X$ and located at $x$. It is given by:

$$\varphi(u) = \beta(u - u^*),$$

where $\beta > 0$ is some constant that depends on the parameters of the payoff matrix and $u^* \in (0, 1)$ is the fraction of $X$-strategists that corresponds to the mixed strategy equilibrium of the coordination game. In the absence of migration the evolution of $u(x, t)$ is governed by:

$$\frac{\partial u}{\partial t} = u(1 - u)\varphi(u). \tag{3.5}$$

Equation (3.5) is known as the replicator dynamics. It states that the rate of change of the fraction of the individuals playing a certain strategy is proportional to the difference between the payoff they earn and the average payoff earned by a representative individual in the population.

To introduce migration, consider a compact set $V \subset \Omega$ with a smooth boundary $\Sigma$. The change of the measure of the individuals playing strategy $X$ and located within $V$ occurs due to differential replication and migration. Therefore, assuming that the rate of differential replication is given by the right hand side of (3.5), one can write

$$\int \frac{\partial u}{\partial t} \mathrm{d}V = \int u(1 - u)\varphi(u)\mathrm{d}V + \oint \boldsymbol{m}\mathrm{d}\Sigma \tag{3.6}$$

Here vector $\boldsymbol{m}$ is the net migration flow through $\Sigma$ of the individuals playing strategy $X$. Assume that the migration decision is not strategic. In that case, the net outflow of the migrants playing strategy $X$ from a particular location will be proportional to the size of the population at that location playing strategy *X*. Hence, the migration will tend to equalize the fraction of the individuals playing strategy *X* across the locations, i.e. the migration flow will be proportional to the gradient of $u(\cdot)$, i.e.

$$\boldsymbol{m} = \gamma \nabla u.$$

Coefficient $\gamma \geq 0$ measures the degree of mobility of the population. Small values of $\gamma$ correspond to barriers to travels, such as mountainous terrains in the context of our hunter-gathering ancestors and migration restrictions in more modern context.

Using the divergence theorem, transform the second term on the right hand side of (3.6) in the following way:

$$\oint \boldsymbol{m} \mathrm{d}\Sigma = \int \mathrm{div}(\boldsymbol{m}) \mathrm{d}V,$$

where the divergence of $\boldsymbol{m}$ is defined by:

$$\mathrm{div}(\boldsymbol{m}) = \sum_{i=1}^{n} \frac{\partial m_i}{\partial x_i}$$

Taking into account that

$$\mathrm{div}(\nabla u) = \Delta u \equiv \sum_{i=1}^{n} \frac{\partial^2 u}{\partial x_i^2}$$

and that (3.6) should hold for any compact set with a smooth boundary, one obtains:

$$\frac{\partial u}{\partial t} = f(u) + \gamma \Delta u, \tag{3.7}$$

where

$$f(u) = u(1-u)\varphi(u)$$

If strategic considerations partially affect migration decisions, one can modify migration flow to become:

$$m = \gamma[(1-\alpha)\nabla u + \alpha\beta \nabla u],$$

where parameter $\alpha \in [0, 1]$ measures the strength of the strategic motive. Then $u(x, t)$ will be governed by an equation similar to (3.7) but with $\gamma$ replaced with $\gamma' = \gamma(1 - \alpha + \alpha\beta)$.

To proceed with a formal analysis of Eq. (3.7) let us define a function

$$V(u) = \int_0^u f(z)\mathrm{d}z,$$

and a functional:

$$F(u) = \int \left[\frac{\gamma}{2}\|\nabla u\|^2 - V(u)\right]\mathrm{d}V,$$

where $\|\cdot\|$ denotes the Euclidean norm of a vector. The first think to notice that the value of functional $F(\cdot)$ is nonincreasing along the solutions of Eq. (3.7). Indeed, Eq. (3.7) can be re-written as:

$$\frac{\partial u}{\partial t} = -\frac{\delta F}{\delta u}$$

where the right hand side is the variational derivative[3] of $F$. Therefore, using the chain rule

$$\frac{\mathrm{d}F(u(t))}{\mathrm{d}t} = -\left(\frac{\partial u}{\partial t}\right)^2 \leq 0.$$

This is by itself is a purely technical result that can be easily extended to the case of spatially heterogeneous payoffs. Its main role is that it enables us to analyze the stability of certain solutions. In particular, its simple corollary is that if the region populated by the agents has a finite positive Lebesgue measure then a stationary uniform solution with value of $u(x,t) = u^*$, where $u^*$ is a strict local maximum of $V(\cdot)$ is locally asymptotically stable.

To see it let us for simplicity assume normalize the Lebesgue measure of the region the agent populate to be one and define function:

$$L(t) = F(u(t)) + V(u^*).$$

Then

$$L(t) = \int \left[\frac{\gamma}{2}\|\nabla u\|^2 + V(u^*) - V(u)\right]\mathrm{d}V \geq 0,$$

with strict inequality if $u$ differs from $u^*$ on a set of a positive Lebesgue measure. Moreover, $L'(t) \leq 0$ with strict inequality for any $u$ such that $f(u)$ is not zero. Therefore, $L(t)$ is a Lyapounov function for (3.7) and $u^*$ is locally asymptotically stable.

---

[3]For a definition of the variational derivative see, for example, Gelfand and Fomin (2000).

Since the Nash equilibria can be found from the condition

$$V'(u) = 0$$

function $V(\cdot)$ can be interpreted as a potential of the game. Below, I will argue that it can also be interpreted as the stochastic potential, in the sense of Foster and Young (1990).

I will call the local maxima of $V(u)$ the medium-run outcomes. Note that though all medium-run outcomes are Nash equilibria of the underlying coordination game the reverse is not true. Apparently, a medium-run outcome that will eventually be reached by the population is history dependent.

#### 3.3.1.1 The Long-Run Outcome

Let us study the spatially stable solution of Eq. (3.7), which I refer to as the long-run outcome and the dynamics of convergence to it. Recall that intuitively the spatially stable solution is defined in the following way: assume a strategy profile corresponds to a spatial equilibrium if the bubble of players that play this profile will eventually cover the entire population. The spatial stability of the risk dominant equilibrium was first proved by HHV (1997). Their proof works for any learning process; however it does not allow calculating explicitly the speed of propagation of the switching wave. The contribution of this subsection is twofold. First, I assume that the learning process can be captured by the replicator dynamics and provide a different proof of the stability of the risk dominant equilibrium, which as a by-product allows us to arrive at the speed of propagation of new conventions. I also establish that the speed of propagation of new conventions is proportional to the square root of openness of the economy for any deterministic dynamics and estimate the life time of the risk-dominated convention. Second, I demonstrate that while in the one-dimensional world the risk-dominant convention will spread as soon as sufficient fraction of population at a given location switches to it, in a two-dimensional world it requires some area of a minimal size to switch to a new convention before it can spread.

To begin the formal analysis as a first observation note that function $V(\cdot)$ achieves its local maxima for the monomorphic populations ($u = 0$ or $u = 1$). Indeed, from the definition of $V(\cdot)$:

$$V'(u) = \beta u(1 - u)(u - u^*)$$
$$V''(u) = \beta(2(1 + u^*)u - 3u^2 - u^*).$$

Therefore,

$$\begin{aligned} V'(0) &= V'(1) = 0, \\ V''(0) &= -u^* < 0 \\ V''(1) &= u^* - 1 < 0, \end{aligned}$$

which implies that both monomorphic states are locally stable. Assume, however, that in an initially monomorphic population once in a while some nontrivial fraction of the population mutates, i.e. switches to an alternative strategy. A sufficiently big exogenous disturbance of this kind can take the population away from a local maximum to the global one. A steady state, which delivers the *global* maximum to $V$ is called stable, while the other local maximum is called metastable.

Let us prove the claim made in the previous paragraph, i.e., establish that in the long-run the population will switch from the metastable steady state to the stable one. In the process of demonstration we will see that the switching does not occur simultaneously at all locations, but rather travels along the population in a form of a switching wave.

Formally, once has to establish that Eq. (3.7) has a particular kind of solutions, known as wave solutions. Let us first consider the case $n = 1$ and look for a solution of Eq. (3.7) of the form:

$$u(x, t) = u(x - ct) \tag{3.8}$$

satisfying the boundary conditions:

$$\lim_{y \to +\infty} u(y) = 0, \lim_{y \to -\infty} u(y) = 1. \tag{3.9}$$

Substituting (3.8) into (3.7) one obtains:

$$\gamma u'' = -f(u) - cu'.$$

Now multiply both sides of this equation by $u'$ and integrate from $-\infty$ to $+\infty$ to arrive at:

$$\gamma \int_{-\infty}^{+\infty} u'(y)u''(y)\mathrm{d}y = -\int_{-\infty}^{+\infty} f(u(y))u'(y)\mathrm{d}y - c\int_{-\infty}^{+\infty} [u'(y)]^2\mathrm{d}y.$$

Taking into account the boundary conditions (3.9) and the fact that

$$f(u) = \beta u(1 - u)(u - u^*)$$

one obtains

$$c\int_{-\infty}^{+\infty}[u'(y)]^2\mathrm{d}y=\frac{\beta}{12}(1-2u^*).$$

Equation (3.8) implies that as long as $c>0$ there exists a switching wave that starts at equilibrium $(Y,Y)$ and moves the population to equilibrium $(X,X)$. In that case $(X,X)$ is called a spatial equilibrium. Otherwise, $(Y,Y)$ is the spatial equilibrium. Intuitively, the spatial equilibrium is an asymptotically stable steady state that is also stable against finite perturbations, i.e. the mutations that make a finite set of players at a neighborhood of particular location to change their strategies.

Note that $c>0$ if and only if $u^*<1/2$. Therefore, the spatial equilibrium coincides with the risk-dominant equilibrium in the sense of Harsanyi and Selten (1988). For a special case when $c=0$, corresponding to $u^*=1/2$, the spatial equilibrium is given by a standing wave

$$u(x)=\frac{1}{1+\exp\left(\sqrt{\frac{\beta}{2\gamma}}(x-x^0)\right)},$$

where $x_0$ is an arbitrary constant reflecting that with spatially homogeneous payoffs any point can serve as the origin. This case is, however, not generic. Moreover, this solution is not asymptotically stable.

To find the value of c let us introduce a notation

$$p(u)=u'(y).$$

Function $p(\cdot)$ gives the derivative of u with respect to $y$ as a function of $u$ at point$y$. Differentiating the above formula with respect to y one obtains:

$$u''=p'(u)u'=p\prime(u)p(u).$$

Therefore, systems (3.8), (3.9) can be written as:

$$\gamma pp'=-\beta u(1-u)(u-u^*)-cp$$
$$p(0)=p(1)=0.$$

Let us look for its solution in the form

$$p=Au(u-1).$$

Substituting it into the above equation, simplifying, and collecting coefficients before the same powers of $u$ one obtains the following system:

$$\begin{cases} 2\gamma A^2 = \beta \\ \gamma A^2 = 2\gamma A^2 u^* + cA \end{cases}.$$

Solving for $c$ one obtains:

$$c = \sqrt{\frac{\beta}{2\gamma}}(1 - 2u^*).$$

One can verify by a direct calculation that $c > 0$ if and only if

$$V(0) > V(1),$$

hence in the long run the population will adopt a convention with a higher value of $V$. The above analysis shows that generically the long-run outcome is unique. However, if $V(1) = V(0)$ then $c = 0$ and both steady states can coexist in the long-run. At the point of switching $u$ will change with a jump.

One can also see that $c > 0$ if and only if $u^* < 1/2$. This implies that if the society was in the risk-dominant equilibrium any mutation that affects a subset of the population with the measure less than one will eventually die out. Hence, assuming the probability of a mutation affecting almost all the population is zero, the society will remain at the vicinity of the risk-dominant equilibrium forever with probability one, once this equilibrium is reached. On the other hand, if the society started from the risk-dominated equilibrium a mutation has a chance of spreading and driving it to the risk-dominant one, provided it is big enough. It is worth noting that function $V(\cdot)$ coincides with the stochastic potential of Foster and Young (1990).

Note also that the speed of the switching wave is increasing in the degree of mobility, $\gamma$, and is proportional to its square root of the openness. This conclusion is universal. Universality here has a double meaning. First, it does not depend on the functional form of $\varphi(\cdot)$, i.e., it will still hold if replicator dynamics in is replaced by some other payoff monotone dynamics. Second, it does not depend on the dimensionality of space.

Basov (2007) also estimated the minimal size of disturbance necessary to initiate the switch to the risk-dominant equilibrium and the typical time such a switch will take.

For the case $n = 2$ most results are similar. One crucial difference, however, that for the risk-dominant convention to spread it should initially take hold in an area with some minimal radius, given by:

$$R = \frac{\gamma}{c}.$$

It will imply that for a custom of a tribe to spread it is not enough for it to be numerous, it should cover sufficiently large area. For a modern example of this phenomenon, assume that a populous but compact city adopts a new driving convention. Then, everybody else traveling between two different locations can simply avoid driving through the city. For this to become too costly the city should have a very large spread. Avoiding the city is, however, not an option impossible in the one-dimensional world.

#### 3.3.1.2 The Medium-Run Outcomes

I have already proved that spatially uniform solutions corresponding to all players at all locations playing the same pure strategy Nash equilibrium are asymptotically stable. In this subsection I prove that these are all asymptotically stable steady states. I call them medium-run outcomes. Moreover, I argue that the medium-run outcome reached by the population is determined only by the spatial average of the initial state. This spatial average is equal to the fraction of population that plays strategy X worldwide. For the sake of simplicity, I will give a proof for $n = 1$. Generalization to the case $n > 1$ is straightforward.

If $n = 1$, without loss of generality, assume $\Omega = [0, 1]$. Let us expand $u(x, t)$ in the Fourier series:

$$u(x,t) = \sum_{n=-\infty}^{+\infty} u_n(t)\exp(2\pi \mathrm{inx})$$

where $i$ is the imaginary unit ($i^2 = -1$), and $u_k(t)$ is defined by

$$u_k(t) = \int_0^1 u(x,t)\exp(-2\pi \mathrm{ikx})\,\mathrm{d}x.$$

Substituting the Fourier expansion in Eq. (3.7) it is straightforward to obtain an infinite system of ordinary differential equations for the Fourier components. Basov (2007) analyzed the system and proved that $u_0(t)$ will converge generically to one of the local maxima of $V(u^0)$, while all other Fourier components will converge to zero. Moreover, the local maximum to which $u^0(t)$ will eventually converge depends only on $u_0(0)$. Hence, any initial distribution of the strategies converges to a spatially uniform stationary outcome. Since $u_0(t)$ is the spatial average of $u(x, t)$ at time $t$, the medium-run outcome is determined by the spatial average of the initial distribution only.

Note that the medium-run outcome is spatially uniform, provided payoffs do not depend on x. This implies that for customs and conventions to differ across the locations (for example, for the national cultures to exist) in the medium-run one has to postulate that the payoffs for some strategy profile differ across the locations.

#### 3.3.1.3 The Model with Spatially Heterogeneous Payoffs

So far I have assumed that the payoffs in the underlying coordination game are the same at all locations. Now I am going to relax the last assumption. For an example of such situation, assume that you live in a hunter-gathering society and agreed to meet with one of your tribesmen for a deer hunt. You have two choices, to honor the agreement or to break it. If both you and your partner choose to honor the agreement, then you will end up catching the deer and get payoff of one each. If both of you break your word and go fishing (assume it is the second best thing to do) both of you will get payoff zero. If you honor the agreement and your partner breaks his word and goes fishing, he will get zero, while it will be too late for you to go fishing (you are too far from the pond), so you will have to settle for a rabbit. Your payoff will, in general, depend on the density of the rabbit population at the location you leave. Normalize payoffs in the following way:

$$\begin{aligned}\pi(X,X) &= 1\\ \pi(Y,X) &= \pi(Y,Y) = 0\\ \pi(X,Y) &= -v(x) < 0.\end{aligned}$$

Let $u^*(x)$ be the probability with which strategy $X$ is played in the mixed strategy equilibrium. Then function $u(x,t)$ satisfies the following nonlinear PDE:

$$\frac{\partial u}{\partial t} = u(1-u)(u-u^*(x)) + \gamma\Delta u(x).$$

Let us assume that $n = 1, \gamma = 1/4$ and

$$u^*(x) = \frac{1-\tanh(x)}{2},$$

where the hyperbolic tangent is defined by

$$\tanh(x) = \frac{\exp(x)-\exp(-x)}{\exp(x)+\exp(-x)}.$$

There corresponding off diagonal payoff is:

$$v(x) = \exp(-2x).$$

Note that equilibrium $(X,X)$ is risk-dominant for $x > 0$, while $(Y,Y)$ is risk-dominant for $x<0$. It is straightforward to check that

$$u_0(x) = \frac{1+\tanh(x)}{2}$$

solves the evolution PDE. Note that the solution converges to the risk-dominant equilibrium as the absolute value of $x$ goes to infinity. However, for any finite $x$ both $X$ and $Y$ strategists are present at the location. Moreover, there share does not correspond to any equilibrium share apart from point $x = 0$. Basov (2007) proves that this solution is asymptotically stable.

Are such solutions a result of a fine-tuning of the parameters of the model or are they quite typical? The first step in answering this question is to establish the existence of stationary spatially nonuniform solutions of the evolution equation. It turns out that existence can be established under rather general condition on both finite and infinite domains (see, for example, Bernfeld and Lakshmikantham 1974). Let $u_0(x)$ be such a solution. Basov (2007) proved that to analyze its stability one has to study the eigenvalues of the linear differential operator

$$H = -(1/2)((d^2)/(dx^2)) + V(x)$$

where

$$V(x) = \frac{2}{\gamma} f_u(u_0(x), x)$$

and subscript denotes partial differentiation. The solution is stable if and only if all eigenvalues of operator $H$ are negative. Operators of this form are known as Schrödinger operators. They are well studied and operators with negative eigenvalues are by no means exceptional (see, for example, Landau and Lifshitz 1958). Therefore, the situation described in the example is rather typical.

I described techniques that can be used to study evolution of social norms using as example well-developed literature on evolution of conventions. Similar techniques can be used to analyze evolution of more general social norms. Similar questions can arise: can different social norms coexist, how fast do they spread from one location to the other, and want determines their ultimate long-term survival.

## 3.4 On Coevolution of Preferences, Social Norms, and Decision Rules

Above I have described models that allow studying evolution of preferences, decision rules of boundedly rational decision-making, and social norms on its own. One can, however, try to deal with a more challenging task and try to merge the model of evolution of preferences with an evolutionary model of boundedly rational behavior. For this purpose, notice that given that utility deviates from inclusive fitness, there might be evolutionary advantage to ambiguity aversion, since it will prevent individuals from taking undue risks. On the other hand, given that individuals are ambiguity-averse, bounded rationality may prove beneficial, since it will prompt agents to try choices that they would have otherwise avoided. On the other hand, as we have already seen, bounded rationality leads to deviation of the preferences from the inclusive fitness. Therefore, bounded rationality, ambiguity aversion, and the wedge between the utility and fitness may reinforce each other.

Assume, for example, that a hunter-gather tribe lives along a river. They can spend the day finishing, which will result in a random fish catch, governed by a known probability distribution (situation of risk) or venture on a hunting expedition, where they will face uncertain outcome. Assume that hunting provides a slightly higher expected fitness than fishing according to the true (but unknown to the decision makers) probability distribution.

Assume that the decision makers are boundedly rational. Then the model discussed above suggests the decision makers will evolve to put much higher utility on hunting than on fishing. This behavior will be adaptive as long as the environment is stable. However, should the payoffs change, for example, should the hunting grounds become invaded by a dangerous predator, and such preferences can prove disastrous. Ambiguity aversion will make the individuals less likely to take the uncertain option, protecting them from such an unexpected change.[4] On the other hand, given the individuals are ambiguity-averse, bounded rationality can prove beneficial, since it will make individuals experiment more often preventing them from getting stuck with old ways past their expiration dates. Moreover, ambiguity aversion may reinforce preference biases in a part of population, creating a group of individuals with direct preferences for novelty, experimentators, and another group of more conservative individuals, imitators.[5]

Ambiguity aversion may also evolve to counterbalance the preferences for excessive risk taking. Dekel and Scotchmer (1999) argued that since in many species a winner-take-all game determines the males' right to reproduce, males will evolve to be risk-takers. They also point out that psychological and sociological evidence gives extra support to the argument that males are more risk taking than females. Such preferences may be less beneficial once the environment changes and winner takes it all feature is no longer relevant. Ambiguity aversion could have evolved to partially offset preference for excessive risk taking.

The main concern of this book is to investigate how ambiguity aversion, social norms, and bounded rationality affect optimal contracts, rather than to investigate their coevolution. However, I believe brief thoughts shared in this Section can provided a basis for future research in this area.

---

[4]Alternatively, caution against a particular gamble can be enforced by a social norm.

[5]See Gale and Rosenthal (1999) on learning outcomes in such a society.

## References


Akerlof, G. A. (1976). The economics of caste, the rat race, and the other woeful tales. *Quarterly Journal of Economics, 90*, 599–617.

Akerlof, G. A. (1982). Labor contracts as partial gift exchange. *Quarterly Journal of Economics, 97*, 543–569.

Anderlini, L., & Ianni, A. (1996). Path dependence and learning from neighbors. *Games and Economic Behavior, 13*, 141–177.

Anwar, A. W. (2002). On the coexistence of conventions. *Journal of Economic Theory, 107*, 145–155.

Basov, S., Blanckenberg, L., & Gangadharan, L. (2007). Behavioral Anomalies, Bounded Rationality and Simple Heuristics, Department of Economics, Working Papers Series 1012, The University of Melbourne.

Basov, S. (2007). *Partial differential equation in economics and finance*. New York: Nova Publishers.

Bendor, J. B., Kumar, S., & Siegel, D. A. (2009) Satisficing: A 'Pretty Good' Heuristic. *The B.E. Journal of Theoretical Economics (Advances), 9*(1), article 9.

Bernfeld S. R., & Lakshmikantham, V. (1974). *An introduction to nonlinear boundary value problems*. New York, NY: Academic Press.

Bernheim, B. D. (1994). A theory of conformity. *Journal of Political Economy, 102*, 841–877.

Bhaskar, V., & Vega-Redondo, F. (2004). Migration and the evolution of conventions. *Journal of Economic Behavior & Organization, 55*, 397–418.

Blume, A., & Temzelides, T. (2003). On the geography of conventions. *Economic Theory, 22*, 863–873.

Blume, L. (1993). The statistical mechanics of strategic interaction. *Games and Economic Behavior, 5*, 387–423.

Blume, L. (1995). The statistical mechanics of best response strategy revision. *Games and Economic Behavior, 11*, 111–145.

Bohnet, I., Frey, B. S., & Huck, S. (2001). More order with less law: On contract enforcement, trust, and crowding. *The American Political Science Review, 95*, 131–144.

Dekel, E., & Scotchmer, S. (1999). On the evolution of attitudes towards risk in winner-take-all games. *Journal of Economic Theory, 87*, 125–143.

Dieckmann, T. (1998). The evolution of conventions with mobile players. *Journal of Economic Behavior & Organization, 38*, 93–111.

Ellison, G. (1993). Learning, local interaction, and coordination. *Econometrica, 61*, 1047–1071.

Ely, J. (2002). Local conventions. *Advances in Theoretical Economics, 2*, 1–30.

Fehr, E. (2000). Do incentive contracts crowd out voluntary cooperation?. Institute for Empirical Research in Economics of University of Zurich, Working Paper #34. http://www.iew.uzh.ch/wp/iewwp034.pdf

Fehr, E., & Gächter, S. (2000). Cooperation and punishment in public goods experiments. *American Economic Review, 90*, 980–994.

Fehr, E., & Schmidt, K. M. (2000). Theories of fairness and reciprocity—evidence and economic applications. In M. Dewartripont, L. P. Hansen, & S. Turnovsky (Eds.), *Advances in economic theory, eighth world congress of econometric society*. Cambridge, UK: Cambridge University Press.

Fehr, E., & Schmidt, K. (1999). A theory of fairness, incentives, and contractual choices. *Quarterly Journal of Economics, 114*, 817–868.

Foster, D., & Young, P. (1990). Stochastic evolutionary game dynamics. *Theoretical Population Biology, 38*, 219–232.

Gale, D., & Rosenthal, R. W. (1999). Experimentation, imitation, and stochastic stability. *Journal of Economic Theory, 84*, 1–40. I. M.

Gelfand, I. M., & Fomin, S. V. (2000). *Calculus of Variations*. Mineola, NY: Courier Dover Publications.

Gigerenzer, G., & Selten, R. (2001). *Bounded rationality: Adaptive toolbox*. Cambridge, MA, USA: The MIT Press.

Hansen, P. S., & Kaarbøe, O. M. (2002). *Equilibrium selection in coordination games with simultaneous play*. Economic Theory, 20, 793–807.

Harsanyi, J., & Selten, R. (1988). *A general theory of equilibrium selection in games*. Cambridge, MA: MIT Press.

Hofbauer, J., Hutson, V., & Vickers, G. T. (1997). Travelling waves for games in economics and biology. *Nonlinear Analysis, Theory, Methods, and Applications, 30*, 1235–1244.

Kandori, M., Mailath, G., & Rob, R. (1993). Learning, mutation and long run equilibria in games. *Econometrica, 61*, 29–56.

Landau, L. D., & Lifshitz, E. M. (1958). *Quantum mechanics, non-relativistic theory*. London, UK: Pergamon Press.

Luce, R. D. (1959). Individual choice behavior, New York, NY, USA: Wiley.

Mailath, G., Samuelson, L., & Shaked, A. (2001). Endogenous interactions, in The evolution of economic diversity, A. Nicita, & U. Pagano (Eds.), New York, NY, USA: Routledge.

Oechssler, J. (1999). Competition among conventions. *Mathematical and Computational Organization Theory, 5*, 31–44.

Robson, A. (2001). Why would nature give individuals utility functions? *Journal of Political Economy, 109*, 900–914.

Robson, A., & Samuelson, L. (2011). The evolutionary foundations of preferences. In A. Bisin, & M. Jackson (Eds.), *Handbook of social economics*. North-Holland.

Samuelson, L. (1997). *Evolutionary games and equilibrium selection*. Cambridge, MA: MIT Press.

Simon, H. A. (1956). *Reply: Surrogates for uncertain decision problems*. Office of Naval Research.

Simon, H. A. (1955). A behavioral model of rational choice. *Quarterly Journal of Economics, 69*, 99–188.

Thaler, R. H. (1991). *Quasi-rational economics*, New York, NY, USA: Russell Sage Foundation.

Young, P. (1993). The evolution of conventions. *Econometrica, 61*, 57–84.

Young, P. (1999). Diffusion in social networks, Center on Social and Economic Dynamics, Working Paper #2.

# Chapter 4
# Complexity Constraints and Optimal Contracts

Optimal mechanisms considered in the literature are often rather complex. Traditional approach ignores complexity costs and concentrates solely on provision of optimal incentives. This is a complete reversal of the earlier trend in mechanism design literature, which dealt with the size of communication necessary to implement a particular mechanism, while completely ignoring incentives. For early papers that utilized this approach, see Mount and Reiter (1974) and Hurwicz (1977). Some papers, mentioned in the Introduction, try to address both types of concerns.

Complexity of the optimal contacts is often argued to underlie the fact that most real life contracts are incomplete, i.e., they do not specify actions to be taken to the party in every possible state of the world. The employment contracts are the prime example of contractual incompleteness. When contracts are incomplete many important decisions have to be negotiated in the future, which leads to holdup problems. So, it is important to understand why despite the costs imposed by holdup problem contractual incompleteness is ubiquitous in the real world. In particular, it is often argued that the main reason for contractual incompleteness is high cost of listing every contingency and precisely specifying expected behavior of the parties.

An early paper in this tradition is Dye (1985), who assumes that the cost of writing a contract is increasing in the number of its contingencies. Therefore, two contracts with the same number of mutually exclusive contingencies have the same cost according to Dye. For example, contract that specifies a certain payoff if and only if event $A$ occurs will have the same complexity that a similar contract with $A$ replaced by other event $B$. This does not take into account that description of $B$ can be more complex than description of $A$. For an example of a situation where it is likely to happen, consider the case when $A$ is a subset of $B$.

Anderlini and Felli (1994, 1998) address the latter difficulty and assume that the state space has cardinality of continuum and contracts correspond to computable functions. They argue that for the computability constraint to be able to preclude an approximate first best, the decision process used to select the contract is also



S. Basov, *Social Norms, Bounded Rationality and Optimal Contracts*,
Studies in Economic Theory 30, DOI 10.1007/978-981-10-1041-5_4

constrained to be algorithmic. In that case the resulting optimal contract is incomplete. A similar approach is taken by Krasa and Williams (2000), however, they assume that the number of relevant contingencies is countably infinite. They also require that the contractual outcome can depend only on a finite number of contingencies.

Battigalli and Maggi (2002) build on the earlier work of Dye (1985), Anderlini and Felli (1994, 1998) and Krasa and Williams (2000). However, they impose more structure and get shaper predictions from the model. In this chapter we will provide a more detailed discussion of the paper by Battigalli and Maggi (2002). Segal (1999) models complexity in a simpler way assuming that there are *n* widgets that can be traded on a future date, but only one of them, special widget, will turn out to be useful.

In this chapter, I review the papers of Anderlini and Felli (1994), Battigalli and Maggi (2002), and Segal (1999). I also compare results obtained by Segal with those obtained by Mukerji (1998) and Grant et al. (2006).

## 4.1 A Model of Computational Complexity

Anderlini and Felli (1994) assume that a contract in order to be written has to be algorithmic in nature and explore whether the incompleteness of contracts can be explained by this restriction. They are motivated by the idea that in order for the contract to be enforceable in a court of law, the mapping it provides from the states of nature into outcomes should be computable by a Turing machine. They argue that this requirement together with the requirement that the contracting parties selection process endogenously generates incomplete contracts.

Their argument proceeds along the following lines. Think of a contact as a finite list of clauses. Once the state of nature is realized, the parties have to examine which clauses apply to the given circumstances and what actions are prescribed by the contract. In order for the parties or the enforcement agency to be able to perform the task, the relation between the states of the world and the actions prescribed should be of the algorithmic nature. The formal notion of algorithmic adopted by Anderlini and Felli (1994) is that of a general recursive function. Intuitively, a function is recursive if a Turing machine capable of computing it in finite time exists.

It is a well-known mathematical fact that not all functions are computable. It is easy to understand on the cardinality grounds. There are an uncountable number of functions, but only countably many algorithms. In this context this implies that not all contracts can be written. Indeed, assume the state of nature can take uncountable many value and consider a contract that prescribes two distinct outcomes according to whether the particular state of nature is realized. In this case a computable description of the contract necessarily contains an exact description of the critical state. But, by the previous argument, some states will not be computable.

Impossibility to write arbitrary contracts is, however, not sufficient to generate endogenously incomplete contracts, since it turns out that even if the first best contract is not computable, it can be approximated by a sequence of computable contracts.[1] To achieve endogenous incompleteness Anderlini and Felli assumed that feature of the process of contract selection is itself algorithmic. When this additional restriction is imposed, they were able to show that the parties may choose to write an endogenously incomplete contract.

Indeed, consider the contracting problem for which the first best requires to identify a critical state of nature, which is not computable. One can always find a non-computable state that cannot be approximated in a computable way. Anderlini and Felli call such states undescribable and assume that the critical state has this property. Now consider a sequence of computable contacts that approximate the first best. Computability restriction on the selection process will imply that this sequence is itself computable. Therefore, there must exist a computable approximation of critical state.

## 4.1.1 A Formal Model

Anderlini and Felli consider the following contracting problem. Two risk-averse parties face some common risk and enter a contract to share it. They denote the common consequence $c \in R$ and assume that the parties have utilities $V_i(c), i \in \{1, 2\}$. The randomness of the environment is captured by $s \in [0, 1]$. The purpose of the contract is to specify a sharing rule $x(\cdot)$ of the realized surplus. The sharing rule and the state of nature determine the consequence for party $i$ to be $f_i(x(s); s)$. The sharing rule defines the indirect utility function according to:

$$U_i(x(s), s) = V_i(f_i(x(s); s)),$$

which is assumed to be bounded and continuous in $x$ for any given $s$. Anderlini and Felli also assume that both parties have symmetric, but incomplete information of the state of nature, i.e., they have a common prior.

An optimal sharing rule can be found by maximizing utility of one of the parties, holding the utility of the other party constant. Another way to obtain an optimal sharing rule is to maximize a social welfare function, increasing in the utilities of the participants. Anderlini and Felli fix such (sufficiently well behaved) social welfare function and call the allocation induced by the optimal sharing rule, $x^*(s)$, is known as the first best. They assume that the first best is well defined, and can be approximated with an arbitrary precision by a step function with finitely many values.

[1] This is similar to possibility to approximate any of uncountable number of real number by a sequence of rational numbers, which belong to a countable set.

A written contract is a finite set of clauses that, given a realization of the state of nature, yields an outcome in a finite number of steps. These steps can be thought as a program ran by a Turing machine,[2] which is identified by its program. A program is a finite string of instructions written in a formal programming language. One can order such programs, for example, alphabetically creating in this way a computable one to one correspondence between programs and the natural numbers. The Gödel number[3] is defined as the number that corresponds to a program in this ordering.

A program, identified by its Gödel number, is applied to a contract in a following way: the realized state of nature, $s$, provides the input for the program in the following way. Consider the binary expansion of $s$,[4] which can be thought of as the evidence about the realization of the state.[5] Since the program has to terminate in finite time it cannot read the entire sequence describing the state of the nature. Instead, only a finite portion of it will.

Given the input, the contract has to specify *an information-gathering procedure*, which decides which portion of description of the state is to be used, and an *outcome determination procedure* that determines the value of the sharing rule. The information-gathering procedure determines which characteristics (digits of the binary expansion of $s$) to scan first. Then, depending on the result of the first round of scanning, where to look next, and so on, for some number of rounds. It also must eventually Holt, after finite number of rounds. The information gathered at this stage now becomes an input for the outcome determination procedure, which computes the value of the sharing rule. Computability restrictions on both procedures imply that the final outcome is a binary rational number with a finite number of nonzero digits. Anderlini and Felli call them regular rational numbers. This description implies that the set of sharing rules that can be implemented via this two-stage procedure is equivalent to the set of sharing rules that can be computed using a Turing machine.

The above considerations imply that the sharing rules the parties can implement using the described procedure are step functions, having as their ends regular binary rational numbers. Therefore, a computable contract will partition state space [0, 1] into intervals, each of which corresponds to a particular value of the sharing rule. The authors' convention about resolving the ambiguities of the binary expansions will also imply that intervals will be closed below but open above. The reverse also turns out to be true, given a set of intervals, satisfying the above-mentioned conditions, one can find a computable contract generating this partition.

---

[2]Turing machine is essentially an idealized version of a computer with an infinite memory.

[3]See, for example, Cutland (1980).

[4]Some real numbers allow for two different binary expansions, for example, 0.1(0) and 0.0(1), where (*a*) denotes an infinite series of *a*, both correspond to 0.5 in the decimal notation. In this case the authors use the one with biggest number of zeros, in this case the first one.

[5]For example, one can think of the potential state as a countably infinite set of characteristics, each of which can be either present or absent in the realized state.

For a simple example of a first best sharing rule that cannot be implemented by a computable contract, let us follow Anderlini and Felli, and consider a coinsurance problem with the first best sharing rule taking the value $l > 0$ for any state of nature on the unit interval except for the state $s'$, while

$$x(s') = h < l.$$

Since $x(\cdot)$ does not provide an admissible partition described above, it cannot be implemented by a computable contract.

Anderlini and Felli proceed to define incomplete contracts as the ones that induce the partition of the state space, which is not as fine or finer, than the partition induced by the first best contract.[6] They argue that the algorithmic nature of contracts is not enough by itself to generate any substantial incompleteness. More precisely, the first best utilities can be approximated to any desirable degree by a computable contract. This happens because the set of regular rationals is everywhere dense in [0, 1].[7] To generate endogenously incomplete contracts, we need to introduce further restrictions. To understand the nature of these restrictions, assume that the agents try to approximate the first best via a sequence of computable contracts. It is reasonable to require for this sequence itself to be computable.

To formalize the above restriction, Anderlini and Felli define the choice criterion by a requirement that when faced with two possible contracts the parties will also choose one that results in more efficient outcome, provided they can computably verify the latter assertion. One can think of it in a following way: start with a particular contract and compare its performance with another one. Should the new contract be a better one, discard the current contract from the computer's memory, replace it with a new one, and repeat. One can then define a sequence of computable contracts, where contract $x_n$ is followed by $x_{n+1}$, where $x_{n+1}$ is the contract with the lowest Gödel number, which is an improvement on $x_n$.

Each contract in the sequence induces a partition of the state space. Anderlini and Felli than proceed to show that there are simple coinsurance problems such that for any sensible choice criterion, the partition generated by the limit of the above-defined contract is incomplete. Moreover, partitions defined for all contracts in the sequence, with a possible exception of a finite number, are incomplete. Incompleteness results from inability to describe ex-ante in an algorithmic contract some relevant states of nature, and therefore formalizes the reasons that where informally advanced in Grossman and Hart (1986) and Hart and Moore (1990). Note that in this paper incompleteness emerges without the need for any transaction costs, however, small. However, it requires infinite (in fact, uncountable) state space.

---

[6]This definition at first glance seems different from a more standard definition that defines a contract to be incomplete if it does not prescribe actions in some states of nature. See, Anderlini and Felli (1994) for a thorough response to this critique.

[7]Some additional care should be taken if the agents' common prior is not absolutely continuous with respect to Lebesgue measure, but this is a purely technical consideration that should not concern as here.

## 4.2 A Model of Linguistic Complexity

In the model of linguistic complexity, developed by Battigalli and Maggi (2002) language consists of two types of sentences. Sentences in set $\Pi^e$ with a generic element $e_i$ are used to describe events, while sentences in the set $\Pi^a$ with a generic element $a_i$ are used to describe action. Sentences that belong to set $\Pi = \Pi^e \cup \Pi^a$ are called primitive. Using primitive sentences and logical operations $\vee$ (or), $\wedge$ (and), $\neg$ (not), $\rightarrow$ (implication), and the logical constant T (tautology), we can form new sentences in the language. If all primitive sentences that were used to construct sentence $s$ belong to $\Pi^e$, we say that $s$ describes a contingency and write $s \in \Lambda^e$. If all primitive sentences that were used to construct sentence $s$ belong to $\Pi^a$ we say that $s$ describes an action and write $s \in \Lambda^a$.

**Definition** A contract is a pair $(g, t)$ such that $g = \wedge(e_k \rightarrow a_k)$, where $e_k \in \Lambda^e$, $a_k \in \Lambda^a$, and $t \in R$.

In words, a contract specifies action for any contingency and the overall payment. Since Battigalli and Maggi (2002) assume that states and behavior are verifiable, all parties and risk neutral, and contracts are perfectly enforceable, there is no reason to allow the transfer to depend on the contingency. Finally, they assume that the cost of writing a contract is proportional to the number of different primitive sentences used to write a contract, with a cost of adding a primitive sentence being $c > 0$. They also assume that the cost of writing logical connectives (*and, or, implies, not*), the logical constant, and the transfer is zero. Under these assumptions they show that when the potential surplus from engaging into a relation is sufficiently small relative to the writing costs, the optimal contract leaves substantial discretion to the agent. Discretion of agent disappears as the surplus rises or the writing costs vanish. Another interesting result is that uncertainty of the environment leads to higher degree of discretion.

Let us illustrate some of these conclusions by a simple example. Suppose that principal hires an agent to perform a task for her. Performing the task requires exerting costly effort $a$, with cost of effort given by:

$$C(a) = \frac{a^2}{2}$$

Assume that effort can take two values, i.e., $a \in \{\theta_H, \theta_L\}$. Assume also that two possible events could happen: $e_1$ and $e_2$. If event $e_1$ happens then the marginal productivity of effort is $\theta_H$, i.e., the output is $\theta_H a$, while if event $e_2$ happens then the marginal productivity of effort is $\theta_L$, i.e. the output is $\theta_L a$. For example, let us assume that the agent is an agricultural employee, event $e_1$ is having a rainy summer, and event $e_2$ corresponds to a draught. The output corresponds to the harvest produced by the agent.

Let $p$ be the probability that event $e_1$ occurs. If the cost of writing a contract is zero the optimal contract will take the form:

$$\left((e_1 \to \theta_H) \wedge (e_2 \to \theta_L), p\frac{\theta_H^2}{2} + (1-p)\frac{\theta_L^2}{2}\right),$$

i.e., it will require the agent to exert high effort if the summer is rainy, low effort in the case of draught, and pay the expected cost of effort. However, under the assumptions made by Battigalli and Maggi, this contract will incur cost $4c$. The expected profits to the principal net of costs of writing the contract are:

$$p\frac{\theta_H^2}{2} + (1-p)\frac{\theta_L^2}{2} - 4c.$$

Let us compare this with a contract

$$\left(\theta_H, \frac{\theta_H^2}{2}\right),$$

i.e., to a contract that requires the agent to always work hard and compensates for this effort. Such a contract exhibits *rigidity* in terms of Battigalli and Maggi, i.e., obligations of the agent are not sufficiently contingent on the state of nature.

The cost of writing such a contract is $c$ and the expected profits to the principal are:

$$(2p-1)\frac{\theta_H^2}{2} + (1-p)\theta_H\theta_L - c.$$

It is easy to verify that the fully contingent contract dominates the rigid one if:

$$(1-p)(\theta_H - \theta_L)^2 \geq 6c.$$

Finally, let us consider contract

$$\left(T, \frac{\theta_L^2}{2}\right),$$

i.e., the contract does not specify any action and promises to compensate for the cost of low effort. The cost of writing such a contract is zero. This contract will exhibit discretion in terms of Battigalli and Maggi, i.e., it does not specify the agent's behavior in sufficient detail. Note, that since the effort is costly and the agent is free to choose any level, she will exert low effort and the profits to the principal will be:

$$(1-2p)\frac{\theta_L^2}{2}+p\theta_H\theta_L.$$

The fully contingent contract will dominate the discretionary one if and only if:

$$p(\theta_H+\theta_L)^2 \geq 8c.$$

These results show that fully contingent contracts are preferable if costs of writing a contract are small and potential surplus from inducing the correct action is large. Also note that when uncertainty of the environment is low, i.e., $p$ is close either to one or the zero, fully contingent contract is not optimal. Intuitively, in these scenarios the principal is almost sure of the state of the world and therefore will specify the action of the agent relevant for this state as if the state will occur with certainty, saving on the costs of writing a contingent contract.

In a subsequent paper Battigalli and Maggi (2008) extended the model to a dynamic setting by allowing the contracting parties to interact repeatedly and modify contracts at any point in time. They found that tasks characterized by a higher degree of uncertainty are more likely to be governed by contingent clauses, i.e., by more complete contracts, while lower-uncertainty tasks are more likely to be governed by a spot approach, i.e., renegotiation is likely to play significant role, leading to holdup problems. They also predicted that the fraction of tasks governed by spot contracting should be higher when the external environment is more stable.

## 4.3 Complexity as the Number of Unforeseen Contingencies

Finally, in the papers by Hart and Moore (1999) and Segal (1999) complexity is modeled as the number of unforeseen contingencies at the moment the contract is drafted. Here I will present the simpler Hart and Moore's version. Hart and Moore assume that parties meet, sign a contract, make a relation-specific investment, and finally trade. For simplicity of exposition here it is assumed that only the seller invests, though generalization for the case when both parties can invest is straightforward. The reader is referred to the Appendix of Hart and Moore's paper for that case.

Following Hart and Moore (1999), assume that at date the parties will find it efficient to trade in one and only one of $N$ potential goods, referred below as widgets, but they cannot know in advance, which one will be suitable for trade. It is assumed that a priori any widget has an equal probability to be the special widget. The widget that should be traded is referred to as the special widget. It is worth $v$ to the buyer. The production cost of the special widget $c \in \{c_L, c_H\}$, where $v > c_H > c_L > 0$, and the probability $\pi(\cdot)$ that $c = c_L$ is strictly increasing in the seller's investment, $\sigma$, which is assumed to be noncontractable. Investment is made after the parties have signed a contract, but before the special widget is revealed. It is assumed that $\pi(\cdot)$ is twice differentiable, with $\pi'(\sigma) > 0, \pi''(\sigma) < 0$. The other widgets are generic. Their production costs are assumed to be located between $c_L$ and $c_H$ in increments of $1/N$, i.e., the $k$th lowest cost of a generic widget is:

$$c_k = c_L + \frac{k}{n}(c_H - c_L). \tag{4.1}$$

Once the state of nature, i.e., the identity of the special widget and the cost to the seller are realized, they are observed by both parties, but cannot be observed by an external enforcer.

The first best allocation solves:

$$\max_{\sigma}[\pi(\sigma)(v - c_L) + (1 - \pi(\sigma))(v - c_H) - \sigma].$$

Note that if parties can agree not to renegotiate at the final date, the first best can be easily achieved by seller making the buyer a take it or leave it offer to buy the special widget at price $v$. Note that implementability of the first best does not depend on the parties' ability to costlessly describe widgets at the initial date. However, if it is impossible to commit not the renegotiate, the first best can no longer be implemented. What is more, even if the parties are able to completely describe the widgets ex-ante, the value of the optimal contract based on such a description goes to zero as the complexity of the environment, parametrized as the number of widgets goes to infinity. Therefore, if signing an optimal contract involves even small transaction costs, the parties will prefer to sign a null contract.

Complexity plays in this argument the role similar to that ambiguity played in the paper by Mukerji (1998), which I described earlier in this chapter. It is not enough by itself to justify the contractual incompleteness, however, it significantly reduces the value of the optimal compete contract and one needs to invoke only very small transaction costs to justify the ultimate incomplete (null) contract. In Chap. 6 of this book, I will describe a hidden action model under bounded rationality due to Basov (2003), where the agents end up choosing the effort with an error. I will argue that the value of the optimal contract decreases to zero as the variance of error term increases. Taking the variance of error term to be a measure of complexity of the environment, one can draw some parallels between that model and the model of Hart and Moore.

Battigalli and Maggi (2002), on the other hand need a non-infinitesimal cost of adding an extra clause to a contract to make the optimal contract incomplete. Note, however, that all these models are capable to generate optimal incompleteness allowing for a finite set of the states of the world. Anderlini and Felli (1994), on the other hand, are able to generate optimally incomplete contracts without invoking the notion of transaction costs, but at a cost of requiring an uncountable infinity of the states of the world.

The Hart and Moore's argument proceeds as follows. First they note that since each widget has an equal a priori probability to be special widget symmetry requires that the expected payment to the parties will depend only on the cost realization for the production of the special widget and not on its identity. Also note that due to the ability of ex-post renegotiation one can assume that it is always the special widget that is traded and the full ex-post surplus is captured.

Assume parties play an abstract mechanism $M$ Let $p(L, \Gamma)$ be the overall expected payment[8] the buyer makes to the seller, when the realization of the cost[9] is $c_L$ and generic widgets are arranged according to some permutation $\Gamma$. Then the buyer's and the seller's equilibrium expected payoffs are $v - p(L, \Gamma)$ and $p(L, \Gamma) - c_L$, respectively. Similarly, if $p(H, \Gamma^*)$ is the overall expected payment the buyer makes to the seller, when the realization of the cost is $c_H$, and generic widgets are arranged according to some permutation $\Gamma^*$, the buyer's and the seller's equilibrium expected payoffs are $v - p(H, \Gamma^*)$ and $p(H, \Gamma^*) - c_H$.

The revelation principle implies that it is sufficient to restrict attention to mechanisms where buyer and seller announce the state of the world and require that both parties find it optimal to announce the truth. Now suppose the buyer and seller make incompatible claims: the buyer claims that the state is $\{c_H, \Gamma^*\}$ and the seller that it is $\{c_L, \Gamma\}$. Assume that if this is the case the mechanism specifies that the buyer pays seller some amount $q$ and widget $k$ is traded with probability $\alpha_k \geq 0$. It also prescribes that there is no trade with probability:

$$\alpha_0 = 1 - \sum_{k=1}^{N} \alpha_k \geq 0.$$

The incentive compatibility constraint for the seller in state $\{c_H, \Gamma^*\}$ is:

$$q - \sum_{k=1}^{N-1} \alpha_k c_k - \alpha_N c_H \leq p(H, \Gamma^*) - c_H.$$

The incentive compatibility constraint for the buyer in state $\{c_L, \Gamma\}$ is[10]:

$$q - \alpha_1 c_L - \sum_{k=2}^{N} \alpha_k c_k \geq p(L, \Gamma) - c_L.$$

Rearranging these two inequalities and taking into account (4.1) one obtains:

$$p(H, \Gamma^*) - p(L, \Gamma) \geq \frac{N-1}{N}(c_H - c_L),$$

[8]Due to risk neutrality of the parties only the expected payments matter.

[9]From here on by *cost* I mean the cost of production of the special widget, unless specified otherwise.

[10]The constraint is expressed in terms of the seller's payoffs. This can be done since the sum of the seller's and buyer's payoffs conditional on the cost realization is fixed.

which is equivalent to:

$$p(L, \Gamma) - c_L \leq p(H, \Gamma^*) - c_H + \frac{1}{N}(c_H - c_L).$$

This implies that the seller can capture at most $1/N$th of the cost reduction and as the number of widgets goes to infinity any incentive to invest in the cost reduction disappears.

## 4.4 Complexity and Economics: A Summary

Complexity can prevent individuals from making optimal decisions in two different ways: it can make thinking or drafting of complete agreements too costly and make agents to fall back on heuristics (situation be described in Chap. 3) or erode the value of the complete contract and make agents sign incomplete contracts (situation described in Battigalli and Maggi 2002, and reviewed in this chapter). Model of Anderlini and Felli (1994) can be viewed as a special case of the model with direct complexity costs, the costs being zero for the computable contracts and infinity for non-computable ones. Alternatively, one can assume that there are no direct computational costs associated with complexity, but it erodes the value of the complete optimal contract. The models that utilize this notion of complexity were developed by Hart and Moore (1999) and Segal (1999). In these models complexity alone is not enough to affect the outcome of economic transactions, but it will lead to extreme contractual incompleteness in conjunction with even trivial transaction costs. In Chap. 7, I present an alternative view of complexity and the magnitude of mistakes made by the agents in response to the contract devised by the principal and show that it also has an effect of eroding the value of the complete optimal contract. However, instead of invoking transaction cost, I rely on the social norm of reciprocity and an efficiency wage model to explain insensitivity of the wage to performance measures.

To summarize, complexity of the environment can be an important part of explanation of reliance on heuristics in decision-making, persistent mistakes, and structure of optimal contracts. However, the remaining challenge is how one should model complexity. The concept has different meanings in different areas of science. For example, in computational complexity theory, it refers to the amount of resources required for the execution of algorithms that is studied. This allows classifying computational problems by complexity class, such as, for example, $P$, problems that can be solved in polynomial time, or NP, problems for which one can verify a proposed solution in polynomial time.[11] In algorithmic information theory, the Kolmogorov complexity (also called descriptive complexity, algorithmic complexity or algorithmic entropy) of a string is the length of the shortest binary

[11]It is still an open question in the computer science whether $P = \text{NP}$.

program that outputs that string. Minimum message length is a practical application of this approach. In information processing, complexity is a measure of the total number of properties transmitted by an object and detected by an observer. In physical systems, complexity is a measure of the probability of the state vector of the system. In network theory, complexity is the product of richness in the connections between components of a system. There are many more definitions of complexity used in other areas of science. It remains to be seen which one of these definitions, if any, has to prove most fruitful in mechanism design applications.

## References

Anderlini, L., & Felli, L. (1994). Incomplete written contracts: undescribable states of nature. *Quarterly Journal of Economics, 109*, 1085–1124.

Anderlini, L., & Felli, L. (1998). Describability and agency problems. *European Economic Review, 42*, 35–59.

Basov, S. (2003). Incentives for boundedly rational agents, 2003. *The BE Journal in Theoretical Economics (Topics), 3*, 1–14.

Battigalli, P., & Maggi, G. (2002). Rigidity, discretion, and the costs of writing contracts. *American Economic Review, 92*, 798–817.

Battigalli, P., Maggi, G. (2008). Costly Contracting in a Long-Term Relationship. *RAND Journal of Economics, Summer 2008*, 39(2), 352–377.

Cutland, N. J. (1980). *Computability: An introduction to recursive function theory*. Cambridge, UK: Cambridge University Press.

Dye, R. A. (1985). Costly contract contingencies. *International Economic Review, 26*, 233–250.

Grant, S., Kline, J., & Quiggin, (2006). *Lost in translation*. Business Papers: Bond University.

Grossman, O. Hart. (1986). The costs and benefits of ownership: A theory of lateral and vertical integration. *Journal of Political Economy, 94*, 691–719.

Hart, O., & Moore, J. (1990). Property rights and the nature of the firm. *Journal of Political Economy, 98*, 1119–1158.

Hart, O., & Moore, J. (1999). Foundations of incomplete contracts. *Review of Economic Studies, 66*, 115–139.

Hurwicz, L. (1977). On the dimensional requirements of informationally decentralized Pareto satisfactory adjustment processes. In Studies in resource allocation, K. J. Arrow, & L. Hurwicz (Eds.), Cambridge, UK: Cambridge University Press.

Krasa, S., & Williams, S. R. (2000). *Incompleteness as a constraint in contract design*, University of Illinois, Working Paper.

Mount, & Reiter, S. (1974). The informational size of message spaces. *Journal of Economic Theory, 8*, 161–192.

Mukerji, S. (1998). Ambiguity aversion and incompleteness of contractual form. *American Economic Review, 88*, 1207–1231.

Segal, I. (1999). Complexity and renegotiation: A foundation for incomplete contracts. *Review of Economic Studies, 66*, 57–82.

# Chapter 5
# Probabilistic Choice and Optimal Contracts

In previous chapter I discussed the problem of optimal contracting when the parties face complexity cost. While existence of complexity costs can be seen as a form of bounded rationality, the agents in this type of models still follow maximizing behavior. In this and subsequent chapters I will consider more drastic deviations from the conventional model by assuming that the agents do not follow maximizing behavior. Models of bounded rationality that deviate from maximizing paradigm can be divided into two groups: static and dynamic. In the first type of models it is usually assumed that the choice behavior is probabilistic, i.e., the probability of choosing a particular option depends on its utility. In most models it is assumed that this dependence is monotonic, i.e., options with higher utilities are chosen with higher probabilities. However, as demonstrated by Basov (2005a), the latter assumption is not innocuous if one considers probability distributions of static models as steady states of a learning process.

Models of bounded rationality that model the learning process explicitly are known as dynamic models. From the point of view of a mechanism designer, dynamic models present an additional difficulty, since the choice of a mechanism will affect not only the final choice probabilities, but also the speed and effectiveness of learning. I will consider some such models in the next chapter. In this chapter I will concentrate on the static models.

## 5.1 Trembling Hands and Optimal Screening

This section is based on Laffont and Martimort (2002), who developed a hidden information model where the agents can be of two types, efficient and inefficient. The principal offers a menu of contracts. When the agent makes a choice between contracts she might miscalculate payoffs by $\varepsilon$ and choose the wrong contract. Agents are ex ante rational and take the possibility of the mistake into account when making their participation decisions. If the support of mistakes is small the only



S. Basov, *Social Norms, Bounded Rationality and Optimal Contracts*,
Studies in Economic Theory 30, DOI 10.1007/978-981-10-1041-5_5

mistakes are by efficient agents behaving as if they were of inefficient type. Therefore, the apparent proportion of low-type agents increases. As a result the utilities of both the principal and agents of efficient type decrease.

Before formulating the model of Laffont and Martimort, let us briefly remind the reader the basic monopolistic screening model with two types. Assume a monopolist can produce a unit of good with quality $x$ at a cost $c(x)$, where $c(\cdot)$ is a strictly convex, twice differentiable function. Monopolist is risk neutral. Preferences of a consumer over a unit of good with quality $x$ are given by

$$v(\theta, x, m) = u(\theta, x) + m,$$

where $u(\theta, x)$ is a twice continuously differentiable utility function.

Each consumer wants to buy at most one unit of the monopolist's goods. Type $\theta$ is private information of a consumer. However, it is common knowledge that $\theta \in \{\theta_H, \theta_L\}$, with $\theta_H > \theta_L$ and probability that $\theta = \theta_H$ is equal to $p_H \in (0, 1)$. If consumer does not purchase a good from the monopolist she receives utility $u_0(\theta)$. For simplicity assume it does not depend on type and normalize it to be zero. Finally, assume that $u_1 > 0$, $u_2 > 0$, $u_{12} > 0$. Here $u_i$ denotes the derivative of $u$ with respect to the $i$th argument, and $u_{12}$ is the cross-partial derivative with respect to $\theta$ and $x$. The positivity of this cross-partial derivative is known as the Spence–Mirrlees condition or the single-crossing property.

It is a standard result in the mechanism design theory that, assuming full rationality of the consumers, without loss of generality one can restrict the mechanisms used by the monopolist to be a menu of two contracts: one designed for the low type and the other designed for the high type. The contracts should satisfy two types of the constraints: participation constraints that ensure that each type of a consumer chooses to buy the product from the monopolist and the incentive constraints that ensure that each type of consumer chooses the contract designed for her.

Formally, the monopolist offers a pair of contracts: $(x_L, t_L)$ and $(x_H, t_H)$ designed for the low and high types, respectively, to solve the following maximization problem:

$$\max(p_H(t_H - c(x_H)) + (1 - p_H)(t_L - c(x_L))$$

subject to

$$\begin{aligned} &u(\theta_L, x_L) - t_L \geq 0 \\ &u(\theta_H, x_H) - t_H \geq 0 \\ &u(\theta_L, x_L) - t_L \geq u(\theta_L, x_H) - t_H \geq 0 \\ &u(\theta_H, x_H) - t_H \geq u(\theta_H, x_L) - t_L \end{aligned}$$

The first two constraints state that both types would like to buy the good from the monopolist and are known as the individual rationality constraints. The last two constraints, known as the incentive compatibility constraints, ensure that no one would like to choose the contract meant for the other type.

One of the basic results in the monopolistic screening model is Stole's constraint reduction theorem that states that under the single-crossing property only two of these constraints bind: the participation constraint for the low type, i.e., this type gets her reservation utility (in this case, zero) and the incentive compatibility for the high type, i.e., the high type is indifferent between her contract and that of the low type. Note that it implies that the high type gets the information rent, i.e., her utility exceeds the value of the outside option.

Using the binding constraints to exclude tariffs and solving the monopolist's problem, it is easy to see that quality provided to the high type can be found from

$$u_2(\theta_H, x_H) = c'(x_H).$$

Therefore, the high type is provided with the good of the efficient quality, this is the well-known "no distortions at the top" property that holds in the unidimensional screening models.[1]

The quality consumed by the low type satisfies

$$u_2(\theta_L, x_L) - c'(x_L) = \frac{p_H}{1 - p_H}(u_2(\theta_H, x_L) - u_2(\theta_L, x_L)) > 0. \tag{5.1}$$

Therefore, $x_L$ is below the efficient level. Corresponding tariffs can be found from the binding constraints.

Let $\pi(p_H)$ denote the monopolist's profits as a function of the probability of high type. Then, using the envelope theorem it is straightforward to show that

$$\pi'(p_H) = \int_{x_L}^{x_H} (u_2(\theta_H, q) - c'(q))dq > 0,$$

where the inequality follows from the first-order conditions and the single-crossing property. Therefore, the monopolist's profits increase in the proportion of high types.

Now let us follow Laffont and Martimort (2002) and assume that though consumers are ex ante rational, they can make a mistake ex post and choose a contract designed for the other type. Ex ante rationality means that the agents are aware of the possibility that they may make a mistake and take it into account when deciding whether to purchase the good in the first place. If we assume that mistakes are modeled by an additive random term $\varepsilon$, drawn from a cumulative distribution

[1]Situation is more complicated in the multidimensional models. The concept of top type is not well-defined for such models. If the number of quality dimensions equals the dimensionality of type one can prove under some technical conditions that there are not distortions on the boundary of type set in the direction normal to the boundary (Basov 2005b).

function $G(\cdot)$ with a compact and sufficiently small support, then the only kind of wrong decision will be the high type choosing a contract designed for the low type.

Let $U_i$ denote the utility of type $i \in \{H, L\}$ when she chooses the contract designed for her. Then type $H$ chooses the proper contract if and only if

$$U_H \geq U_L + (\theta_H - \theta_L)x_L + \varepsilon.$$

Let $\varepsilon^*$ be the highest value of $\varepsilon$ for which the high type will still choose the contract designed for her. Then going through the same argument as above one can show that the high type is still served efficiently, while the quality supplied to the low type is given by formula (5.1) but with $p_H$ been replaced by $p_H G(\varepsilon^*)$. Therefore, effectively the fraction of high types decreases and so do the profits of the monopolist.

Several comments are due about this result. First, the way bounded rationality is introduced in the model does not invalidate the revelation principle. Therefore, when looking for the optimal mechanism, one can still restrict oneself to a menu of contracts. Laffont and Martimort (2002) discussed another way of introducing bounded rationality, assuming that the agents are satisfying rather than maximizing, but this conclusion still holds. Later in this chapter, I will introduce a model of bounded rationality that violates the revelation principle and leads to a more drastic deviation from the optimal contract. Second, in this model it is the monopolist who carries the burden of boundedly rational behavior of the consumers. Therefore, she will have incentives to educate the consumers or to make the choice easier for them by providing a better description of the product. Below in this chapter I will present several models, where the seller or sellers benefit from irrational behavior of the buyers and have incentives to engage in obfuscating activities. I will also argue that competition has the power to decrease obfuscation.

## 5.2 Nonlinear Pricing Under Bounded Rationality

This section is based on Basov and Mirrlees (2009) and introduces bounded rationality into the standard Mussa and Rosen (1978) model of nonlinear pricing. Nonlinear tariffs are ubiquitous in the real world. Such tariffs are charged by utility companies, auctions, and governments in a form of taxes. Mechanism design theory and, in particular, the theory of nonlinear pricing provides the main tool for analyzing such situations. Often, however, optimal contracts obtained in this way look very complex. Therefore, insistence on the hypothesis of rational behavior becomes less compelling and modeling-bounded rationality on the side of the agents becomes desirable.

Similar to Laffont and Martimort, Basov and Mirrlees modeled bounded rationality as a possibility of mistake. However, unlike Laffont and Martimort, they have continuum of types and all agents have a continuum of choices and are faced with a nonlinear tariff rather than a menu of choices. More importantly, we do not assume ex ante rationality, i.e., the agents may end up with a utility level below that of their outside option. They find the integro-differential equation for the optimal tariff and solve it for some particular cases. We show that the optimal tariff remains almost the same for the consumers who purchase the high quality good, but exhibits irregular behavior at low qualities. Intuitively, since the optimal tariff is convex, the monopolist benefits from the erratic behavior of the consumers. But she has to trade this off against the extraction of the surplus generated by underlying preferences and technology. Since under perfect rationality the profits obtained by the monopolist by selling a good of the particular quality increase in quality, the monopolist's incentives to deviate from the tariff obtained under perfect rationality decreases with quality.

Before formulating the model of Basov and Mirrlees we briefly revisit Mussa and Rosen (1978). The approach here follows Wilson (1993) and differs from the standard account in that we exclude the consumer's private information from the model and obtain a calculus of variations problem for the optimal tariff and product line. This formulation is the most convenient one for introducing bounded rationality.

### 5.2.1 Mussa and Rosen Model Revisited

Consider a continuum of consumers and assume that each of them is interested in buying at most one unit of an indivisible good. Different units of the goods may differ in quality, $x$. The marginal rate of substitution between quality and money, $\alpha$, does not depend on quality but differs across the consumers, i.e., utility takes the form

$$u(\alpha, x, t) = \alpha x - t,$$

where $t$ is the amount paid to the monopolist. Parameter $\alpha$ is private information of the consumer. It is common knowledge that $\alpha$ is distributed on $[\beta, \infty]$ according to a twice continuously differentiable, everywhere positive density $f(\alpha)$. The cumulative distribution function corresponding to density $f(\cdot)$ is denoted $F(\cdot)$. Define the virtual type by

$$v(\alpha) = \alpha - \frac{1 - F(\alpha)}{f(\alpha)}$$

and assume that it is strictly increasing in $\alpha$, continuously differentiable, and unbounded from above, and that $v(\beta) \leq 0$. These assumptions guarantee that the optimal product line is $[0, \infty)$ and that the convexity constraint on the optimal tariff does not bind. The utility of the outside option is the same across consumers and is normalized to be zero. The cost of production is additive across goods and convex in quality. It is given by a twice differentiable, strictly increasing, convex function $c(x)$. It is assumed that $c(0) = c'(0) = 0$.

The monopolist selects a tariff $p(\cdot)$ to maximize profits, i.e., the monopolist solves

$$\max_{p(\cdot)} \int_0^\infty (p(x(\alpha)) - c(x(\alpha)))\mathrm{d}F(\alpha)$$

subject to

$$\begin{aligned} &x(\alpha) \in \operatorname{argmax}(\alpha x - p(x)) \\ &\max(\alpha x - p(x)) \geq 0 \end{aligned} \tag{5.2}$$

Under the above assumptions the optimal tariff exists and is twice continuously differentiable and convex for all $x > 0$. The first of the conditions (5.1), known as the incentive compatibility constraint, implies the following first-order condition:

$$\alpha = p'(x). \tag{5.3}$$

It is well known that if the virtual type is strictly increasing the second-order condition for the incentive compatibility, stating that $p(\cdot)$ is convex, is never binding. Therefore, one can use (5.3) to change the variable of integration in the monopolist's objective to $x$ and rewrite the monopolist's objective as

$$\max_{p(\cdot)} \int_0^\infty (p(x) - c(x))f(p'(x))p''(x)\mathrm{d}x$$

subject to

$$p(0) = 0$$

Performing integration by parts one can transform the monopolist's objective to be

$$\max_{p(\cdot)} \int_0^\infty (p'(x) - c'(x))(1 - F(p'(x))\mathrm{d}x.$$

The Euler–Lagrange equation is given by

$$\frac{\mathrm{d}}{\mathrm{d}x}\{(p'(x) - c'(x))f(p'(x)) - [1 - F(p'(x))]\} = 0.$$

Integrating it and taking into account the transversality condition one obtains

$$v(p'(x)) = c'(x), \tag{5.4}$$

where $v(p'(x))$ is the virtual type evaluated at the marginal tariff. The latter equation should be solved subject to the participation constraint $p(0) = 0$. This is a Cauchy problem for the tariff. Therefore, given our assumptions on $v(\cdot)$, the solution exists and is unique. Moreover, under our assumption on the cost and the virtual type, $p'(x)$ is increasing; therefore the convexity constraint is satisfied.

Consider, for example, the case when the distribution of types is exponential on $[\beta, \infty]$, with $\beta \leq 1$, i.e.,

$$f(\alpha) = \exp(\beta - \alpha)$$

on the support and zero everywhere else.

Then the Cauchy problem for Eq. (5.4) can be solved explicitly and the solution is

$$p(x) = c(x) + x. \tag{5.5}$$

It is straightforward to see that some consumers will choose not to purchase the good, i.e., they will belong to the so-called exclusion region, which is given by

$$\alpha \leq p'(0) = 1.$$

### 5.2.2 *Introducing Bounded Rationality in the Mussa and Rosen Model*

Basov and Mirrlees introduced bounded rationality in the Mussa and Rosen's model by assuming that consumers compute their optimal quality with a mistake. Note that this is different from the assumption made by Laffont and Martimort, who assume that the consumers make a mistake while evaluating the utility of the contract. Another difference is that in this model one allows for a continuum of types, while Laffont and Martimort work with a discrete type set.

Formally, Basov and Mirrlees assume that a consumer whose optimal quality is $y$ computes his desired quality to be $x$, where $x$ is a random variable with a probability density $g(x, y)$, and corresponding cumulative distribution function $G(x, y)$. It is assumed that all consumers make the same kind of mistakes: the distribution of mistakes does not explicitly depend on type, though it depends on it implicitly, through $y$. The monopolist is aware of the possibility that the consumer may make a mistake and takes it into account when devising the optimal contract, i.e., she solves

$$\max \int_{0}^{+\infty} E[p(x) - c(x)|y] \mathrm{d}F(p'(y))$$

subject to

$$p(0) = 0.$$

Here the expected profit of producing a good of quality $x$ conditional on $y$ is

$$E[p(x) - c(x)|y] = \int_{-\infty}^{+\infty} (p(x) - c(x))g(x, y)\mathrm{d}x.$$

In most applications it is assumed that

$$g(x, y) = 0 \text{ for } x < 0,$$

i.e., it is impossible to choose a negative quality. However, in some examples it will be convenient to allow for negative qualities to be chosen by mistake, though the optimal quality is always positive. To accommodate this case the limits of integration are chosen to be from negative to positive infinity.

An important result, summarized in the theorem below is that under some technical assumptions, the most important of which is that the consumers' mistakes are unbiased, the monopolist will benefit from the bounded rationality of the consumers. The intuition is rather simple. As we discussed above, given the structure of the preferences, the optimal tariff in the Mussa and Rosen's problem with rational consumers will be convex. Therefore, if the monopolist simply offers the same tariff to the boundedly rational consumers as she would have offered to the rational ones, the revenues will increase due to the Jensen's inequality. Additional assumptions make sure that the tariff is more convex than the cost, so not only the revenues, but also the profits increase.

**Theorem 5.1** *Assume that the consumers' preferences, distribution of types and the cost satisfy all the assumptions made above and that also the following assumptions hold:*

$$E(x|y) = y$$
$$H(\alpha) \equiv \frac{(1 - F(\alpha))f'(\alpha)}{(f(\alpha))^2} \leq -1$$

*for almost all y according to the Lebesgue measure. Then the monopolist will earn higher profits if the consumers are boundedly rational than when they are rational.*

The first of the assumptions of the theorem implies that the consumers' mistakes are unbiased, i.e., they choose the correct quality in expectation. The second assumption is technical in nature and ensures that the optimal tariff offered to rational consumers is more convex than the cost. Though this assumption is somewhat strong, it holds for some reasonable distributions. For example, it holds as a strong inequality for the Pareto distributions, with the exponential one being the boundary case for which the condition holds as equality.

*Proof* Define $\pi^*$ as the monopolist's maximum profit and let $r(\cdot)$ be the optimal tariff when there are no mistakes. Since the monopolist is always free to offer tariff $r(\cdot)$ to the consumers one must have

$$\pi^* \geq \int_0^{+\infty} E(r(x) - c(x)|y)f(r'(y))r''(y)\mathrm{d}y. \tag{5.6}$$

First, let us demonstrate that our assumptions imply that $r(x) - c(x)$ is convex in $x$. Indeed, evaluating the derivative of virtual type, one can show that

$$v'(\alpha) = 2 + H(\alpha) \leq 1$$

under the assumptions of the theorem, and therefore, since Eq. (5.4) implies that

$$\frac{\mathrm{d}(r'(x) - c'(x))}{\mathrm{d}c'(x)} = \frac{1}{v(r'(x))} - 1 > 0,$$

i.e., $r'(x) - c'(x)$ is a nondecreasing function of $c'(x)$, which itself is a nondecreasing function of $x$. Thus $r'(x) - c'(x)$ is nondecreasing in $x$, which is equivalent to $r(x) - c(x)$ being convex in $x$. Equation (5.5) and the Jensen's inequality then imply that

$$\pi^* \geq \int_0^{+\infty} (r(y) - c(y))f(r'(y))r''(y)\mathrm{d}y,$$

which is the monopolist's profit in the absence of mistakes. ■

Theorem 5.1 shows that under some conditions the monopolist may benefit from the bounded rationality of the consumers. This result is in contrast with the result obtained by Laffont and Martimort. The source of this ambiguity in hidden information models is that bounded rationality has two effects: it erodes the total social surplus but also prevents agents from being able to extract their information rents.

The monopolist will prefer less rational consumers if the latter effect dominates the former. In this case the monopolist may have incentives to obfuscate consumers, for example, via uninformative advertisements, to increase the probability of mistakes.

Preferences for obfuscation are not limited to hidden information models and may arise even when consumers do not possess any private information. I will discuss a model along these lines later in the book. However, without information rents it is hard to imagine how the principal can benefit from bounded rationality of consumers in a long-term relationship as long as we assume that even boundedly rational agents do not stay for long in a relationship that gives them utility below their reservation level. As a result, in the hidden action models the cost of boundedly rational behavior is born solely by the principal. An example of such a model will be described later in the book.

The next step is to derive the first-order condition that characterizes the optimal tariff under bounded rationality. It is convenient to express the monopolist's objective in terms of the function $q(x) = p'(x)$. Function $q(\cdot)$ represents the value of marginal increase in quality. After some obvious transformations, the monopolist's profits can be expressed as

$$\pi = \int_{0}^{+\infty} (1 - F(q(y))(\int_{-\infty}^{+\infty} (q(x) - c'(x))G_2(x,y)\mathrm{d}x)\mathrm{d}y$$

To find the optimal $q(\cdot)$ take any integrable function $h(\cdot)$ and define a real-valued function $V(\cdot)$ by

$$V(t;h) = \int_{0}^{+\infty} (1 - F(q(y) + th(y))\left( \int_{-\infty}^{+\infty} (q(x) + th(x) - c'(x))G_2(x,y)\mathrm{d}x \right)\mathrm{d}y$$

Since $q(\cdot)$ is optimal, the derivative of $V(\cdot)$ with respect to $t$ at zero should be zero, i.e.,

$$\int_{0}^{+\infty}\int_{-\infty}^{+\infty} [(1 - F(q(y)))h(x) - (q(x) - c'(x))f(q(y))h(y)]G_2(x,y)\mathrm{d}x\mathrm{d}y = 0.$$

After standard manipulations and taking into account that this equation must hold for all integrable test functions $h(\cdot)$ one obtains the following integral equation for $q(\cdot)$:

$$\int_{-\infty}^{+\infty} \{G_2(y,x)(1 - F(q(x)) - (q(x) - c'(x))G_2(x,y)f(q(y))\}\mathrm{d}x = 0. \tag{5.7}$$

This is an integral equation for the marginal tariff $q(\cdot)$. For the details of derivation, see Basov and Mirrlees (2009), who also proved existence of the solution under certain regularity conditions. They establish that the solution exists as long as the consumers are not too irrational. When solution exists, it can be approached using the method of successive approximations.

Suppose for some particular combination of fundamentals one can find the explicit solution $q_0(\cdot)$. If the fundamentals in the problem of interest differ only slightly from the ones for which the problem is explicitly solvable, then starting with $q_0(\cdot)$, one can construct series of successive approximations employing the following procedure. Given $q_k(\cdot)$, one can find $q_{k+1}(\cdot)$ by solving a linear integral Fredholm equation of the first kind, i.e.,

$$\int_0^{+\infty} G_2(x,y)q_{k+1}(x)\mathrm{d}x = \chi(y) + \int_0^{+\infty} \frac{1-F(q_k(x))}{f(q_k(y))}G_2(y,x)\mathrm{d}x,$$

where

$$\chi(y) = \int_0^{+\infty} c'(x)G_2(x,y)\mathrm{d}x.$$

For example, if consumers are nearly rational, $q_0(\cdot)$ can be chosen to be the solution to the problem with rational consumers. For a detailed discussion of this case the reader is referred to Basov and Mirrlees (2009). Below I provide another example where the closed-form solution can be found explicitly.

*Example* Assume that the cost is quadratic and distribution of types is exponential and the mistake is additive, i.e.,

$$f(\alpha) = \exp(-\alpha), c(x) = \frac{x^2}{2}.$$

Let us also assume that

$$x = y + \varepsilon,$$

where $\varepsilon$ is a random variable with zero mean and finite variance, distributed according to a probability density function $\phi(\cdot)$. Note that this specification allows for negative qualities to be chosen by mistake. However, Chebyshev's inequality guarantees that the probability of such a choice is nonnegligible only for low types, for which $y$ does not significantly exceed the variance of $\varepsilon$. Moreover, it can provide a good approximation for random choice rule, which does not allow for negative $x$ for sufficiently large $y$. Further, assume that

$$\mathrm{E}(\exp(-\varepsilon)) = \int_{-\infty}^{+\infty} \exp(-z)\phi(z)\mathrm{d}z = t < \infty$$

This condition will be satisfied, for example, for the normal distribution and for any distribution with compact support. Note that convexity of the exponential function and Jensen's inequality imply that $t \geq 1$, moreover, $t = 1$ if and only if the distribution of $\varepsilon$ degenerates, i.e., if the agents are rational. It is straightforward to check that

$$q(x) = x + t$$

solves Eq. (5.7). The corresponding tariff is

$$p(x) = c(x) + tx.$$

Note that it coincides with tariff (5.5) for $t = 1$, i.e., if and only if the consumers are rational. Also, note that boundedly rational consumers always pay a higher price and the optimal tariff is steeper. In particular, if the noise is normal with variance $\sigma^2$ than

$$t = \exp\left(\frac{\sigma^2}{2}\right).$$

The last observation implies that bounded rationality exacerbates distortions and diminishes the available social surplus. Since Theorem 5.1 implies that the monopolist will in this case be at least as good under bounded rationality as she were under perfect rationality, the result implies that the burden of boundedly rational behavior is born by consumers. Consumers suffer twice: they face a less favorable tariff and choose suboptimally given the tariff.

Another interesting specification is the one where mistakes are multiplicative. The reader is referred to Basov and Mirrlees (2009) for the analysis of that case.

The model developed in this section belongs to the class of hidden information models, i.e., models where one party possesses some private information (in this model the marginal valuation of quality) at a stage prior to contracting, i.e., before the tariff is designed. It is important to point out that in this model the cost of bounded rationality is born by the boundedly rational agents themselves, i.e., consumers. The monopolist, on the other hand, might benefit from the bounded rationality of consumers.

The result on the incidence of the cost of bounded rationality in this model is in a sharp contrast with that of Laffont and Martimort (2002). The difference is driven by the fact that in the latter model the mistakes of the agents do not interfere with their a priori ability to extract information rents.

It also stands in sharp contrast with a result on incidence of bounded rationality in a hidden action situation. In the latter case, bounded rationality increases the noise-to-output ratio and, therefore, dissipates the social surplus. I will discuss such a model below in this book.

The last three decades have witnessed the considerable progress in the models of multidimensional screening. Basov (2005b) contains an exposition of mathematical techniques and results in the area. Since in most interesting situations private information of the consumers is multidimensional (for example, consumers may have different slopes and intercepts of their demand curves); a natural question is: To what extend the model developed here generalizes to the multidimensional case. There are two kinds of difficulties one has to overcome in order to address this question. First, screening models become rather technically intricate in that case. Moreover, there is no simple condition on the fundamentals of the model that will prevent bunching, though recent research (see, Basov 2005b) shows that it is less likely to occur when the consumers' utility is concave in types. This implies that the optimal tariff need not be everywhere differentiable and one should exercise caution in characterizing the solution of the monopolist's problem. Furthermore, most intuitions gained in the unidimensional case, such as the "no distortions at the top" property fail to hold. Second, as argued by Basov (2005b) the steady state distributions of choices of boundedly rational agents are unlikely to possess any reasonable properties. Therefore, the learning process should be modeled explicitly and the proper model should be dynamic. Though it seems unlikely that such a model will be amenable to the analytic solution, I believe that a numerical simulation and study of the properties of the solution is possible. Moreover, since the agents continue to earn information rates in the multidimensional case, one might conjecture that the result on the incidence of the cost of boundedly rational behavior will continue to hold for these models.

## 5.3 Bounded Rationality and the Revelation Principle

In the models I presented in this chapter so far, the monopolist faced with boundedly rational consumers relied on the same type of contracts when faced with boundedly rational consumers as when she faced the rational ones. Laffont and Martimort continue to offer consumers a menu of contracts with cardinality equal to that of the type space, while Basov and Mirrlees solve for the optimal nonlinear tariffs. In this section I ask a question whether bounded rationality can lead to more drastic deviations from the optimal behavior under full rationality.

For this purpose, in this section, based on Basov (2009), I revisit the monopolistic screening problem for the case of two types, the framework employed by Laffont and Martimort, and assuming that consumers are boundedly rational. However, I model bounded rationality differently from those authors, assuming that the choice of consumers is governed by Luce's model of probabilistic choice (Luce 1959), in which the degree of rationality can be captured by a single parameter, $\lambda$. In this model the revelation principle[2] does not apply and the choice of the selling mechanism is with a loss of generality. I show that if the monopolist restricts attention to mechanisms, which offer menus of two choices, the profits are lower than in the case of full rationality by the terms of order $\lambda/n\lambda$, where $\lambda$ is the degree of irrationality of the consumers. The monopolist, however, can approximate the profits she earns under assumption of full rationality, using a more elaborate message game.

The revelation principle allows a researcher to restrict her attention to direct mechanisms when searching for the optimal mechanism. Once the optimal direct mechanism is found, any other mechanism (not necessarily direct), which reproduces its payoffs is also optimal. An important assumption that underlies the revelation principle is that of sufficiently high degree of rationality on the part of the participants, which allows us to employ the Bayes–Nash equilibrium as the solution concept. Therefore, one should expect that revelation principle does not apply in general under bounded rationality. Below, I show that this is indeed the case and the consequences for the optimal contracting of even small deviations from rationality can be quite drastic.

There are two natural responses to the failure of the revelation principle in this context. The first is to search for some generalized version of the principle, which will allow restricting the set of the mechanisms for the new solution concept. The second is to restrict attention to a particular class of mechanisms, e.g., nonlinear tariffs, and look for the optimal mechanism in this class. Though the second approach does not guarantee that one will arrive at the optimal mechanism, it is much more manageable than the first and is practically important; therefore I limit myself here to it, leaving the first approach to the future research.

In this section I consider a particular problem, which served as an important example of a general mechanism design problem: monopolistic screening. Assume a monopolist can produce a unit of good of different quality. Consumer's marginal utility of quality is unknown to the monopolist, but she knows that it can take one of two commonly known values with some commonly known probabilities. Assuming full rationality on the side of the monopolist and the consumers' one can prove that without loss of generality the monopolist can restrict her choice of a mechanism to a choice of a nonlinear tariff.

Since the set of types is finite, the equilibrium will be characterized by a discrete set of qualities purchased and transfers made, with cardinality equal to the cardinality of the type space, i.e., consumers of each type will select a quality-transfer pair, which will maximize their utility. Therefore, nonlinear tariff defined over all possible qualities will produce the same equilibrium outcome as a direct revelation mechanism.

---

[2]For a textbook exposition of the Revelation Principle, see Mas-Colell et al. (1995).

This equivalence will, however, be broken if the consumers are boundedly rational. I will model bounded rationality using Luce (1959) model. Consumers behaving in accordance with this model will purchase any quality offered with positive probability. Therefore, a nonlinear tariff with connected product line will produce a different behavior from the direct revelation mechanism. I will show that offering a pair of contracts and allowing the consumers to choose freely among them, offering a nonlinear tariff over a connected product line, and playing an elaborate message game with only two payoff relevant outcomes will produce different behavior under bounded rationality, while all three mechanisms are equivalent under full rationality.

Basov and Danilkina (2007a) analyze a particular message game where each payoff relevant outcome is presented in different multiplicities, called flavors. They show that if flavor proliferation is costless one can approach the optimal outcome under full rationality with exponential precision. In this paper I calculate the optimal pair of contracts, and compare the performance of this mechanism with the one presented in Basov and Danilkina (2007a). This allows me to establish the bounds on the costs of proliferation, which can be alternatively interpreted as complexity costs, for which the principal should look for more sophisticated contracts.

The formal model is similar to the one developed in Sect. 5.1. Assume a monopolist can produce a unit of good with quality $x$ at a cost

$$c(x) = \frac{x^2}{2}.$$

The marginal rate of substitution between quality and money, $\theta$, does not depend on quality but differs across the consumers, i.e., utility takes the form

$$u(\alpha, x, t) = \theta x - t,$$

where $t$ is the amount paid to the monopolist. Parameter $\theta$ is private information of the consumer.

However, it is commonly known that $\theta \in \{\theta_L, \theta_H\}$ and that probability that $\theta = \theta_H$ is equal to $p_H$. I assume that

$$p_H < \frac{\theta_L}{\theta_H}, \tag{5.8}$$

so both types get served in equilibrium. I also assume that the utility of the outside option is independent of the type and normalize it to be zero.

The task of the monopolist is to devise a mechanism to maximize her expected profits. To do this she has first to make some assumptions about the consumer's behavior. The standard assumption is that the consumer is rational. The solution in that case is well known. I reviewed this case in Sect. 5.1. Recall that high type is supplied at the efficient level (no distortions at the top) and quality supplied to the low type is downward biased, i.e., it is below the efficient level. I will assume below that fraction of the high types is sufficiently small, so both types of the consumer are served in the rational equilibrium.[3] Corresponding tariffs are

$$t_L = \theta_L x_L$$

$$t_H = t_L + \frac{\theta_H}{1 - p_H}(\theta_H - \theta_L),$$

where

$$x_L = \theta_L - \frac{p_H}{1 - p_H}(\theta_H - \theta_L).$$

Note that the same outcome can be implemented by offering a connected product line $X = [0, a]$ and the following tariff $t$: $X \to R$:

$$t(x) = \begin{cases} \theta_L x, & \text{for } x < x_L \\ \theta_L x + \theta_H(x - x_L), & \text{for } x_L \leq x \leq a. \end{cases}$$

where $a \in [x_H, +\infty)$. Therefore, under assumption of perfect rationality, using the optimal nonlinear tariff is equivalent to using the optimal menu of choices. We will see that this equivalence breaks down under bounded rationality.

### 5.3.1 A Model of Boundedly Rational Behavior

No let us assume that the consumers are boundedly rational. In particular, I will follow Basov (2011) and assume that the behavior of the consumers is governed by Luce's model (see, Luce 1959).[4] In that model the choice probabilities can be represented by

$$p_i = \frac{\exp\left(\frac{u_i}{\lambda}\right)}{\sum_{j=1}^{n} \exp\left(\frac{u_j}{\lambda}\right)}.$$

We have already encountered the Luce's model in Chap. 3. Recall that here $n$ is the number of alternatives, $p_i$ is the probability that alternative $i$ is chosen, and $u_i$ is

[3]Recall that the major trade-off is between inefficient provision of the low type and information rents paid to the high type. If the high type is sufficiently numerous it is advantageous to exclude low type completely to avoid paying information rents to the high type.

[4]The Luce's probabilities are also known in Industrial Organization (IO) as the logit probabilities. However, while in the IO literature the justification for probabilistic choice comes from horizontal heterogeneity in the consumers' tastes, Luce justified it appealing to the bounded rationality of the decision makers.

the utility associated with alternative $i$. Note that according to this model any two alternatives that have the same utility are selected with the same probabilities. Parameter $\lambda$, which changes from zero to infinity, can be usefully thought to represent the degree of irrationality on the side of the decision maker.

If $\lambda = 0$ then the choice is rational, i.e., it assigns positive probability only to utility maximizing options and if there are several such options equal probability is assigned to all of them. Note that rationality, as usually understood, does not require that all optimal choices have the same probability. Therefore, if one considers probability of choice as a correspondence in $\lambda$, it will not be lower semicontinuous at zero. It is this lack of lower semicontinuity that makes the optimal mechanism for nearly rational agents substantially different from the one used for the rational ones and breaks the equivalence (even approximate one) between menus of choices and nonlinear tariffs.

At the other extreme, as $\lambda \to \infty$ the choice probabilities converge to $1/n$, i.e., the choice becomes totally random independent of the utility level. This corresponds to completely irrational behavior.

### 5.3.2 The Optimal Menu of Contracts and a Comparison with Some Other Mechanisms

Let us first assume that the consumers and boundedly rational in the sense described above and ask what is the optimal two item menu for the monopolist? This means that we are restricting the monopolist to offer menu consisting of two contracts $(x_L, t_L)$ and $(x_H, t_H)$ and allow the consumers to choose freely between these contracts and the option of not participating. For simplicity of exposition, I will also assume that (5.8) holds, i.e., under full rationality both types of consumers are served at the equilibrium. The assumption of near rationality implies that we can assume that low-type consumers are randomizing between their contract and the option of not participating, while the high-type consumers are randomizing between their contract and the contract designed for the low type[5] and neglect the probabilities that high type of consumers choose not to participate of that low type of the consumers will choose the contract designed for the high types. Let $\Delta$ be the minimal slack in nonbinding constraints. Then, neglecting the terms of order $O(\exp(-\Delta/\lambda))$, the monopolist's profits are given by

$$\pi = \gamma_L(t_L - c(x_L)) + (1 - p_H)\frac{(t_H - c(x_H))\exp\left(\frac{(\theta_H x_H - t_H)}{\lambda}\right)}{\exp\left(\frac{(\theta_H x_H - t_H)}{\lambda}\right) + \exp\left(\frac{(\theta_H x_L - t_L)}{\lambda}\right)},$$

[5]Recall that the binding constraints are the individual rationality for the low type and the incentive compatibility for the high type.

where

$$\gamma_L = \frac{(1-p_H)\exp\left(\frac{(\theta_L x_L - t_L)}{\lambda}\right)}{1+\exp\left(\frac{(\theta_L x_L - t_L)}{\lambda}\right)} + \frac{p_H \exp\left(\frac{(\theta_H x_L - t_L)}{\lambda}\right)}{\exp\left(\frac{(\theta_H x_H - t_H)}{\lambda}\right) + \exp\left(\frac{(\theta_H x_L - t_L)}{\lambda}\right)}.$$

The first term in expression for $\gamma_L$ captures the fraction of low types that choose the contract designed for them, while the second term captures the fraction of high types who choose the contract designed for the low types.

Note that if the monopolist offers exactly the same contract as would have been offered to the rational consumers exactly half of low types would have dropped out and exactly half of high types would have chosen to behave as if they were low types. Therefore, though the degree of irrationality is assumed to be small, the losses would have been of order of $O(1)$, rather than $O(\lambda)$. Basov (2009) shows that the monopolist will instead choose to create slack in the previously binding constraints of order of $O(\lambda)$. The high type will still be served efficiently, and the low-type quality will also be the same up to terms of order of $O(\lambda)$. Therefore, in the main approximation with respect to $\lambda$ the monopolist offers the same qualities, she would have offered to the rational consumers, but adjusts the tariffs by terms of order of $O(\lambda \ln(\lambda))$. This implies that the probability of a wrong choice by both types of the consumers is of order $O(\lambda)$. Therefore, using the optimal two contract menu the monopolist earns lower profits against nearly rational consumers than she would have earned against the fully rational ones and the magnitude of the loss is $O(\lambda \ln \lambda)$.

Note that this outcome cannot be implemented by tariff of type defined over a connected product line $[0, a]$, since under bounded rationality the distribution of choices will have a continuous rather than binary support. Therefore, two mechanisms equivalent under full rationality will be no longer equivalent under bounded rationality.

It can be shown that using continuous tariffs will decrease the profits of the monopolist comparatively to a binary menu. Next I am going to ask: can the monopolist improve her profits using more elaborate mechanism? I argue that the answer is yes, if there are no complexity costs. In particular, in this case it is possible to achieve profits, which are exponentially close to the profits under the assumption of full rationality.

Let us consider the following message game: the set of all possible massages is divided into three groups. The default group consists of just a single message; the low group consists of $m_L$ messages and the high group of $m_H$ messages. The consumer is asked to send a message and is not assigned any good if she sends the default message, is offered the contract devised for the low-type rational consumers if she sends the message belonging to the low group and the contract devised for the high-type rational consumers if she sends the message belonging to the high group. The probability that the low-type consumer will by mistake choose to not participate is $1/m_l$, while the probability that the high type will accidentally choose the problem designed for the low type is $m_l/(m_l + m_H)$. By choosing $m_l$ and $m_H$ sufficiently large both of these probabilities can be made arbitrary close to zero.

Note that though the message game described above allows the monopolist to achieve profits exponentially close the profits she would have earned against rational consumers, it does it at the cost of expanding the cardinality of the strategy set of a consumer. One can restrict values of $m_l$ and $m_H$ by assuming that the consumers, when making decisions, experience complexity costs. Alternatively, one may assume that the monopolist will experience menu costs. The last approach was taken in Basov (2009) to explain flavor proliferation with quality. Basov et al. (2011) apply this model to explain some empirical regularities of the Australian car market. In particular, they found that the number of flavors indeed increases with quality for low qualities as the model suggests. The eventual drop of the number of flavors with quality at the high end can be explained by thinning of the market for the luxury cars.

The above analysis shows that the structure of optimal contract changes discontinuously, once a small degree of irrationality is introduced. This happens because correspondence from degree of irrationality into choice probabilities is not lower semicontinuous as the degree of irrationality reaches zero as long as set of utility maximizers is not singleton. This is a general property of most probabilistic choice models, whether those models are justified on axiomatic grounds or are seen as the steady states of dynamic learning model, since such models typically map any utility profile into the unique probability distribution for a positive irrationality parameter, but prescribe any probability distribution supported by the set of utility maximizers as the decision maker becomes rational. I have chosen the Luce's model to make this point. One objection to the use of Luce's model is that the comparative statics pattern produced by it is often criticized in the discrete choice literature, using an example known as the blue bus–red bus paradox (see, for example, Ben-Akiva and Lerman 1985). The latter consists of the following observation: suppose a decision maker has to decide whether to drive to work or to take a bus. If the bus alternative is replaced by two bus alternatives that differ in some irrelevant aspect, such as color of the bus (blue bus vs red bus), the Luce's model predicts the probability of a car trip decreases. While this conclusion seems unnatural in the above context (hence, it is called a paradox), one can easily come up with a context where it seems more intuitive. Suppose, for example, a buyer walks into a car dealership and seems two cars on display: a Mercedes-Benz and a BMW. Suppose, given the prices, the buyer is indifferent between the alternatives. It is natural to assume that she will choose each with 50 % probability. Now, assume that she sees a red Mercedes-Benz, a blue Mercedes-Benz, and a BMW. Even if upon reflection she is indifferent between colors of a car, it seems less unnatural to think that the total probability of buying a Mercedes-Benz might increase. This is captured in the recent generalization of the logit model by

Mattsson and Weibull (2002). They showed that under plausible assumptions choice probabilities can be written as

$$p_i = \frac{q_i \exp\left(\frac{u_i}{\lambda}\right)}{\sum_{j=1}^{n} q_j \exp\left(\frac{u_j}{\lambda}\right)}$$

where $q_i$ can be thought of as a default probability of alternative $i$, i.e., the probability the decision maker will choose alternative $i$ without trying to compute utilities of different alternatives. In the blue bus–red bus scenario it is reasonable to assume that $q_{\mathrm{B}} = q_{\mathrm{Br}} + q_{\mathrm{Bb}}$, i.e., the default probability of choosing a bus is the sum of the default probabilities of choosing red bus or blue bus, which avoids the paradox. In the car dealership example, it is more natural to assume that default probabilities assign an increased likelihood to choosing the car with more varieties. The Luce model captures this effect in the simplest possible way. However, note that in the more general model of Mattsson and Weibull, the mechanism described above is still as default probabilities of choosing higher quality goods increase in variety. The latter property is robust in the Mattsson and Weibull class of models and Berger et al. (2007) provide some empirical evidence that this is indeed may be the case.

Since the Revelation Principle does not hold under bounded rationality, the choice of a class of mechanisms is with a loss of generality. I demonstrated an example of such a situation here. An important feature of the example is that allowing several messages to map in the same allocation allows the monopolist to manipulate probabilities without manipulating the payoffs, and in particular it allows the monopolist to push the probability of the "right" choice arbitrary close to one. This feature allows one to hypothesize that a mechanism that reproduces the good of the given quality in different flavors can approximate arbitrary mechanism with arbitrary precision. The idea is to start with an arbitrary message game and find the equilibrium probabilities of different choices made by different types in a QRE. Then consider a direct revelation mechanism. In general, the probabilities of different choices will not match those of the QRE, but now the principal can use flavor proliferation to adjust probabilities. Note that the hypothesis, if correct, does not rely on the degree of irrationality of the consumers.

## 5.4 Oligopoly, Bounded Rationality, and Optimal Obfuscation

Recently, there emerged considerable interest in studying the consequences of boundedly rational behavior on the oligopolistic pricing and other activities of the firms. See Ellison (2006) for a detailed review of this literature. Here we will mention only a few papers related to the current topic. Of particular importance is the question of the incidence of burden of boundedly rational behavior. We saw that in the monopolistic screening setting depending on the way of modeling bounded rationality and particular realization of the fundamentals the burden can be born either by the monopolist, as in Laffont and Martimort (2002) or by the consumers as in Basov and Mirrlees (2009). If the degree of rationality of the consumers can be manipulated by the monopolist, then depending on the incidence of the burden, the monopolist will have incentives either to educate the consumers, i.e., help them make more rational decisions, for example, by revealing to them all the relevant information, or obfuscate them, i.e., try to make their decisions less rational, for example, by withholding relevant information and supplying irrelevant one. In the case of oligopolistic market, these incentives are confounded by strategic interaction among the firms.

In the early contributions to the literature, Grossman (1981) and Milgrom (1981) demonstrated that if information disclosure is costless the firms will reveal all the relevant information, i.e., they will educate rather than obfuscate the consumers. This prediction was examined empirically by Ellison and Ellison (2009), who on the basis of their study of price elasticities on the Internet, argued that this prediction is not born out by many real-world observations. To explain obfuscation in the real-life markets, Ellison and Wolitzky (2012) developed a model where it is theoretically justified in a search-theoretic framework.

Obfuscation, in Ellison and Wolitzky, takes a form of an unobservable action that makes it more difficult for consumers to inspect the product and learn its price or quality. One way to think about it is to assume that the consumers have to spend time to make a product selection. They go through the list of product's characteristics to determine its value. If the list is too long they may end up making a mistake in their assessment. By devising concise and relevant description of the product a firm may ease the task of the consumer, thereby decreasing the probability of mistake. On the contrary, by putting a lot of irrelevant characteristics on the list or by engaging in a uninformative advertising, firms can make it more difficult for the consumers to go through the product description, increasing the probability of an error. One just needs to remember the plethora of different mobile plans to see the point. The complexity of different rates and features leaves most consumers being unable to compare mobile plans, let alone to choose the best one.

Ellison and Wolitzky describe several scenarios for achieving obfuscation. For example, they suggest that in online shopping application the firm can choose the number of screens the consumer has to go through to find all the relevant information and they may instruct the salespeople how long to talk to consumers in face-to-face shopping. They assumed that consumers go sequentially through description of products supplied by the firms and face search costs that depend on the sum of obfuscation levels chosen by the firms that the consumer has chosen to visit. Consumers have rational expectations about the obfuscation levels and can rationally choose to stop the search.

The latest contribution to the literature was made by Basov and Danilkina (2015). I will review this contribution in more detail below. The model developed by Basov and Danilkina is similar in spirit to Ellison and Wolitzky (2012), however, instead of assuming that consumers experience direct costs from going through the products description and learning relevant information about their quality and price, they assumed that this process affects quality of consumers decision-making, the longer and more confusing the product description the lower the quality of decision-making. The crucial difference of this assumption from the one used by Ellison and Wolitzky is that while in the latter model the consumers are fully aware of the search costs and will rationally stop search at some point, while in Basov and Danilkina consumers are not aware of the effect of obfuscation on the quality of the decision-making. For example, a consumer who already has spent a couple of hours at a computer screen reading through description of different house insurance policies, will still continue going through the exhaustive list, since she does not experience direct costs from search and is not aware that the very act of continuing the search will decrease the quality of decision-making.

Since the consumer will always go through the exhaustive set of the alternatives, which will affect the overall quality of choice, a decision of one firm to increase level of obfuscation will affect the relative probabilities of all choices.

To formalize the idea of quality of choice Basov and Danilkina use Luce's model of probabilistic choice with irrationality parameter $\lambda$, which we have already encountered in this book. The important property of this model is that probabilities of different choices are sensitive to differences in utilities. This creates a relationship between price differences and buyer mistakes, which can explain negative relation between buyers' mistakes and price differences and lack of correlation between high prices and higher complexity, observed and experiments better than do the alternative models, according to Kalayci (2015a). Another important conclusion reached by Basov and Danilkina is that aggregate obfuscation level decreases and consumer surplus increases with the number of firms in a market. This result is in agreement with experimental findings by Kalayci (2015b). Previous theoretical work, such as Gabaix and Laibson (2004), Carlin (2009), on the contrary, predicted that increasing the number of sellers in a market might lead to more obfuscation.

### 5.4.1 The Bertrand Model with Boundedly Rational Consumers

Following Basov and Danilkina, I start with a model of Bertrand completion between $n$ firms who face boundedly rational consumers. Firm $i$ produces a homogenous good at marginal cost $c$, and posts price, $p_i$, of the unit of the good. A consumer is interested in buying at most one unit of a good, i.e., is faced with $(n + 1)$ different alternatives, to buy from one of the firms or not to buy at all. Utility of buying the good is equal to the value of the good, $v$, which is the same for all consumers, minus the purchase price. The consumers' choices among the alternatives are governed by the Luce model with irrationality parameter $\lambda$, which we have already encountered in this chapter and earlier in Chap. 3. Therefore, the demand share of firm $i$ is given by

$$q_i = \frac{\exp\left(\frac{v-p_i}{\lambda}\right)}{1 + \sum_{j=1}^{n} \exp\left(\frac{v-p_j}{\lambda}\right)}.$$

Note that unlike the Hotelling model, where the demand shares depend only on price differences as long as the consumers' value is sufficiently high, so that all consumers purchase the good at equilibrium, in this model this is also true asymptotically as the consumers' value converges to infinity. Since the sum of the market shares is always less than one, for any profile of prices and any finite $v$ some consumers will choose not to purchase the good.

The profits of firm $i$ are given by

$$\pi_i = (p_i - c)q_i.$$

Let $p^n$ denote the equilibrium price when there are $n$ firms on the market. It is straightforward to show that it satisfies

$$p^n = F(p^n) \equiv c + \frac{\lambda\left(1 + n\exp\left(\frac{v-p^n}{\lambda}\right)\right)}{1 + (n-1)\sum_{j=1}^{n} \exp\left(\frac{v-p^n}{\lambda}\right)}. \tag{5.9}$$

Basov and Danilkina (2015) have shown that this equation has the unique solution. They have also shown that as the number of firms increases the equilibrium price decreases from the monopoly level $p^1$ to $c + \lambda$, while always staying above the marginal cost.

Let us for a moment consider in more detail the case of the monopoly, i.e., assume $n = 1$. To simplify notation, I will drop superscript 1 and rewrite Eqs. (5.9 and 5.10) as

$$\frac{v-c}{\lambda} = \psi\left(\frac{v-p}{\lambda}\right),$$

where

$$\psi(x) = 1 + x + \exp(x).$$

Then the equilibrium monopoly price is given by[6]

$$p = v - \lambda\psi^{-1}\left(\frac{v-c}{\lambda}\right).$$

[6]Since $\psi(\cdot)$ is strictly increasing, the inverse function $\psi^{-1}(\cdot)$ exists.

In particular, the monopoly price can be above the consumers' value if the consumers are sufficiently irrational.

To study how social welfare changes depending on the number of firms, first note that since $v > c$, the social efficiency requires that all consumers buy a unit of the good. Therefore, the welfare loss is proportional to $q_0$, the fraction of the consumers who do not buy the good, where

$$q_0 = \frac{1}{1 + \sum_{j=1}^{n} \exp\left(\frac{v - p_j}{\lambda}\right)}.$$

Recall that under perfect rationality social welfare in the Bertrand model increases as the industry structure changes from a monopoly to a duopoly, but is at the maximum value independent of the number of firms as long as there are at least two competitors. However, if the consumers are boundedly rational both the total welfare and the consumer surplus increase when there are more firms in a Bertrand competitive industry. Indeed, as I argued above, the increase in number of firms leads to a decrease in equilibrium price. It is also easy to see that it leads to an increase of consumer participation via two channels. First, it increases number of options associated with participation, and second it makes each of this options more attractive. Therefore, it raises both the social welfare and the consumer surplus.

So far I assumed that the irrationality parameter is fixed. Let us now extend the model by assuming that the consumers are rational at default ($\lambda = 0$); however, the firms can spend resources to confuse the consumers. This will lead to an increase in the value of $\lambda$.

The structure of the game is as follows. At date one all firms simultaneously decide on the amount of resources they spend confusing the consumers. If firm $i$ devotes resources $z_i$ to the obfuscating activities, then

$$\lambda = \varphi\left(\sum_{i=1}^{n} z_i\right),$$

where $\varphi(\cdot)$ is a twice differentiable, strictly increasing, concave function, such that $\varphi(0) = 0$, and satisfying the Inada conditions. We will refer to it as an "obfuscating technology." At the beginning of date two the firms observe $\lambda$ and play the simultaneous Bertrand game, described above.

One can solve for subgame perfect equilibrium of this game by backward induction. Let $p^n(\lambda)$ be the equilibrium price found at stage two and define

$$G(\lambda, n) = \pi_i(\lambda, n, p^n(\lambda)).$$

Basov and Danilkina showed that the level of obfuscation $z^n$ *is* chosen by the competitors when there are $n$ firms on the market is determined by

$$G_\lambda(\varphi(nz^n, n))\varphi'(nz^n) = 1,$$

where subscript denotes partial derivative with respect to the appropriate variable. Inada conditions guarantee that if at default consumers are rational, the equilibrium amount of obfuscation is positive. They have further shown that as the number of firms increases toward infinity, the total amount of obfuscation converges to zero. If instead of assuming that consumers are rational at default one assumes that they are characterized by some positive $\lambda_0$, there will exist $n_0 \in N$ such that whenever number of firms is at least $n_0$ no resources are spent on obfuscation in equilibrium. Value of $n_0$ can be one if $\lambda_0$ is sufficiently large, in which case no resources will be spent on obfuscation at all.

Intuitively, the obfuscation is a public good, from the point of view of the firms, and the firms tend to free ride at each other's expenses. Therefore, in this framework competition has two beneficial effects from the social point of view: it increases the chance that a consumer will buy the product and decreases the amount of obfuscation. From the consumers' point of view, there is another beneficial effect of competition—it leads to a decrease in price.

## 5.5 Emotional Temperature and the Power of Optimal Incentives

In the models considered so far in this chapter, the principal(s) had either to take the boundedly rational behavior of the agents as given as in Laffont and Martimort (2002), Basov and Mirrlees (2009), Basov (2009) or manipulate the degree of bounded directly as in Basov and Danilkina (2015). In this section I am going to present a model, based on Basov (2013), where the principal's choice of contract will affect a variable which affects the effective degree or rationality in a non-monotone way: the *emotional temperature*.

There exists a long tradition in western thought going back to Plato (see, Plato 1902) that assumes that proper reasoning can only be clouded by emotional arousal. As a result, emotions often have been regarded as a dangerous threat to morality and rationality and Desecrates (1968) noted that "those that are most agitated by their passions are not those who know them best." Fully rational individual was supposed to be completely free of emotions.

Modern psychological research revealed a more complex role emotions play in decision-making. For example, Damasio (2005) argued that though emotions indeed interfere with the ability to evaluate the objective consequences of the choices, they also allow the decision maker to feel the difference in utility arising from those choices. A completely emotionless individual will be in a better position to predict consequences of her choices, but will not feel any difference between the consequences and therefore will not be motivated to make a good decision. The best known example of such an individual is Phineas Gage, an American railroad construction foreman, now remembered for his improbable survival of an accident in which a large iron rod was driven completely through his head. Following the accident Gage was perfectly capable of evaluating the results of his actions, but was unable to make even simplest decisions. Damasio (2005) uses Gage's case to illustrate that emotions are instrumental in translating evaluations into motivations and through it affecting the decision-making.

On the other extreme, if an individual feels a very strong emotion, then according to APET[7] model recently developed by neuroscientists, his brains can automatically shut down the rational process entirely and the individual may find himself acting entirely on impulse.

To formalize the intuition that strong emotion makes you care more about the outcome, but also clouds your thinking, Basov (2013) introduced the concept of an *emotional temperature*, which characterizes the degree of emotional arousal. In line with the two effects of emotional arousal described above emotional temperature plays a dual role in the model. On one hand, stronger emotion provides us with stronger motivation to make a correct choice. On the other, it interferes with our ability to figure out this correct choice. Therefore, though increase in emotional temperature makes agents less rational in a sense that their choices are noisier given the level of utilities, it also scales up the level of utilities and therefore *effective degree of rationality* depends in a nonmonotone way on the degree of emotional arousal. To simplify technical exposition, I will again make use of Luce's model of probabilistic choice, already employed several times in this book, and assume that emotional temperature affects both scale of utility and the probability that the expected monetary payoff of a particular action is miscalculated. The choice of the Luce's model is motivated by analytical convenience. Any other probabilistic choice model, for example a probit model, where the degree of miscalculation is captured by a single parameter will lead to similar results.

First result of this model is that for each agent there exists a positive optimal emotional temperature, which leads to an irreducible positive probability of sub-optimal choices. One should also distinguish between the optimal *objective emotional temperature*, which maximizes the expected monetary payoff of the decision maker and the *optimal subjective temperature*, which maximizes her feeling of well-being. The optimal objective emotional temperature depends on the cardinal difference between the utilities of different alternatives, but not on the arbitrary selected origin, i.e., utility is defined up to an additive constant. It is a common property of many models of bounded rationality: both static and dynamic that units of utility have meaning, i.e., the utility is defined up to an additive constant, rather than up to an affine transformation as is the case in the expected utility theory. The optimal subjective emotional temperature, on the other hand, does depend on the

[7]In APET A stands for actions activating agents, P for pattern match, E for emotion, and T for thought. For an exposition of the model, see Griffin and Tyrrell (2003).

choice of the origin of utilities. One may fix the origin by requiring the optimal objective and subjective optimal temperatures coincide, making utility fully cardinal. This is the first model that allows ascribing fully cardinal meaning to the utilities.

To apply this model to the contract theory one has to assume that emotional temperature can depend on the choice of a contract/mechanism. Basov (2013) considers a model of optimal incentive provisions in the principal–agent model with hidden action and assumes that emotional temperature responds to the power of incentives. The stronger the power of incentives, the more anxious the agent becomes and the higher is her emotional temperature. Under these conditions the power of incentives has double effect: it motivates the agent and affects the probability of the correct decision. Whether this makes the power of the optimal incentives weaker or stronger depends on the initial state of the agent. If she is initially very cold, incentives are likely to be stronger since they will provide motivation to work and reduce the chance of an error. On the other hand, if the initial temperature is close to the optimal objective temperature and the agent is sufficiently rational at this temperature, such that the principal finds it optimal to provide the utility level at least equal to the outside option, then the sensitivity of the emotional temperature to the power of incentives will lower the power of optimal incentives.

One might also speculate that if the emotional temperature decreases with experience, the power of optimal incentives should increase, so a CEO should face more powerful incentives than a junior manager. For another application of this result, assume that agents with lower emotional temperature select for themselves the low pressure jobs, e.g., a bureaucrat or a civil servant, while individuals with high emotional temperature select for themselves the high pressure managerial jobs. Then, when designing optimal incentives, one should attempt to increase the emotional temperature of bureaucrats and civil servants, but to decrease the emotional temperature of managerial staff. It would imply that bureaucrats and civil servants should face higher power incentives than the standard theory recommends, while managers should face lower power incentives. Another interesting application will arises in auction theory. If one assumes that conducting open format auction raises emotional temperature compared to strategically equivalent closed value format, two otherwise strategically equivalent auctions (e.g., sealed-bid first price and Dutch or sealed-bid second price and English in an independent private value environment) will lead to different bidding behaviors.

### 5.5.1 Optimal Emotional Temperature

Let us assume that the individual faces a choice among $n$ alternatives, utility of alternative $i$ is $u_i$, and the choice probabilities are governed by Luce's model with irrationality parameter $\lambda$. Basov (2013) further assumes that both utilities of different choices and $\lambda$ are functions of some parameter $T$, the emotional temperature. In particular,

$$u_i = Tv_i,$$

where $v_i$ depends on objective characteristics of alternative $i$, and can be thought of as the utility experienced by an economic agent with a typical (e.g., population average) emotional temperature, which is normalized to be one. Value $u_i$, on the other hand, is the subjective experienced utility. Note that subjective experienced utility is assumed to be proportional to the objective value of the alternative. Emotional temperature is defined as coefficient of proportionality. This captures the intuition that emotions makes us feel stronger about issues. However, the choice of a perfectly rational decision maker does not depend on $T$, as long as $T > 0$.

On the other hand, following a tradition going back to Plato and Descartes, Basov assumes that emotions interfere with rational judgment. To model it, he postulates that $\lambda$ is a strictly increasing function of $T$, i.e., the irrationality parameter increases in the emotional temperature. Let us introduce *effective degree of rationality*, $\varphi(\cdot)$, by

$$\varphi(T) = \frac{T}{\lambda(T)},$$

and make the following assumption:

**Assumption 5.1** Function $\varphi(\cdot)$: $[0, +\infty) \to [0, +\infty)$ is differentiable,[8] single peaked, and

$$\lim_{T \to +\infty} \varphi(T) = \lim_{T \to +0} \varphi(T) = 0.$$

Assumption 5.1 implies that individuals with too low or too high emotional temperature both make poor decisions, but for different reasons: individuals with the low emotional temperature do not care enough about consequences of their decisions, while the ones with high emotional temperature make significant computational mistakes. It is in line with the Yerkes–Dodson law (Yerkes and Dodson, 1908), which states that performance increases with physiological or mental arousal, but only up to a point. When level of arousal becomes too high, performance decreases.

Assumption 5.1 allows one to prove the following useful result.

**Lemma 5.1** *There exists constant* $K > 0$ *such that* $T\varphi'(T) > -K$.

The proof is straightforward. See, Basov (2013) for detail.

[8]At $t = 0$ differentiability is understood as differentiability from the right.

Following Basov let us introduce objective expected utility, $U_O$, by

$$U_O(T) = \sum_{i=1}^{n} v_i p_i(T),$$

where $p_i(T)$ are Luce's choice probabilities, depending on emotional temperature, $T$, through $\lambda$. It measures the quality of choices, but not how the decision maker feels about them. For example, if $v_i$ is measured in monetary terms, $U_O$ measures the expected profits. To capture the decision maker's feeling about different choices, let us introduce the subjective expected utility, $U_S$, by

$$U_S(T) = \sum_{i=1}^{n} u_i p_i(T).$$

Note that

$$U_S(T) = TU_O(T).$$

Basov then argued in a straightforward way that Assumption 5.1 implies that there exists the unique value of emotional temperature that maximizes the objective expected utility, provided that not all objective payoffs are the same. He calls this value critical temperature and denotes it by $T_c$. Notice that

$$U'_S(T) = TU'_O(T) + U_O(T).$$

Assume that $U_O(T_c) > 0$,[9] then $U'_S(T_c) > 0$, therefore the emotional temperature that maximizes subjective expected utility is above $T_c$, i.e., the happiest people are not the best decision makers. Objective and subjective optimal temperatures are the same if $U_O(T_c) = 0$. One may speculate that if the subjective feeling of happiness helps one to attract mates, the evolution would have selected for higher emotional temperature than needed for the best decision-making in safe environments and to a lower one in harsh ones.

It is worth noting that comparison between optimal subjective and objective emotional temperatures endows utilities with cardinal meaning. It is part of a general pattern that the further one deviates from the model of purely rational behavior by introducing psychological elements in the decision-making, the more cardinal meaning is acquired by the utilities. Indeed, in the basic von Neumann–Morgenstern framework Bernoulli utilities are defined up to a positive affine transformation, i.e., both the origin and the units of the utility can be rescaled arbitrarily. Luce probabilities do depend on the units, but still allow to choose the

[9]This assumption can be interpreted as saying that the environment is sufficiently safe.

origin arbitrarily (i.e., one can shift all the utility levels by the same arbitrary constant without affecting the choice probabilities). The reason for this is that the variance of the error term provides a natural measure for the units of utility. The difference between optimal objective and subjective emotional temperatures depends on how an agent feels about the average choice for at the critical emotional temperature. This feeling can be good, bad, or neutral, depending on the value of $U_O(T_c)$, which fixes the origin of the utility. One can argue that evolutionary pressure tends to equalize the optimal subjective and objective temperatures. It implies that the origin of the utility is found from $U_O(T_c) = 0$.

For example, assume a decision maker faces two choices and $v_1 = a$, $v_2 = a + 1$. Note that no observation either in rational choice or in Luce model can allow one to fix value of $a$. Indeed, in the Luce model the probabilities of the two choices do not depend on $a$ and are given by

$$p_1 = \frac{1}{1 + \exp(\varphi(T))}, p_2 = \frac{\exp(\varphi(T))}{1 + \exp(\varphi(T))}.$$

However, the requirement that the objective and the subjective optimal temperatures coincide will allow us to pin down the value of $a$. For the sake of concreteness, assume $\lambda(T) = \exp(\alpha T)$. It is easy to check that the resulting function $\varphi(\cdot)$ satisfies Assumption 5.1 and $T_c = 1/\alpha$. It is straightforward to evaluate that

$$U^0(T_c) = \frac{a\left(1 + \exp\left(\frac{1}{\alpha e}\right) + 1\right)}{\left(1 + \exp\left(\frac{1}{\alpha e}\right)\right)}.$$

Therefore, the subjective and the objective optimal emotional temperatures coincide if and only if

$$a = -\frac{1}{1 + \exp\left(\frac{1}{\alpha e}\right)}.$$

### 5.5.2 *Effect of Emotional Temperature on the Power of Optimal Incentives*

Let us apply the developed model to the problem of devising of the optimal incentive scheme. For this purpose, let us endogenise the emotional temperature. In particular, following Basov (2013), let us assume that the higher the power of incentives (i.e., the pressure put on the agent), the higher is her emotional temperature. For simplicity, I will concentrate here on the principal–agent model with two outcomes. For application of this ideas to a model with a continuum of outcomes, see Basov (2013).

Suppose an agent can undertake a positive level of effort, $e$, when employed by the principal. The cost of effort is $c > 0$ and it generates profit $\pi >$ c with certainty. If the agent shirks it costs her nothing and generates zero profits with certainty. Therefore, the total surplus from the relationship is

$$x = \pi - c > 0.$$

To simplify matters, let us also assume that there is no outside option available to the agent, but the principal is constraint to offer a nonnegative wage. Note, that under full rationality any wage $w \in [c, \pi]$, paid if and only if the agent succeeds, will generate positive effort and result in nonnegative profits. If the principal has all the bargaining power (the usual assumption in the principal–agent models) then she will offer wage $w = c$ for output $\pi$ and wage zero for output zero and the agent will exert effort $e$. The contract can be seen as a base wage of zero and a bonus, $c$, for success. Under bounded rationality the optimal contract will similarly consist of a zero base wage plus a bonus, $w$, for success, but $w$ will not be necessarily equal to $c$. It will elicit positive effort with probability $p$ given by

$$p = \frac{\exp(\varphi(T)w)}{(\exp(\varphi(T)c) + \exp(\varphi(T)w)}.$$

Let us further assume that the emotional temperature itself is an increasing differentiable function of $w$ and define

$$\phi(w) = \varphi(T(w)).$$

Then the principal's profits are given by

$$\Pi(\varphi(w), w) = \frac{(\pi - w)exp(\phi(w)w)}{\exp(\phi(w)c) + exp(\phi(w)w)}.$$

The profit should be maximized subject to $w \geq 0$. Ignoring the last constraint for a moment, the first-order condition is

$$\Pi_\phi \phi'(w) + \Pi_w = 0,$$

where subscripts, as usual, denote derivatives. Straightforward algebra implies

$$(\pi - w)((w - c)\phi'(w) + \phi(w)) = 1 + \exp\{(w - c)\phi(w)\}.$$

Let us start investigating the case when $\phi(w) = \phi_0$, i.e., the emotional temperature does not depend on the incentives. In this case principal simply faces a boundedly rational agent whose behavior is described by the Luce's model. In that case the first-order condition becomes

$$(\pi - w)\phi_0 = 1 + \exp[(w - c)\phi_0].$$

Note that the optimal bonus is unique and satisfies $w<\pi$, i.e., the principal always earns positive profits. If

$$1 + \exp(-c\phi_0) \geq \pi\phi_0,$$

then the constraint $w \geq 0$ is binding and the optimal bonus is zero. Otherwise, there exists the unique positive optimal bonus. If the agent is sufficiently rational, i.e., $(\pi - c)\phi_0 > 2$, then the optimal bonus covers the cost of effort, i.e., $w > c$ and both parties share in the surplus. It is straightforward to show that the optimal bonus increases in the surplus inherit in the relationship, while the relationship between $w$ and $\phi_0$ is not monotonic. The optimal wage is zero for small values of $\phi_0$, starts to rise at $\phi_0$ given by

$$1 + \exp(-c\phi_0) = \pi\phi_0,$$

reaches value $c$ at

$$\varphi^0 = \frac{2}{\pi - c}$$

and continues to rise for a while, reaching maximum at the point $(w, \phi_0)$, where

$$\phi_0 = \frac{z\exp(z)}{\pi - c}, w = c + \exp(-z) * (\pi - c)$$

and $z \approx 1.28$ is the unique solution to equation

$$1 + \exp(z) - z\exp(z) = 0.$$

As $\phi_0$ continues to increase, the bonus drops from its maximum value to value $w = c$ as $\phi_0$ approaches infinity.

Let us return to the analysis of a more general case, where the optimal bonus satisfies equation and assume that the emotional temperature rises linearly in the power of incentives, i.e., it is given by

$$T = T_c + \delta w$$

for some $\delta > 0$, where $T_c$ is the critical temperature. Therefore, in the absence of incentives the agent has optimal objective emotional temperature but has no reason to exert effort. Bonus motivates the agent to exert effort but also increases the chance of wrong decision. Therefore, one may expect that the optimal value of the bonus decreases in the sensitivity of the emotional temperature to the power of incentives, as long as the optimal bonus is above the cost of effort. If the value of $\delta$ is sufficiently small one can find the approximate optimal solution, following procedure outlined in Basov (2013). First, expand $\varphi(T)$ in Taylor series around $T_c$

$$\varphi(T) = \varphi(T_c) - \frac{\gamma}{2}(T - T_c)^2 + o\left((T - T_c)^2\right)$$

Definition of the critical temperature and the second-order condition imply that $\gamma \geq 0$. We assume that the inequality is strict.

Introducing notation

$$\varphi^0 = \varphi(T_c), k = \frac{\gamma\delta^2}{2},$$

the first-order condition becomes

$$(\pi - w)\left(\varphi^0 - 3kw^2 + 2kwc\right) = 1 + \exp\left[(w - c)\left(\varphi^0 - kw^2\right)\right].$$

Analyzing this first-order condition Basov (2013) has shown that for sufficiently small value of $k$ the optimal bonus is decreasing in $k$. The reason for this is that for positive value of $k$ bonus, while eliciting effort also increases the probability that the wrong decision will be taken. Basov has also shown that similar conclusions can be reached in the linear–exponential model with continuum of possible effort choices.

It is important to note that in this model the lower power of incentives is driven by their effect on the emotional temperature rather than by bounded rationality per se. This is in contrast with the model of the optimal incentive provision for boundedly rational agents participating in social learning, developed by Basov (2003), which I will discuss later in this book.

The lesson one can learn from the above exercise is that if the degree of emotional arousal is determined by economic environment, e.g., power of incentives, and it in turn affects the quality of the decision-making, then this fact should be taken into account when designing different mechanisms.

Another interesting application of the developed model is auction design. For example, uncertainty about payment a winning bidder will have to make in the second-price sealed-bid auction may make bidders more anxious than when participating in the first-price sealed-bid auction and affect their emotional temperature. A more interesting observation is that if one assumes that conducting open format auction raises emotional temperature compared to strategically equivalent closed value format, two otherwise strategically equivalent auctions (e.g., sealed-bid first price and Dutch or sealed-bid second price and English in an independent private value environment) will lead to different bidding behavior. This will lead to the violation of the Revenue Equivalence Theorem, though it is hard to say a priori in what direction. To determine how emotional considerations will affect revenues of the different auctions a further study is needed. To pave the way to such study, I will start by introducing the model of all-pay auctions with boundedly rational bidders, developed by Anderson et al. (1998).

## 5.6 All-Pay Auctions with Boundedly Rational Bidders

In this section I will consider application of the Luce model to a situation, which entails strategic interaction among agents. While standard Luce model recognizes that the choice probabilities are affected by utilities, the strategic nature of equilibrium implies that the probabilities of choices made by agents, in turn, affects expected utilities. Therefore, the equilibrium probability of choices must be defined as the fixed point of this mapping.

Anderson et al. (1998), referred hereafter as AGH, applied this logic[10] to the study of all-pay auctions. They have shown that an equilibrium defined as above exists, is unique, and has intuitive properties. In particular, rent dissipation increases with the number of players and rent overdissipation, a phenomenon observed in laboratory but ruled out by the rational choice model, is possible.

In an all-pay auction among $n$ bidders, each bidder receives her value, $v_i$, of a prize. Following AGH, we will assume that all values are publicly observed. The bidders simultaneously submit their bids, the highest bidder wins the auction, but all bidders are required to pay their bids. All-pay auctions are often hailed as good models of political competition, where all candidates have to spend on the campaign but only one can take the offices, or of the legal battles, where all parties pay their legal fees. AGH also assumed that there exists a maximal allowed bid, $B$, but that it is sufficiently large, i.e., bigger than the highest possible valuation.

Such assumption would have entailed no loss of generality in the rational model, as long as $B$ is sufficiently large, since no bidder will bid above her value. However, as we will see below, in the quantal response equilibrium (QRE) model employed by AGH the bid can exceed the value for the bidder with positive probability. We have already observed a similar kind of error in Basov and Danilkina (2015), where consumers were making a purchase with positive probability, even when the price of the good exceeded the value.

Before discussing the boundedly rational case, it is useful to mention that in the case of rational bidders and identical values the game possesses the unique symmetrical mixed strategy equilibrium, where each bidder selects her bid from a the distribution with density $f(b)$ and support $[0, v]$, where

$$f(b) = \frac{1}{\sqrt[n-1]{v}} b^{(2-n)/(n-1)}.$$

[10]This logic is a special case of application of the concept of quantal response equilibrium, developed by McKelvey and Palfrey (1996).

For a derivation, see Baye et al. (1996). Note that the corresponding cumulative distribution function is

$$F(b) = \frac{1}{(n-1)\sqrt[n-1]{v}} b^{1/(n-1)}$$

To describe equilibrium in the case of bounded rationality, assume that player $j$ selects her bid at random from a cumulative distribution $F_j(\cdot)$. Then the expected payoff of player $i$ who submits bid $b$ is given by

$$\pi_i(b) = v_i \prod_{j \neq i} F_j(b) - b. \tag{5.10}$$

This determines a mapping from the vector of cumulative distributions into the vector of expected payoffs. To close the model we will assume that the mapping from expected payoffs into the vector of the densities of choices is determined by

$$f_i(b) = k_i \exp\left(\frac{\pi_i(b)}{\lambda}\right), \tag{5.11}$$

where $f_i(b)$ is the probability density corresponding to cumulative distribution $F_i(b)$ and $k_i$ is a normalization constant, given by

$$k_i = \left[\int_0^B \exp\left(\frac{\pi_i(x)}{\lambda}\right) dx\right]^{-1}.$$

Formula (5.11) is a straightforward generalization of Luce probabilities (3.4) for the case where the choice set is a measurable subset of the real line[11] with cardinality of continuum. Composition of mappings defined by (5.10) and (5.11) determines a mapping from set of cumulative distributions into itself. The QRE is determined as the fixed point of this mapping.

AGH invoked Schauder's Fixed Point Theorem, which generalizes Brower's Fixed Point Theorem to arbitrary normed vector spaces, to prove that the equilibrium bid density $f(b)$ exists and satisfies the following equation:

$$f_i(b) = f_i(0) \exp\left( \left(v_i \prod_{j \neq i} F_j(b) - b\right) / \lambda \right). \tag{5.12}$$

The last equation can be easily obtained combining Eqs. (5.10), and (5.11) and observing that $f_i(0) = k_i$. Note that for $\lambda \to 0$ the argument in the exponent of

[11] Generalization to measurable subsets of arbitrary measure space proceeds in a similar way.

(5.12) converges to zero. Therefore, in the symmetrical equilibrium[12] cumulative distribution function converges to the one obtained for rational bidders. It is also interesting to observe that for $B = v$ and $n = 2$ the equilibrium density is given by

$$f(b) = \frac{b}{v}$$

and is independent from $\lambda$. Therefore, in this case the bounded rationality of the bidders does not affect the equilibrium distribution of bids. Note, however, that we ruled out overdissipation of rents by assumption. For the case of general $B$ one can easily show using (5.12) that[13]

$$f(b) = \frac{1}{v\left(1 - K \exp\left(\frac{b}{\lambda}\right)\right)}, \tag{5.13}$$

where

$$K = \frac{\exp\left(\frac{v-B}{\lambda}\right) - 1}{\exp\left(\frac{v}{\lambda}\right) - 1}.$$

Let us concentrate on the opposite case and assume that $B \to +\infty$. Let us also assume that there are only two symmetric bidders and that $\lambda$ is small. Then integrating (5.13) one obtains

$$F(b;\lambda) = \frac{b - \lambda \ln\left(1 + \exp\left(\frac{b-v}{\lambda}\right)\right)}{v} + O(\lambda).$$

Straightforward differentiation implies that

$$\frac{\mathrm{d}F(b;\lambda)}{\mathrm{d}\lambda} = \frac{(b-v)\exp\left(\frac{b-v}{\lambda}\right)}{\lambda v\left(1 + \exp\left(\frac{b-v}{\lambda}\right)\right)} - \frac{\ln\left(1 + \exp\left(\frac{b-v}{\lambda}\right)\right)}{v}. \tag{5.14}$$

Let us introduce notation

$$x = \exp\left(\frac{b-v}{\lambda}\right).$$

---

[12]See AGH for a proof that at any equilibrium bidders with identical valuation choose their bids from the same distribution.

[13]Just recall that $F'(b) = f(b)$. Then (5.11) is a first-order differential equation for cumulative distribution function. General solution will depend on arbitrary constant, $K$, the value of which is determined from the normalization condition.

Then one can rewrite (5.14) as

$$\frac{\mathrm{d}F(b;\lambda)}{\mathrm{d}\lambda}=\frac{1}{v}\left(\frac{x}{1+x}\ln x-\ln(1+x)\right)<0.$$

Therefore, if the bidders are nearly rational increase in the degree of irrationality will increase the bids in the sense of the first-order stochastic dominance. A revenue maximizing auctioneer will, therefore, choose to obfuscate nearly rational bidders.

Notice that a pattern seems to emerge. First, the principal (auctioneer, seller) is more likely to benefit from bounded rationality of the agents (bidders, consumers) if the latter were to earn information rents under full rationality. This usually happens in hidden information models, therefore in such situations obfuscation is more likely to occur. Another important observation is that if there are several principals, for example, competing oligopolists, then competition will tend to reduce obfuscation, since from the point of view of the principals the latter is a public good. This last insight is due to Basov and Danilkina (2015) and provides an important lesson for the design of the optimal institutions. In the next chapter I will discuss a hidden action model, in which rational agents will always get utility equal to their outside option. In such a model, unless agents are too irrational and stay for a long period of time in an unprofitable relationship, the cost of bounded rationality is borne by the principal, who may choose to educate the agents and will never choose to obfuscate.

## References

Anderson, S. P., Goeree, J. K., Holt, C. A. (1998). Rent seeking with bounded rationality: an analysis of all-pay auction. Journal of Political Economy, 106, 828-853.

Basov, S. (2003). Incentives for boundedly rational agents. The BE Journal in Theoretical Economics (Topics), 3: 1–14.

Basov, S. (2005a). Bounded rationality: Static versus dynamic approach. *Economic Theory, 25*, 871–885.

Basov, S. (2005b). *Multidimensional screening, studies in economic theory* (Vol. 22). Berlin: Springer-Verlag.

Basov, S. (2009). Monopolistic screening with boundedly rational consumers. *The Economic Record, 85*, S29–S33.

Basov, S. (2013). Emotional temperature, probabilistic choice, and the optimal power of incentives. *The Economic Record, 89*(s), 84–94.

Basov, S., Danilkina, S. (2007). Bounded rationality, taxation, and prohibition. In: Proceedings of the Econometric Society Australasian Meeting. https://editorialexpress.com/cgi-bin/conference/download.cgi?db_name=ESAM07&paper_id=159

Basov, S., & Danilkina, S. (2015). Bertrand oligopoly with boundedly rational consumers. *The BE Journal for Theoretical Economics (Topics), 15*, 107–123.

Basov, S., Mirrlees, J. A. (2009). Nonlinear pricing under bounded rationality. SSRN Electronic Journal. http://papers.ssrn.com/sol3/papers.cfm?abstract_id=1399924

Basov, S., Danilkina, S., Prentice, D. (2011). When does variety increase with quality? SSRN Electronic Journal. http://papers.ssrn.com/sol3/papers.cfm?abstract_id=1242662

Baye, M. R., Kovenock, D., de Vries, C. G. (1996). The all-pay auctions with complete information. Economic Theory, 8, 291–305.

Ben-Akiva, M., & Lerman, S. R. (1985). *Discrete choice theory: theory and application to travel demand*. Cambridge, MA, USA: MIT Press.

Berger, J., Draganska, M., & Simonson, I. (2007). The influence of product variety on brand perception and choice. *Marketing Science, 26*, 460–472.

Carlin, B. I. (2009). Strategic price complexity in retail financial markets. *Journal of Financial Economics, 91*, 278–287.

Damasio, A. R. (2005). *Desecrates error: emotions, reason, and the human brain*. Penguin Books: Harmondsworth, UK.

Desecrates, R. (1968) . Discourse on method; And the meditations. Harmondsworth, UK: Penguin Books.

Ellison, G., & Ellison, S. F. (2009). Search, obfuscation, and price elasticities on the internet. *Econometrica, 77*, 427–452.

Ellison, G., & Wolitzky, A. (2012). A search cost model of obfuscation. *RAND Journal of Economics, 43*, 417–441.

Gabaix, X., & Laibson, D. (2004). *Competition and consumer confusion*. Mimeo, Harvard University and MIT.

Griffin, J. & Tyrrell, I. (2003). Human givens. East Sussex, UK: Human Givens Publishing.

Grossman, S. (1981). The role of warranties and private disclosure about product quality. *Journal of Law and Economics, 24*, 461–483.

Kalayci, K. (2015a). Price complexity and buyer confusion in markets. *Journal of Economic Behavior & Organization, 111*, 154–168.

Kalayci, K. (2015b). Confusopoly: competition and obfuscation in markets. *Experimental Economics, 18*, 1–18.

Laffont, J. J., & Martimort, D. (2002). *The theory of incentives*. Princeton, NJ, USA: Princeton University Press.

Luce, R. D. (1959). *Individual choice behavior*. Wiley: New York, NY, USA.

Mas-Colell, A., Whinston, M. D., & Green, J. R. (1995). Microeconomic theory, Oxford, UK: Oxford University Press.

Mattsson, L. G., & Weibull, J. W. (2002). Probabilistic choice and procedurally bounded rationality. *Games and Economic Behavior, 41*, 61–78.

McKelvey, R. D., Palfrey, T. R. (1996). A statistical theory of equilibrium in games, *The Japanese Economic Review*, 47: 186–209.

Milgrom, P. (1981). Good news and bad news: representation theorems and applications. *Bell Journal of Economics, 12*, 380–391.

Mussa, M., & Rosen, S. (1978). Monopoly and product quality. *Journal of Economic Theory, 18*, 301–317.

Plato, (1902). *The republic*. Cambridge, UK: Cambridge University Press.

Wilson, R. (1993). *Non linear pricing*, Oxford, UK: Oxford University Press.

Yerkes, R. M., & Dodson, J. D. (1908). 'The relation of strength of stimulus to rapidity of habit-formation'. *Journal of Comparative Neurology and Psychology*, 18, 459–82.

# Chapter 6
# Bounded Rationality, Learning, and Optimal Contracts

In the models considered so far economic agents do not change their decision-making procedure with time. In the language adopted by Basov (2005) the models of bounded rationality we employed so far are static. Bounded rationality of the agents was captured in these models by assuming that the choice is probabilistic. Though static models provided important insights in the nature of optimal contracts and drew our attention to some limitation of rational agent paradigm, they cannot capture some important features of real-life environments. To achieve this, one has to rely on dynamic models.

In dynamic models individuals are assumed to adjust their choices over time in directions that appear beneficial. The dynamic approach originated in the work of Bush and Mosteller (1955), was introduced in economics by Arrow and Hurwicz (1960), and is represented, for example, by papers of Foster and Young (1990), Fudenberg and Harris (1992), Kandori et al. (1993), Young (1993), Friedman and Yellin (1997), Anderson et al. (2004), Friedman (2000), Basov (2003).

The distinctive feature of this type of models is an attempt to capture the fine-grain adjustments made by the individuals on the basis of their current experiences. On a very general level, such adjustments produce a stochastic process on the choice set. The probability distribution of choices of a static model can be naturally viewed as the steady-state distribution of the stochastic process arising from a dynamic model.

There are several reasons why a studying mechanism design problem, while modeling agents' behavior using a dynamic model is important. First, as argued by Basov (2005), if the choice space is multidimensional, the most common probabilistic choice models that assume monotonicity of probabilities in payoffs can be misleading. Second, the choice of mechanism can affect both the rate and direction of learning, and therefore, also the resulting steady state choice probabilities, especially if the latter are not unique, which can happen in the models of social learning. Third, in the models of social learning one may address the question of whether allowing communication between different groups of agents is beneficial for the principal.



S. Basov, *Social Norms, Bounded Rationality and Optimal Contracts*,
Studies in Economic Theory 30, DOI 10.1007/978-981-10-1041-5_6

Note that in such models the communication or lack of it can affect the principal's profits even in the absence of productive synergies between the agents.

While the literature on the dynamic models of bounded rationality is abundant and apart from the papers cited above includes extensive studies on learning in games and evolutionary game theory, little is done in the area of directly applying these models to analyzing the problems in mechanism design. A notable exception is Basov (2003). I will review that paper in this chapter.

Agency relationships form an important part of economic life. In the models we discussed so far, the agents possessed hidden information. In the model I will present below, they undertake hidden action on behalf of the principal. Among the most common examples of such situations are managers acting on behalf of an owner, workers supplying labor to a firm, and customers buying coverage from an insurance company. The common feature of all these examples is that unobservable actions undertaken by one party have payoff relevant consequences for another. This creates a moral hazard problem. The early papers that incorporated agency relationships into formal economic models were Spence and Zeckhauser (1971), Ross (1973), Mirrlees (1974, 1976), Holmström (1979).

Currently, there exists a big body of literature devoted to optimal contract design under hidden action. Although some features of real-life contracts are captured by this literature, several important deviations are worth mentioning. First, most real-life contracts are incomplete. They neither specify actions at each possible contingency nor use all available information. Second, as argued by Jensen and Murphy (1990), incentives in the real world are too low powered. Third, Bertrand and Mullainathan (2000) argue that insufficient noise filtering occurs, that is the basic sufficient statistics result (Holmström 1979, 1982; Shavell 1979; Dewartripont et al. 1999) is violated.

The conventional model is built on the assumptions of full rationality. In this paper I replace this assumption by an assumption of boundedly rational behavior. Introducing bounded rationality into a model of optimal incentives is important for being able to properly address issues of low-powered incentives, insufficient noise filtering, incompleteness of contracts, and robustness of optimal incentive schemes. As Hart and Holmström write: one will have to go outside the Bayesian framework and introduce bounded rationality in order to capture the true sense in which incentive schemes need to be robust in the real world (Holmström and Hart 1987). The model developed in this paper allows us to deal with the first two of these problems. Even though the issues of incompleteness and robustness are not addresses here, I believe that the model developed here can be considered as a first step to addressing these issues as well. Some hints along these lines are made in the paper.

Boundedly rational agents have to learn the optimal behavior. There exists a big body of literature on boundedly rational learning. It originated in the work of Bush and Mosteller (1955). A pioneering economics paper is Arrow and Hurwicz (1960). Some recent papers in this tradition are Foster and Young (1990), Fudenberg and Harris (1992), Kandori et al. (1993), Young (1993), Friedman and Yellin (1997), Anderson et al. (2004), Friedman (2000). The distinctive feature of this line of thought is an attempt to capture the fine-grain adjustments made by the individuals on the basis of their current experiences. On a very general level, such adjustments produce a stochastic process on the choice set.

In the above cited papers individuals adjust their choices based on their own experience. Learning is, however, often a social process. Therefore, it can be considered as a stochastic rule for adjustment of the current behavior that utilizes social information. An interesting model of social learning is a paper by Rosenthal and Gale (1999), where the population is heterogeneous and consists from the experimentalist and imitators. In the model of this paper the population is homogenous and each individual participates in three activities: gradient adjustment, imitation, and experimentation. Such agents can be considered to be procedurally rational; under some conditions the process may converge to the rational outcome. The stochastic component of the rule has the virtue of reducing the probability of getting stuck at a local maximum at a generic environment. I endogenise the random component by making it a function of others' actions. The endogenizing is achieved by making agents experiment more aggressively when there is less agreement in the population about the optimal course of action. This can potentially facilitate convergence, since the agents experiment less when the population as a whole is close to the optimum. I will call this type of behavior imitation of scope.

Note that though the agents in this paper are assumed to behave in a boundedly rational manner, the principal is assumed to be fully rational and to realize the way in which the agents behave. Though bringing bounded rationality on the side of the principal into the model is important, one can argue that the principal should be expected to behave more rationally than the agents, since her stakes are much higher. Since the model is already rather technically it seems a reasonable first approximation to assume that the principal is fully rational.

Basov (2003) finds that when a principal knows that a population of agents behaves according to such a process and plans accordingly, the contracts she offers can be very different from those of standard models, and the resulting behavior of both principal and agents can be more realistic than is depicted in standard models.

The model also allows us to discuss the optimal incentive provision in a multicultural environment. Even though the model of bounded rationality developed in this paper may seem rather specific, it turns out to be a special case of a general social learning rule, studied in Basov (2001). Hence, its predictions hold generically.

Before introducing bounded rationality, let us first briefly remind the reader the standard linear-exponential model which is a work horse of many applications of the contract theory. Assume that a principal hires an agent to perform a task. Let the gross profit of the principal be given by

$$\Pi = z + \varepsilon,$$

where $z$ is effort undertaken by the agent and $\varepsilon$ is normally distributed random noise with zero mean and variance $\sigma^2$.

Let only $\Pi$ be observable by the principal, but not the effort or the average market performance, at least prior to date when the agent is paid. This makes it impossible for the principal to base the payment to her agent on his performance relative to the market.

The Bernoulli utility of the agent who receives payment $w$ is given by

$$U(w,z) = \frac{1 - \exp\left(-\varphi\left(w - \frac{z^2}{2}\right)\right)}{\varphi},$$

i.e., it has CARA form, and the corresponding certainty equivalent is

$$\mathrm{CE} = E(w) - \frac{\varphi}{2}\mathrm{Var}(w) - \frac{z^2}{2},$$

where $w$ is the agent's wage conditioned on $z$ through $\Pi$. Given the wage schedule the agent first decides whether to participate and if he participates he chooses effort level to be

$$z \in \operatorname{argmax}\left(E(w) - \frac{\varphi}{2}\mathrm{Var}(w) - \frac{z^2}{2}\right).$$

The agent participates if

$$\max(E(w) - \frac{\varphi}{2}\mathrm{Var}(w) - \frac{z^2}{2}) \geq 0.$$

Let us restrict our attention to the situation when the principal is restricted to offering affine contracts

$$w = \alpha\Pi + \beta.$$

It is easy to see that given such a wage contract

$$Ew = \alpha z + \beta, \mathrm{Var}(w) = \alpha^2\sigma^2,$$

i.e., increasing the slope of the incentive scheme creates more powerful incentives, but exposes the agent to more risk. A rational agent will choose $z = \alpha$. Taking this into account the principal will choose $\beta$ to ensure that the agent is indifferent between participating and nonparticipating, which implies

$$\beta = \frac{\alpha^2(\varphi\sigma^2 - 1)}{2}.$$

Substituting it into the principal's objective one will obtain

$$E(\Pi - w) = (1-\alpha)\alpha - \frac{\alpha^2(\varphi\sigma^2 - 1)}{2},$$

where I took into account the agent's optimal choice of effort. Maximizing it with respect to $\alpha$ leads to

$$\alpha = \frac{1}{1+\varphi\sigma^2}.$$

The principal's net expected profits are

$$E(\Pi - w) = \frac{1}{2(1+\varphi\sigma^2)}.$$

Now let us suppose that the agent starts with some idea of an appropriate level of effort and gradually adjusts it in the light of her experience. The initial level of effort can be determined by the agent's culture or the way she perceives the social norms of the organization. I will have more to say about the interaction of social norms with the incentive structure in Chap. 7.

Let the general structure of the model be the same as above and let us again restrict our attention to affine compensation schemes. Such schemes exert a constant incentive pressure on the agents, which is a reasonable assumption given that CARA utility function we employ does not allow for income effects. However, now instead of assuming that the agent responds rationally to the incentive scheme, I assume that she conditionally on the decision to participate she starts exerting an effort adjusts it according to the differential equation

$$\frac{dz}{dt} = \alpha(t) - z. \tag{6.1}$$

The function on the right hand side of this equation is the derivative of the agent's certainty equivalent with respect to $z$. It is worth mentioning that units of utility have meaning in this framework since they determine the speed of adaptation. This contrasts with the rational paradigm where utility units are arbitrary.

The agent is therefore boundedly rational when choosing the effort. However, I assume that her participation decision is myopically rational, i.e., she participates if her instantaneous utility at time t is nonnegative, that is if, given her current effort level, $z$

$$\alpha z - \frac{z^2}{2} - \frac{\varphi\alpha^2\sigma^2}{2} + \beta \geq 0. \tag{6.2}$$

Following Basov (2003), assume that the principal seeks to maximize the discounted expected present value of net profits, subject to (6.1) and (6.2). Solving

(6.2) with equality for $\beta$, one gets the following optimal control problem for the principal:

$$V(z_0) = \max \int_0^{+\infty} \exp(-\rho t)\left(z - \frac{z^2}{2} - \frac{\varphi\alpha^2\sigma^2}{2}\right)dt$$

subject to (6.1) and the initial condition $z = z_0$, where $\rho > 0$ is the principal's discount factor. This is a straightforward optimal control problem, and the solution can be easily found to be[1]

$$\alpha(t) = \frac{1}{1+\varphi\sigma^2(1+\rho)} + \left(z^0 - \frac{1}{1+\varphi\sigma^2(1+\rho)}\right)(1-\gamma)\exp(-\gamma t)$$

$$z(t) = \frac{1}{1+\varphi\sigma^2(1+\rho)} + \left(z_0 - \frac{1}{1+\varphi\sigma^2(1+\rho)}\right)\exp(-\gamma t)$$

where

$$\gamma = \frac{\sqrt{(\rho+2)^2 + \frac{4}{\varphi\sigma^2}} - \rho}{2}.$$

Two things are worth mentioning here. First, the slope of the compensation scheme, $\alpha(t)$, converges to a stationary value, which coincides with the slope of the optimal compensation scheme for a rational agent in the static model if $\rho = +0$. However, if $\rho > 0$ the optimal long-run incentives will be weaker than those for a rational agent. This result seems surprising at first. The intuition is, nevertheless, straightforward. Since instantaneous effort is insensitive to the slope of the wage schedule the principal has an incentive to offer flat wage and realize efficiency gains. She, however, has to trade this off against the decrease of the effort in the future. Therefore, the optimal power of the incentive scheme should be in between zero and that for a rational agent. Second, on the dynamic path $z(t) > \alpha(t)$ provided that $z_0$ is greater than the steady-state level; that is, the agent exerts more effort than would be myopically optimal, though the difference shrinks in time.

It is also easy to see that the present value of net expected profits of the principal as a function of the initial conditions has the form

$$V(z_0) = Az_0^2 + Bz_0 + C,$$

with $A < 0$ and $C < 0$. This implies that profits would be negative if initial effort is too high. In that case the principal would prefer to stay out of business. This makes intuitive sense since the principal has to compensate the agent for wasted effort due to the participation constraint.

[1]See, Basov (2003) for details.

So far I assumed that the agent adjusts choices based only on her own experiences and that the adjustment process is deterministic. In practice one will find it reasonable to challenge both of these assumptions: agents may from time to time experiment with the choice of effort.[2] They may also sometimes imitate behavior of other agents. Their rate of experimentation can also be affected by the spread of choices in the population.

To take these considerations into account, let us consider the principal's problem of designing the optimal compensation scheme for a population of agents. Assume that there is a continuum of identical agents working for the same principal and that the principal can pay a wage based only on the output produced by an agent but not on relative performance, and is bound to pay different agents the same wage for the same performance. Relative performance evaluation may be suboptimal if the agents cannot be prevented from destroying each other's output. Equal treatment (the same wage for the same performance) can be often required by the law of by a union contract.

Preferences and technology are assumed to be the same as above. But the effort adjustment process in the light of acquired experiences is more complex. Rather than simply climbing the gradient of their certainty equivalent, as assumed above, the agents are involved in three types of adjustment: gradient dynamics, imitation, and a particular form of experimentation: imitation of scope. Intuitively, the imitation of scope can be described in a following way. The agent, whose current choice is $x$, observes the choice of another randomly selected agent in the population, $y$. She than interprets the absolute value of the difference between the choices as a measure of spread of the population choices. The bigger the spread of the choices in the population the further is the society as a whole from the optimal choice, hence the returns to experimentation are potentially high. She interprets spread of the choices in the population indicates that society as a whole does not know the optimal choice, and hence that there may be returns to experimentation. Therefore, the agent opens a search window, the width of which is determined by the degree of disagreement between her current behavior and the observed choice of another agent and randomly selects a choice from this window.

Under these assumptions, Basov (2003) derived an integro-partial-differential equation that governs the evolution of the density of the choices in the population of agents and has shown that there exists a set of parameter values, for which the mean population effort is a fast variable, that follows approximately gradient dynamics (6.1), while the variance changes at a much slower rate and can be taken to be constant in the first approximation. More precisely, the evolution of choices of the population of agents is well approximated by wave packets which converge to quasistationary states. Intuitively, a wave packet is a solution to this integro-differential equation in which the mean moves according to the gradient dynamics

[2] Propensity to experiment may have evolved in our ancestors to prevent them from getting stuck in a local optimum. For example, when looking for the optimal fishing spot along a river, they may have found the one that dominates all the nearby locations, but even a better spot may be located a mile away.

and the variance changes so slowly that in a first-order approximation it can be considered to be constant. As the mean approaches its steady-state value under the gradient dynamics, a wave packet converges to a quasistationary state that is to a distribution with a very slowly changing mean and variance.

To formulate the principal's problem in such an environment, one will need to discuss the participation decision of the agents. Following Basov (2003), assume that each agent observes the variance of the current output in the population, uses it to evaluate wage variance and hence, her expected utility, and participates as long as it is greater than zero. This assumption can be justified in two different ways. First, since an agent is assumed to be boundedly rational, she is assumed to be incapable of evaluating the expected discounted present value of the incentive scheme. However, she realizes that her instantaneous gratification is a poor indicator of her future utility stream and hence, chooses to rely on the population information when evaluating the value of the incentive scheme. Another story is that the participation decision is taken by the workers' union on the basis of the utility of a representative agent.

Denoting it by *v(t)* the slowly changing variance in quasistationary state one can show that the principal faces the following optimal control problem:

$$\max \int_0^{+\infty} \exp(-\rho t)\left(z - \frac{z^2}{2} - \frac{\varphi\alpha^2(\sigma^2 + v(t))}{2}\right)dt$$

subject to (6.1) and the initial condition $z = z_0$. The optimal solution is given by

$$\alpha(t) = \alpha_s(t) + (z_0 - \alpha_s(t))(1 - \gamma_s)\exp(-\gamma_s t)$$

$$z(t) = \alpha_s(t) + (z_0 - \alpha_s(t))\exp(-\gamma_s t)$$

where

$$\alpha_s(t) = \frac{1}{1 + \varphi(\sigma^2 + v(t))(1 + \rho)}.$$

$$\gamma_s = \frac{\sqrt{(\rho + 2)^2 + \frac{4}{\varphi(\sigma^2 + v(t))}} - \rho}{2}.$$

Here $\alpha_s(t)$ is slowly changing function. Though in the very long-run variance *v (t)* will converge to zero and one will obtain the same solution as under pure gradient dynamics, in the medium-run the power of the optimal incentives is weaker and convergence takes longer. Moreover, along the optimal path the average effort exerted by the social learners is always less than the one exerted by purely gradient learners with the same initial mean and the optimal incentives are less powerful. The intuition for this result is straightforward. Social learning injects additional noise onto the system and makes the effort less sensitive to the power of the incentive scheme. As a result the optimal incentive scheme becomes less powerful and the average optimal effort falls. The principal's net expected profits are

$$E(\Pi - w) = \frac{1}{2(1 + \varphi(\sigma^2 + v(t)))}. \tag{6.3}$$

Therefore, that the medium-run profits under bounded rationality are smaller than under full rationality, while our specification of the participation constraint implies that the agents get the same utility on average. Hence, the cost of boundedly rational behavior is completely born by the principal. This implies that in this environment the principal will never obfuscate the agents. On the contrary, she may try to educate them to improve the quality of their decision-making.

The results obtained here can allow us to address interesting questions concerning the design of the optimal work place. For example, assume that there are two distinguishable groups of agents, which differ in their initial effort distributions. Basov (2003) refers to the difference in the initial effort distributions as a difference in culture. The principal has a choice whether to pool the groups, so the members of both groups face the same wage schedule and can observe each other's choices, or to keep them separate so they cannot observe each other and have different wage schedules. I will refer to the last choice as a differential treatment.

Note, that as long as there is no direct skill transmission from one group to another, the conventional rational choice model will predict that the decision whether to pool the groups together makes no difference. This conclusion is still true as long as learning is individualistic, which is the case, for example, under pure gradient dynamics. However, if the learning is a social process of the type described above, one can argue that, in the absence of positive productive externalities, the differential treatment is always optimal. The result follows immediately from (6.3), by observing that the principal's expected profits are convex in $v(t)$ and invoking Jensen's inequality. See, Basov (2003) for details.

Another observation made in Basov (2003) is that one of the main results of conventional contract theory, the sufficient statistics theorem, should be modified. The theorem states that when several signals of effort are observed, optimal contracts should be based on a sufficient statistic for effort. Since in the first best the principal should compensate the agent only for effort, it seems quite intuitive that second-best compensation is based on the best possible estimate of effort available.[3] However, this is not the case when the agents engage in social learning. Intuitively, the reason is that under bounded rationality, effort can be only partly attributed to the incentive scheme. The other part comes from the fact that the choice of effort itself is noisy. Since this noise will affect all the signals equally, one should put more equal weights on different signals than dictated by the sufficient statistics theorem.

[3]This intuition is a little misleading since in the equilibrium the principal knows the effort. However, to create correct incentives, she should pretend that she does not know and behave as a statistician who tries to estimate effort from available data.

Note that though there is a modest literature, some of it described in this book that addresses optimal contracts design in the environment when the agents' behavior is described by static models of bounded rationality; Basov (2003) is the only model, which employs a dynamic framework. It will be interesting to consider generalizations of this model. For example, one line of research is to assume that the rate of experimentation depends on the power of the optimal incentives. Such an assumption can be justified, for example, by assuming that the power of incentives affects the emotional temperature, which in turn affects the degree of experimentation. One can also study it in the context of multitasking. As argued by Basov (2005), it is in multidimensional choice problems, where the explicit modeling of learning is important and reliance of reduced form static models can mislead.

## References


Anderson, S. P., Goeree, J. K., & Holt, C. A. (2004). Noisy directional learning and the logit equilibrium. *The Scandinavian Journal of Economics, 106*, 581–602.

Arrow, K. J., & Hurwicz, L. (1960). Stability of gradient process in n-person games. *Journal of Society of Industrial and Applied Mathematics, 8*, 280–294.

Basov, S. (2001). Bounded rationality, reciprocity, and their economic consequnces. PhD Thesis, Graduate School of Arts and Sciences, Boston University, Boston, MA, USA.

Basov, S. (2003). Incentives for boundedly rational agents, 2003. *The BE Journal in Theoretical Economics (Topics), 3*, 1–14.

Basov, S. (2005). Bounded rationality: Static versus dynamic approach. *Economic Theory, 25*, 871–885.

Bertrand, M. & Mullainathan, S. (2000). *Are CEOs rewarded for luck: A test of performance filtering*. NBER Working Paper 7604.

Bush, R., & Mosteller, F. (1955). *Stochastic models for learning*. New York, NY, USA: Wiley.

Dewartripont, M., Jewitt, I., & Tirole, L. (1999). The economics of career concerns, Part I. *Review of Economic Studies, 66*, 183–198.

Foster, D., & Young, P. (1990). Stochastic evolutionary game dynamics. *Theoretical Population Biology, 38*, 219–232.

Friedman, D. (2000). The evolutionary game model of financial markets. *Quantitative Finance, 1*, 177–185.

Friedman, D., & Yellin, J. (1997). *Evolving landscapes for population games*. University of California Santa Cruz: Mimeo.

Fudenberg, D., & Harris, C. (1992). Evolutionary dynamics with aggregate shocks. *Journal of Economic Theory, 57*, 420–441.

Gale, D., & Rosenthal, R. W. (1999). Experimentation, imitation, and stochastic stability. *Journal of Economic Theory, 84*, 1–40.

Hart, O., & Holmström, B. (1987). The theory of contracts. In T. Bewley (Ed.), *Advances in economic theory: Fifth world congress*. New York, NY, USA: Cambridge University Press.

Holmström, B. (1979). Moral hazard and observability. *Bell Journal of Economics, 10*, 74–91.

Holmström, B. (1982). Moral hazard in teams. *Bell Journal of Economics, 13*, 324–340.

Jensen, M. C., & Murphy, K. J. (1990). Performance pay and top-management incentives. *Journal of Political Economy, 98*, 225–264.

Kandori, M., Mailath, G., & Rob, R. (1993). Learning, mutation and long run equilibria in games. *Econometrica, 61*, 29–56.

Mirrlees, J. A. (1974). Notes on welfare economics, information and uncertainty. In M. Balch, D. McFadden, & S. Wu (Eds.), *Essays in economic behavior under uncertainty*. Amsterdam: North-Holland.

Mirrlees, J. A. (1976). The optimal structure of authority and incentives within an organization. *Bell Journal of Economics, 7*, 105–131.

Ross, S. (1973). The economic theory of agency: The principal's problem. *American Economic Review, 63*, 134–139.

Shavell, S. (1979). Risk sharing and incentives in the principal and agent relationship. *Bell Journal of Economics, 10*, 55–73.

Spence, M., & Zeckhauser, R. (1971). Insurance, information and individual action. *American Economic Review: Papers and Proceedings, 61*, 380–387.

Young, P. (1993). The evolution of conventions. *Econometrica, 61*, 57–84.

# Chapter 7
# Social Norms and Optimal Contracts

Social norms are described by sociologists as informal understandings that govern individuals' behavior in society. Examples include driving on a particular side of the road on exchanging gifts at Christmas. When investigating economic phenomena and interaction of social norms with financial incentives, it is often useful to use a broader definition, adopted by the social psychologists, recognizing that smaller group units, such as a team or an office, may also endorse norms separate or in addition to cultural or societal expectations. Effects of social norms on individual behavior are well-studied in sociology and are known to promote prosocial behavior, for example, are decreasing alcohol use and increasing voter turnout. Social norms have a way of maintaining order and organizing groups.

A type of a social norm that is easier to understand from an economic point of view is convention that is typically modeled by economists as equilibria in a coordination game. Agreement to drive on the left or on the right falls into this group. There is an extensive literature on the evolution of conventions, which I will review later in this chapter and suggest a novel model to describe spatial spread of conventions. Conventions are easy to understand, since once a convention is at place individuals do not have incentives to deviate from it.

Let us consider an example of another social norm: giving gifts at Christmas. An individual has financial incentive to deviate from this norm, i.e., to receive a gift from a friend but not to return one. There are three ways to explain why individuals usually follow the norms like this one. The first assumes that the individual interacts repeatedly with his friend, so if he breaks expectation by not giving a Christmas gift, he will lose Christmas gifts (and possibly other favors) in the future. This explanation effectively states that gift giving is an equilibrium in the repeated game and should therefore be treated as a convention. Another explanation is that the individuals experience psychological pleasure from giving a gift or psychological cost if he fails to give one. This will give rise to a convention upheld by non-standard preferences. Finally, one can assume that reliance on social norm is simply kind of hard-wired heuristic, which will give rise to bounded rationality model of



S. Basov, *Social Norms, Bounded Rationality and Optimal Contracts*,
Studies in Economic Theory 30, DOI 10.1007/978-981-10-1041-5_7

social norms. The last two explanations require extra structure on the top of usual description of possible actions and their financial payoffs.

Recently, economists started to pay more attention to the interaction of social factors and economic incentives. Therefore, research conducted by the economists is converging to that conducted in other social sciences, such as business, psychology, sociology, in acknowledging importance of social norms in governing incentives of workers within firms, managers, and independent agents. A pioneering work in the area was conducted by Akerlof (1976, 1982), marking the birth of the literature that includes social norms in microeconomic analysis, discussed the role the norms of reciprocity and gift exchange. However, mechanism design literature ignored the importance of social norms for almost two decades following these contributions. The interest to the topic was revived after Fehr (2000) demonstrated the existence of reciprocal behavior in a series of controlled experiments, and Fehr and Gächter (2000) discussed the role of reciprocity in the general incomplete contracting framework.

The role of the norms of reciprocity and gift exchange on labor market outcomes is perhaps studied more extensively in the literature than the role of any other social norm. For an example of a reciprocal contract, consider the standard principal–agent framework and assume that the relationship lasts just for one period. Suppose the principal offers a flat wage, $w$. Since the agent will get the wage even if he shirks, the wage can be considered as a gift. Now imagine that agents can be of one of two types, self-interested agents who will choose to shirk, and reciprocal ones who will choose to "return a gift" and exert a positive effort. A self-interested agent will not exert any effort in response to such a contract. A reciprocal agent, on the other hand, will follow the norm of gift exchange and reciprocate in kind by exerting a positive effort, $e(w)$, with $e(\cdot)$ being an increasing function. If the proportion of reciprocal agents in the economy is large enough and the value of the optimal incentive contract is small, the principal may choose to rely on a gift exchange contract, rather than on a conventional one. I will study a model along these lines below.

Some other types of social norms were studied in the literature. For example, Bernheim (1994), explicitly introduced the norm of conformity; Bohnet et al. (2001), studied the importance of trust; and Fehr and Schmidt (1999, 2002), studied the effects of norms of fairness on optimal incentives.

Recent theoretical papers[1] argue that peer effects may also be important in providing motivation to workers. Sliwka (2007) and Fischer and Huddart (2008) developed models where social norms arise endogenously. These papers, however, require an entire population of agents and cannot be applied to the models of bilateral contracts. For a review of the literature on interaction of social norms and incentives, see Festre (2010).

The main lesson to be learned from this literature is that relying on a social norm creates a nontrivial trade-off. On one hand, social norms may be used to mitigate the moral hazard problem. For example, if the agents follow social norm of honesty,

---

[1]See, for example, Kandel and Lazear (1992), Barron and Gjerde (1997), Che and Yoo (2001), Huck and Rey-Biel (2006), and Huck et al. (2010).

risk versus incentive provision trade-off can be avoided by simply making agents to promise to exert the efficient effect, and reciprocal agents can work hard in response to an above-market wage. However, most social norms are more complex than simply honesty or reciprocity. They specify complex code of behavior and may restrict how the economic actors are supposed to share gains or losses, what is the maximal possible repayment on loan, etc. Therefore, social norms restrict the set of allowable contracts that can be signed between agents.

Basov and Bhatti (2013) were the first to study the trade-off between choosing to invoke a social norm to mitigate moral, while simultaneously restricting the set of available contracts, or not invoking a social norm and relying on the optimal incentive contract and concentrated on a composite norm of honesty and trust. In their paper, the agent follows the abstract social norm of honesty; however, this norm should be triggered by the environment. This idea is the main innovation made by Basov and Bhatti. In particular, they assumed that the social norm requires the agent to be honest, but it also requires the principal to exhibit trust by restricting the slope of the incentive scheme. The agent will feel disutility from breaking her promise only as long as the principal demonstrates trust.

In this chapter, I will discuss in detail a model built along similar lines, but applied to the question whether a multinational company should hire a local manager. I will further assume that the international manager is better qualified, but the local one can make workers work harder given the incentive structure by relaying on a social norm, e.g., loyalty. Later, I will also briefly discuss the model of Basov and Bhatti.

## 7.1 A Model of Reciprocal Wage Setting

Akerlof (1982), in his analysis of wage setting in primary labor markets, imposed a social norm of reciprocity which called for above-standard work performance in return for the above-market-clearing wages. He assumed that all agents are reciprocal and considered incentive contract as mean behavior per se. Under these conditions, reciprocal contract will be always optimal. However, experimental evidence suggests that nontrivial proportion of population seems to behave in self-interested way. Moreover, in practice one can observe the use of both incentive and reciprocal contracts. Hence, it is interesting to investigate how the type of an optimal contract depends on economic fundamentals.

Let us start by describing the production technology and the preferences of the economic actors. The model is similar to that in Chap. 6. Assume that a firm consists of a principal and an agent. Let the gross profit of the principal be given by

$$\Pi = z + \varepsilon,$$

where $z$ is effort undertaken by the agent and $\varepsilon$ is normally distributed random noise with zero mean and variance $\sigma^2$.

Let only $\Pi$ be observable by the principal, but not the effort or the average market performance, at least prior to date when the agent is paid. This makes it impossible for the principal to base the payment to her agent on his performance relative to the market.

The utility of the agent is given by

$$U = E(w) - \frac{\varphi}{2}\mathrm{Var}(w) - \frac{z^2}{2},$$

where $w$ is the agent's wage conditioned on $z$ through $\Pi$.

Given an incentive scheme, the agent first decides whether to participate and if he participates he chooses effort level to be

$$z \in \operatorname{argmax}\left(E(w) - \frac{\varphi}{2}\mathrm{Var}(w) - \frac{z^2}{2}\right).$$

The agent participates if

$$\max\left(E(w) - \frac{\varphi}{2}\mathrm{Var}(w) - \frac{z^2}{2}\right) \geq 0.$$

Now, assume that the principal could offer two different types of contracts, an "incentive contract" where the wage is an affine function of the output, i.e.,

$$w = \alpha\Pi + \beta$$

and a "trust contract" where the wage is fixed at some level. An agent could be either self-interested or reciprocal. Let $r$ denote the probability of an agent being reciprocal. Given an incentive contract, both types of agents respond identically[2] and act in accordance model described in Chap. 6. As we found in Chap. 6, the profits in that case are:

$$\Pi = \frac{1}{2(1+\varphi\sigma^2)}.$$

Given a trust contract, a self-interested agent will choose the effort level $z = 0$, while the effort of a reciprocal agent is given by:

$$z(w) = \sqrt{w},$$

[2]This is crucial assumption. It says that incentive contract is not considered as a hostile act per se.

where $w$ is a fixed wage. The fixed wage can be considered as a gift. Hence, the fact that effort increases with the wage reflects the observation that the degree of reciprocity increases with the gift size. If the principal chooses to rely on the trust contract then she will choose the wage, $w$, to solve

$$\max_w\{r(z(w) - w) - (1 - r)w) = r\sqrt{w} - w\}.$$

It is straightforward to show that optimal wage level is given by

$$w = \frac{r^2}{4},$$

while net profits are given by

$$\Pi = \frac{r^3}{4}.$$

To compare the performance of the optimal reciprocal and incentive contacts, let us first, consider the economy without any technological uncertainty, i.e., set $\sigma^2 = 0$. In this, the optimal incentive contract outperforms all reciprocal ones even if all agents in the economy are reciprocal. In the model above, one can see it formally by observing that

$$\frac{1}{2} > \frac{r^3}{4}$$

for any $r \in [0, 1]$. However, this result does not depend on particular functional forms for utility and cost of effort, on degree of risk aversion and the particular model of reciprocity. Indeed, while in a noisy environment reciprocal contract might outperform an incentive contract because it allows economizing on risk premium. However, since all sources of risk are eliminated from environment there is no need to rely on reciprocity. Note, however, that as the technological uncertainty increases, the reciprocal contract will eventually become more attractive as

$$\frac{1}{2(1 + \varphi\sigma^2)} < \frac{r^3}{4},$$

which demonstrates that for reciprocal contracts to become attractive, there should be enough reciprocal agents in the economy and technological uncertainty should play an important role.[3]

[3]As discussed in Chap. 6, bounded rationality can sometimes substitute for technological uncertainty to make reciprocal contracts more attractive. Therefore, one should expect more reliance on reciprocity in a complex environment.

### 7.1.1 An Evolutionary Model of Reciprocity

In the model presented above, the fraction of reciprocal agents was given. However, what determines the fraction of reciprocal agents in population? A pioneering paper that introduced concept of reciprocity to economics is Akerlof (1982), who in his analysis of wage setting in primary labor markets, imposed a social norm of reciprocity which called for above-standard work performance in return for above-market-clearing wages. However, the social norm was imposed exogenously rather than explained. Baker et al. (2002) and Levine (2003), on the other hand, argued that reciprocal behavior can be sustained as equilibrium in a repeated game. Ghosh and Ray (1996) and Kandori (1992) considered some variations of these models that do not assume that fixed set of players are locked in a market interaction, but rather allow for it to arise endogenously. These models explain endogenous cooperation but fail to account for the experimental evidence provided, for example by Fehr (2000), who demonstrated that reciprocal behavior plays an important role even in the absence of repeated game effects.

Cross-cultural studies of the ultimatum game point to an interesting regularity. The probability of reciprocal behavior is insensitive to the size of the stakes involved, but is strongly affected by the stability of the relationships in the group under study. In particular, behavior is influenced by the general level of group cohesion. For a review of cross-cultural studies of the ultimatum game, see Mace (2000). One might argue that similar predictions can be generated by a repeated game model. For a discussion of the evolution of cooperation in a repeated game framework, see Axelrod (1984). Axelrod studied the repeated prisoner's dilemma. Evolutionary models have been suggested as well; see, for example, Gintis (2000). His approach is also based on the idea of a repeated interaction, but there exists a significant difference between the evolutionary and the repeated game models. In the case of a repeated game, an individual behaves reciprocally within a relation but has no reason to reciprocate outside it. The experimental studies show, however, that individuals reciprocate even if a relationship is anonymous, which cannot be explained by a repeated game model. This is anyway the concept of reciprocity I used in the model above. Therefore, I will take the point of view that reciprocity is an inherent trait of individual behavior[4] and ask whether such a trait can survive evolutionary pressure.[5] For this purpose, I will present a sketch of a simple evolutionary model of reciprocity. For a detailed analysis, see Basov (2007).

Consider a world that consists of a continuum of workers and firms that live for two periods. The firms are assumed to be profit maximizers. The workers can be of

[4]One can always assume that some experience psychological cost from breaking trust, while others find it pleasurable, but such an assumption will not add anything to the proposed model.

[5]In an evolutionary framework, Sethi and Somanathan (2003) also show how a population of materialists can be invaded by agents with reciprocal preferences. Their model, however, is too complicated to analyze the dependence of the share of reciprocal agents on the economic fundamentals.

two types: self-interested and reciprocal, and the type does not change during the worker's life. The firms do not observe the type of each worker, but know the distribution of the types in the population. They can offer two types of contracts: incentive contracts and trust contracts. Given an incentive contract, both types of workers react identically by choosing the optimal effort, which generates zero profits for the firms and zero utility for the workers. Given a trust contract, a self-interested worker shirks, generating utility $U_2$ for herself and profit $B$ to the firm; and a trustworthy worker exerts effort, generating utility $U_1$ for herself and profits $A$ to the firm. Assume that

$$A > 0 > B, \quad U_2 > U_1 > 0.$$

After the end of the first period the worker may be fired. The probability of being fired is $p_1^F$ if the worker did not shirk and $p_2^F$ if she did. Assume

$$1 > p_2^F > p_1^F > 0$$

and the firms observe whether the worker was fired in the first period before offering the second period contract. Finally, define

$$\Delta U = (2 - p_1^F)U_1 - (2 - p_2^F)U_2$$

and assume that

$$0 < \Delta U < p_2^F U_2 - p_1^F U_1.$$

After two periods, all workers and firms are replaced by a new generation of workers and firms.

The proportion of reciprocal workers in successive generations is assumed to follow the replicator dynamics, that is, it changes at a rate proportional to the difference between the workers' total two period utility average population utility. Let $r$ be the proportion of reciprocal workers. The firms will offer trust contracts in period one if and only if

$$rA + (1 - r)B \geq 0.$$

Since workers and firms are a priori identical, all workers will receive the same contract in the period one. If firms offer incentive contracts in period one, they will offer incentive contracts in period two as well, since no new information is revealed. Suppose that the firms offered trust contracts in period one. In this case, their behavior in period two is described as follows: if the firms offered a trust contract in period one, they will offer a trust contract in period two to all workers if $r > r^*$ and a trust contract to the workers who were not fired and an incentive contract to the workers who were fired if $r < r^*$, where

$$r^* = \frac{|B|p_2^F}{Ap_1^F + |B|p_2^F}.$$

Indeed, the probability that the worker is reciprocal conditional on the event that she was not fired is given by

$$p(R \mid \text{not fired}) = \frac{\left(1 - p_1^F\right)r}{\left(1 - p_1^F\right)r + \left(1 - p_2^F\right)(1 - r)} > r.$$

Therefore, since the firms found it in their interest to offer a trust contract in period one, they will a fortiori find it in their interest in period two after observing the outcome "not fired." The probability that the worker is reciprocal conditional on the event that she was fired is given by

$$p(R \mid \text{fired}) = \frac{p_1^F r}{p_1^F r + p_2^F(1 - r)}.$$

Hence, the expected payoff to the firm from a trust contract with a worker who was fired is

$$\frac{Ap_1^F r + Bp_2^F(1 - r),}{\left(1 - p_1^F\right)r + \left(1 - p_2^F\right)(1 - r)}$$

which is nonnegative if and only if $r \geq r.^*$ If $r = r^*$, the firms are indifferent between giving an incentive contract and a trust contract to the worker who was fired in period one. I will assume that in this case they mix with probability $q$ given by

$$q = \frac{\Delta U}{p_2^F U_2 - p_1^F U_1}.$$

The evolution of the share of reciprocal agents is assumed to be governed by the following equation:

$$\frac{\mathrm{d}r}{\mathrm{d}t} = \varphi(r),$$

where the function $\varphi(r)$ is defined as

$$\varphi(r) = \begin{cases} 0, \text{ if } r \in [0, \bar{r}] \cup \{r^*\} \\ r(1 - r)\Delta U, \text{ if } \bar{r} < r < r^* \\ 2r(1 - r)(U_1 - U_2), \text{ if } r^* < r \leq 1 \end{cases},$$

where

$$\bar{r} = \frac{|B|}{A + |B|}.$$

This evolution rule is known as the replicator dynamics and it states that the rate of change of the fraction of reciprocal agents equals the difference in payoffs between the reciprocal agents and the average population payoffs. If the fraction of reciprocal agents is small then everyone receives the same incentive contract and therefore there is no difference in payoffs between reciprocal and self-interested agents. If population is dominated by reciprocal agents, everyone receives reciprocal contract and self-interested agents free ride on the reciprocal ones, so the share of the latter decreases. In the intermediate range, reciprocal agents fare better, since they have smaller chance of being fired and therefore are more likely to have a reciprocal contract for both periods.

Note that all states $[0, \bar{r}] \cup \{r^*\}$ are steady states under deterministic replicator dynamics. However, if one allows for random mutations, states in interval $[0, \bar{r}]$ will be subject to random genetic drift and the fraction of reciprocal agents will eventually leave this interval[6] and be carried toward $r^*$. Therefore, the stochastically stable fraction of reciprocal agents is $r^*$.[7]

Some comparative statics results are worth mentioning. First, note that as $p_1^F \to 0$, the share of reciprocal types in the stochastically stable equilibrium converges to one. Hence, if reciprocal workers do not get fired the entire population becomes asymptotically reciprocal. On the other hand, as $p_1^F \to 1$ reciprocity disappears, since $r^* \to \bar{r}$, the boundary of the incentive contracts region. This suggests that in stable economies with low rates of job separation, reciprocity will be a more common phenomenon than in economies where job separation occurs more often. This prediction seems similar to the one that can be generated through a repeated game mechanism. However, there is one significant difference. A repeated game model will predict that workers hired by the firm for life will exhibit reciprocal behavior toward the firm, but they need not exhibit such behavior outside this particular relationship. The model of this chapter, on the contrary, predicts that workers from economies with stable employment will exhibit reciprocal behavior in all their relations.

It is interesting to note that both $r^*$ and $\bar{r}$ are invariant with respect to rescaling of the payoffs, which means that not only long-run behavior, also but the dynamics of the model, is invariant to it. They depend, however, on the probabilities of separation, in particular on $p_1^F$ that can be viewed as a measure of the cohesiveness of the firm–worker relationship. This matches the stylized facts reported in Mace (2000).

[6]If the population contains $N$ agents and each agent mutates with probability $\mu$ during time interval $\tau$, it will take time of order $\left(\frac{\tau N|B|}{(A+|B|)\mu}\right)^2$.

[7]For details of derivation and meaning of stochastic stability, see Basov (2007).

## 7.2 When to Hire a Local?

Consider a multinational company, which opens a division in a developing country. The company has to appoint a manager and hire a worker. Suppose that the company has to hire a worker from the local labor force, but it may choose to hire either a local or an international manager. I will further assume that the international manager is better qualified, but the local one can make workers work harder given the incentive structure by relaying on a social norm, e.g., loyalty. I show that if output is not too noisy indicator of the worker's effort and if the worker is not too risk averse than hiring a foreign manager is preferable. Otherwise, it is better to rely on a domestic manager.

Many firms today operate in different countries, i.e., they become multinational companies (MNC). When opening a division in a foreign country, an MNC is often constrained to hire workers from a local labor force, but can choose to fill top management position either with local or with foreign employees. When choosing the top management an MNC faces a trade-off whether to invite a foreign manager who is better qualified (for example, has an MBA from a prestigious university) or hire a local manager who better understands local social norms and can use them to mitigate the moral hazard problem.

In this section, I concentrate on the norm of loyalty. Workers who are asked and promise to exert a certain noncontractible effort by a manager will feel guilt from breaking the promise if the manager is local, but feel no guilt if the manager is foreign. Alternatively, one may assume that local manager has a nonmonetary means of enforcing her request, for example, reliance on local mafia. As a result, a local manager will have extra instrument at her disposal and will be able to elicit higher effort from the worker for a given power of financial incentives. When deciding whether to hire a local manager, this ability should be traded against her lower qualifications and therefore smaller direct contributions to the profits comparatively to the foreign manager.

I show that if the risk sharing motive is strong enough, i.e., the environment is too noisy of the workers are too risk averse, a local manager what be preferable. These conditions are likely to be satisfied in poor countries with weak legal codes. As the importance of risk sharing decreases (e.g., country becomes richer and develops viable legal codes), hiring more qualified foreign managers becomes preferable.

The formal model goes as follows. Suppose a capitalist would like to open a business in a developing country. To do this, she has to create a firm consisting of a manager and a worker. The worker should belong to the local labor force, while the manager can be domestic or foreign. The profits generated by the firm are

$$\pi = e + a + \varepsilon,$$

where $e$ is the effort exerted by the worker, $a$ is the ability of the manager, and $\varepsilon$ is a normally distributed random variable with zero mean and variance $\sigma^2$. Assume that $a \in \{a_D, a_F\}$, with $a_F > a_D$, and subscript *F*(*D*) standing for foreign (domestic), respectively. Let us also assume the manager is risk neutral and capitalist is weakly risk averse. Then they can perfectly align their incentives. This can be achieved, for example, by offering the manager a wage

$$w_E = \pi - K,$$

where constant $K$ is determined by the outside option of the manager.

The manager, in turn, has to device a contract for the worker. A contract consists of wage schedule as a function of output, $w(\cdot)$, and of a suggested effort, $e^*$. The worker decides whether to accept the contract and if yes, what effort to exert. The manager cannot observe the effort exerted.

Assume that the worker accepts the contract and exerts effort $e$; then his expected utility is given by

$$U(e; w(\cdot), e^*) \equiv \int u(w(x), e, e^*) \mathrm{d}F(x, e),$$

where

$$u(w, e, e^*, i) = v(w(x)) - c(e) - \theta_i c_P(e, e^*),$$

the physical cost of effort, $c(e)$, is given by

$$c(e) = \frac{e^2}{2}$$

the psychological cost from deviating from the recommended effort is given by

$$c_P(e, e^*) = \frac{\theta_i}{2\gamma}(e - e^*)^2$$

$i \in \{D, F\}$ is a binary variable denoting whether the manager is domestic or foreign, $\theta_F = 0$ and $\theta_D = 1$.

The last conditions indicate that the worker feels some loyalty to the domestic manager and experiences a psychological cost from not following her recommendation, but he does not feel any such cost if the manager is foreign.

The manager (foreign or domestic) will choose $w(\cdot)$ and $e^*$ to maximize the expected profits subject to constraints

$$e \in \operatorname{argmax} \mathrm{U}(e; w(\cdot), e^*)$$

$$\max \mathrm{U}(e; w(\cdot), e^*) \geq 0.$$

The first of these constraints is known as an incentive compatibility constraint and determines the choice of effort conditional on participation, while the second constraint, known as the individual rationality constraint, determines whether the agent would like to take the contract.

Note that though both a foreign and a domestic manager could recommend some effort $e^*$, such a recommendation will affect the decision of the worker only if the manager is domestic. As a result, the domestic manager has an extra instrument and generically will be able to elicit higher contribution to the profits from the worker. However, due to the lower ability, her own contribution to the profits will be lower than that of a foreign manager. Therefore, in deciding what kind of a manager to hire the capitalist trades off the manager's own contribution to profits, versus the contribution she can elicit from the worker.

To obtain a closed from solution, let us assume that the worker's utility function is of a CARA form, i.e.,

$$v(y) = ((1 - \exp(-\varphi y))/\varphi)$$

and restrict the set of allowable contracts to be affine in income, i.e.,

$$w(x) = \alpha x + \beta \tag{7.1}$$

for some constants $\alpha$ and $\beta$. Then, for any effort the wage in distributed normally and the agent's certainty equivalent is given by

$$u(w(\cdot), e; \gamma, e^*) = Ew - \left(\frac{\varphi}{2}\right)\mathrm{Var}(w) - c(e) - \theta c_P(e, e^*).$$

It is straightforward to see that

$$Ew = \beta + \alpha e, \quad \mathrm{Var}(w) = \alpha^2\sigma^2.$$

Given contract (7.1) the agent of type $\gamma$ selects the effort according to:

$$e = \left(\frac{e^*}{1+\gamma}\right) + \left(\frac{\gamma\alpha}{1+\gamma}\right). \tag{7.2}$$

The first term on the right hand side of Eq. (7.2) is the part of effort, which is not responsive to the incentive pressure. It decreases in $\gamma$, the degree of opportunism of the agent and helps to mitigate the moral hazard problem. Assuming the value of the outside option to be independent of $\gamma$ and normalizing it to be zero, $\beta$ must satisfy

$$\beta \geq c(e) + \theta c_P(e, e^*) + \frac{\varphi\alpha^2\sigma^2}{2} - \alpha e. \tag{7.3}$$

Let us first consider the problem of the domestic manager. The manager will maximize the capitalist's profits net of wages subject to (7.2) and (7.3). Note that Eq. (7.3) should be satisfied with equality. After using it to solve for $\beta$ and substituting the result into the objective function, the manager will face the problem of selecting $e$ and $\alpha$ to maximize the total certainty equivalent (TCE):

$$\mathrm{TCE} = e - \frac{\varphi\alpha^2\sigma^2}{2} - \frac{e^2}{2} - \gamma\frac{(e-\alpha)^2}{2}. \tag{7.4}$$

In obtaining Eq. (7.4), we used (7.2) to exclude $e^*$ from the psychological cost. Let us introduce a notation $\varphi\sigma^2 = \varphi_0 > 0$. Parameter $\varphi_0$ measures the importance of risk sharing motive and captures both the degree of the agent's risk aversion and the noisiness of the environment. The optimal effort, found by maximizing the TCE, is easily shown to be

$$e = \frac{\gamma^2 + (1+\gamma)\varphi^0 + \gamma}{(1+\gamma)((1+\gamma)\varphi^0 + \gamma)}.$$

The optimal power of incentive and optimal recommended effort in turn are given by

$$\alpha = \frac{\gamma}{(1+\gamma)\varphi_0 + \gamma}, e^* = 1.$$

To obtain optimal implemented effort and the power of optimal incentives for the foreign manager, simply take the limit of $\gamma \to +\infty$, which corresponds to the vanishing psychological costs. Straightforward calculations lead to following expressions for profits obtained by the foreign and domestic manager, respectively

$$\pi_F = \frac{1}{2(1+\varphi_0)} + a_F, \quad \pi_D = \frac{\varphi_0 + \gamma}{2(\gamma + (1+\gamma)\varphi_0)} + a_D.$$

The capitalist will choose a foreign manager if

$$a \equiv a_F - a_D \geq \frac{\varphi_0^2}{(1+\varphi_0)((1+\gamma)\varphi_0 + \gamma)}.$$

Note that the right hand side of this inequality is increasing in $\varphi_0$, which means that riskier the environment higher the skill premium required to justify hiring a foreign manager. The result is intuitive. Indeed, riskier the environment, harder it is to provide financial incentive, and therefore loyalty becomes more important. On the other hand, the right hand side decreases in $\gamma$, i.e., weaker is the loyalty motive lower is the skill premium required to justify hiring a foreign manager. Note, however, that even in case of extremely noisy environment ($\varphi_0 \to +\infty$) and absolute loyalty ($\gamma = 0$) the skill premium remains finite, i.e. $a_{\max} = 1$, which happens because the production technology does not allow for complementarity between the manager's ability and the worker's effort. By continuity, the result will continue to hold if the complementarity is weak.

One of the predictions of this model is that as a country proceeds on along the way of development it will prefer to hire managers based on skill (foreign managers in this model) rather than on the ability to invoke a social norm. Note, however, that in this model the skill premium remains finite, which implies that even if highly uncertain an environment is a sufficiently skilled foreign manager will be preferred to a local. This happens, as I stressed above, because the production technology does not allow for complementarity between the manager's ability and the worker's effort. An important avenue for future research is to study whether this conclusion survives strong complementarity between the manager's ability and the worker's effort.

## 7.3 Optimal Contracting Model in a Social Environment and Trust-Related Psychological Costs

In this chapter, we have discussed how some examples and social norms can shape optimal contracts. We started with a simple model wage setting in the world, where some agents are reciprocal and saw that reciprocity helps to mitigate moral hazard. Some other types of social norms were studied in the literature and have reached similar conclusions. For example, Bernheim (1994), explicitly introduced the norm of conformity; Bohnet et al. (2001), studied the importance of trust; and Fehr and Schmidt (1999, 2002), studied the effects of norms of fairness on optimal incentives.

However, recent theoretical literature argued that the effects of relying on social norm are more complex. Indeed, such reliance creates a nontrivial trade-off. On one hand, social norms may be used to mitigate the moral hazard problem. For example, if the agents follow social norm of honesty, risk versus incentive provision trade-off can be avoided by simply making agents to promise to exert the efficient effect, and reciprocal agents can work hard in response to above-market wage. However, most social norms are more complex than simply honesty or reciprocity. They specify complex code of behavior and may restrict how the economic actors are supposed to share gains or losses, what is the maximal possible repayment on loan, etc. Therefore, social norms restrict the set of allowable contracts that can be signed between agents.

Basov and Bhatti (2013) studied the trade-off between choosing to invoke a social norm to mitigate moral, while simultaneously restricting the set of available contracts, or not invoking a social norm and relying on the optimal incentive contract. They concentrate their attention on an example of a composite norm of honesty and trust. Conceptually, the role of trust in the paper is similar to that in the paper of Sliwka (2007), though the economic environment is very different. The agent is assumed to follow the abstract social norm of honesty, which makes it similar to the earlier papers. However, this norm should be triggered by the environment. The idea that the social norm should be triggered by the environment is the main innovation of this paper. We study it in the context of a bilateral principal–agent relationship. Another reason to concentrate on bilateral contracts is that, as pointed out by Hart (2001), when considering a theory of a firm one has to separate the corporate culture of the firm from the social norms held by its personnel. This difficulty does not arise in a bilateral relationship. Therefore, studying a bilateral contract and assuming that agents follow personal norms is an important first step in building richer models with peer effects.

Basov and Bhatti consider a principal–agent model. The principal contracts with the agent on provision of a task. The success of the task depends on the effort exerted by the agent, which is unobservable. The principal has to choose whether to offer a standard contract, i.e., a wage-profit schedule, or a social contract, which provides the agent with an incentives scheme and also makes him to promise to exert a specified level of effort. The preferences and technology in the model developed by Basov and Bhatti are similar to the one of the previous Section, but psychological costs are triggered by demonstration of trust by providing lower powered incentives. That is, they assume that the social norm requires the agent to be honest, but it also requires the principal to exhibit trust by restricting the slope of the incentive scheme. The agent will feel disutility from breaking her promise only as long as the principal demonstrates trust.

Some restrictions on the slope of the incentive scheme may be dictated by religious laws of various communities. For example, Islamic finance law requires that participants share in any losses proportional to their capital contribution, while profits can be shared in an arbitrary fashion, i.e., the slope of the optimal incentive scheme is restricted for the negative realization of profits. See, for example, Khan and Bhatti (2008) and Kettell (2010) for a discussion.

Gift exchange literature makes an extreme form of this assumption, by assuming that any incentives destroy the reciprocal motive, i.e., it restricts the slope of the incentive scheme to be zero. This is an extreme form of crowding out effect. Benabou and Tirole (2003) provide information-based explanation for crowding out. They make a crucial assumption that the principal has private information about some characteristics of the agent (e.g., ability or cost of effort) that the agent himself does not possess. Though one can easily come up with examples where such an assumption is appropriate, it does not apply to many other situations of interest, for example, shareholders providing incentives for a CEO.

Unlike Benabou and Tirole (2003), Basov and Bhatti do not assume that the principal has any private information concerning the agent's characteristics. Our paper also differs from Benabou and Tirole's in its predictions. While in Benabou and Tirole (2003) crowding out occurs for any level of incentives and high-powered incentives have negative long-term consequences, in our model crowding out occurs only when the power of incentives crosses a critical value. There is no crowding out either to the left or to the right of that value. Also high-powered incentives do not handicap the long-term performance.

Formally, assume that a principal hires an agent to perform a task. The profits generated by the agent are

$$x = e + \varepsilon,$$

where $e$ is the effort exerted by the worker, and $\varepsilon$ is a normally distributed random variable with zero mean and variance $\sigma^2$. The principal does not observe $e$ and therefore is forced to offer a wage schedule $w(x)$. If the agent accepts the contract and exerts effort $e$; then his expected utility is given by

$$U(e; w(\cdot), e^*) \equiv \int u(w(x), e, e^*) \mathrm{d}F(x, e),$$

where

$$u(w, e, e^*, i) = v(w(x) - c(e) - \theta_i c_P(e, e^*)),$$

the physical cost of effort, $c(e)$, is given by

$$c(e) = \frac{e^2}{2}$$

the psychological cost from deviating from the recommended effort is given by

$$c_P(e, e^*) = \frac{\theta_i}{2\gamma}(e - e^*)^2,$$

where

$$\theta_i = 1 \text{ if } \sup(w'(x)) \leq \alpha_c$$

and

$$\theta_i = 0 \text{ if } \sup(w'(x)) > \alpha_c.$$

Again for simplicity let us restrict attention to the situation, when the principal is bound to offer affine contracts, i.e.,

$$w(x) = \alpha x + \beta.$$

First, let us assume that the principal decides to invoke social norm. Going through calculations similar to those in the previous section, one obtains that assuming the agent feels disutility from cheating; then she will choose the effort according to

$$e = \left(\frac{e^*}{1+\gamma}\right) + \left(\frac{\gamma\alpha}{1+\gamma}\right). \tag{7.5}$$

As before, the first term on the right hand side of Eq. (7.5) is the part of effort, which is not responsive to the incentive pressure. It decreases in $\gamma$, the degree of opportunism of the agent, and helps to mitigate the moral hazard problem. Again, one can write the total certainty equivalent (TCE) as

$$\mathrm{TCE} = e - \frac{\varphi\alpha^2\sigma^2}{2} - \frac{e^2}{2} - \gamma\frac{(e-\alpha)^2}{2}. \tag{7.6}$$

As in the previous section, let us introduce a notation $\varphi\sigma^2 = \varphi_0 >$ that measures the importance of risk sharing motive and captures both the degree of the agent's risk aversion and the noisiness of the environment. The optimal effort, found by maximizing the TCE, is easily shown to be

$$e = \frac{\gamma^2 + (1+\gamma)\varphi_0 + \gamma}{(1+\gamma)((1+\gamma)\varphi_0 + \gamma)}. \tag{7.7}$$

The optimal power of incentive and optimal recommended effort in turn are given by

$$\alpha = \frac{\gamma}{(1+\gamma)\varphi^0 + \gamma}, e^* = 1. \tag{7.8}$$

Equations (7.7) and (7.8) provide us with a solution as long as the risk sharing motive is strong enough, i.e.:

$$\varphi_0 > \frac{(1-\alpha_c)\gamma}{(1+\gamma)\alpha_c} = \varphi_0^c. \tag{7.9}$$

We will refer to the right value $\varphi_0^c$ determined by (7.9) as the critical value.

Note that if (7.9) holds, the social norm mitigates the moral hazard problem, i.e., effort is higher than it would have been in the absence of the social norm. In particular, effort remains positive in the limit when the risk sharing motive becomes infinitely important and the power of optimal incentives converges to zero. Note also that the social norm is always invoked if $\alpha_c > 1$ or $\gamma = 0$. If condition (7.9) does not hold the principal has two choices, she can either not invoke the social norm at all and offer the optimal financial contract, which will have $\alpha > \alpha_c$, or she can invoke the social norm and offer a contract with $\alpha = \alpha_c$.

If she chooses not to invoke the social norm then we can use the results from Chap. 6 to obtain

$$\alpha = \frac{1}{1+\varphi_0}.$$

The principal's net expected profits are

$$E(\Pi - w) = \frac{1}{2(1 + \varphi^0)}.$$

If, on the other hand, the principal decides to rely on a social norm, she will set $\alpha = \alpha_c$ and $e^* = 1$. Basov and Bhatti (2013) calculated the profits from this contract[8] and established that at the neighborhood of $\varphi_0^c$ the principal is still better off relying on the social norm. The intuition for this result is quite simple. Assume that $\varphi_0$ is only slightly smaller than $\varphi_0^c$. If the agent continued to feel disutility from breaking his promise irrespective of $\alpha$, the optimal contract would have specified $\alpha$ only slightly above $\alpha_c$. Therefore, specifying $\alpha = \alpha_c$ and still relying on the social norm results in the loss in profits of the order $O(\varphi_0^c - \varphi_0)$. On the other hand, not invoking the social norm and denying oneself the use of instrument $e^*$ will result in the loss of profit of $O(1)$. Therefore, for $\varphi_0$ sufficiently close to the critical value, it is optimal to still rely on the social norm.

This result suggests that one will observe either high-power incentives with

$$\alpha \in \left[\frac{1}{1 + \varphi_0^c}, 1\right]$$

or low power incentives with

$$\alpha \in \left[0, \frac{\gamma}{(1 + \gamma)\varphi_0^c + \gamma}\right].$$

Medium power incentives in the range

$$\alpha \in \left[\frac{\gamma}{(1 + \gamma)\varphi_0^c + \gamma}, \frac{1}{1 + \varphi_0^c}\right]$$

are never observed, i.e., the model predicts a gap in the power of the incentive schemes. Informally, the model can be said to predict emergence of two cultures: bureaucratic culture with lower powered incentives and heavy reliance on the social norms and corporate culture with reliance of high-power incentives, with social norms playing little or no role.

If the opportunism parameter is unobservable, the workers can self-select into different organizations characterized by different cultures. Basov and Bhatti considered an extreme case, when $\varphi_0$ is infinite and therefore financial incentive are completely ineffective. In this situation, it will be impossible to have any production in the world populated by purely opportunistic agents. However, if agents feel guilt from cheating, but do so to a different degree, the principal can offer a menu of

[8]The calculation is tedious but straightforward.

contracts, which will differ in recommended effort and fixed wage. Equivalently, the principal asks the agent to promise to exert effort $e^*$ and offers a wage $\beta(e^*)$, where $\beta(\cdot)$ is an increasing function.

This is a standard screening problem and can be readily handled by techniques developed by Mussa and Rosen (1978). One can show that relatively honest agents select the contracts that ask them to exert low effort and pay low salaries, while more opportunistic agents select the contracts that ask them to exert high efforts and pay higher salaries. The principal will earn positive profits if the agent turns to be sufficiently honest and experiences losses otherwise. Basov and Bhatti provided a numerical example when reliance on the social norm provides the principal with positive expected profits even in the presence of opportunistic agents, while reliance purely on the financial incentives in this environment will have resulted in zero profits.

The case when $\varphi_0$ is finite is more complicated. Formally, it gives rise to a multidimensional screening model with moral hazard, similar to one studied in Basov and Danilkina (2010). One cannot obtain a closed form solution in that case, but the problem can still be studied numerically.

To conclude, I presented here a model, where a principal has a choice between relying on purely financial incentives or on a combination of financial incentives and a social norm of honesty and trust. The cost of invoking the social norm is that it restricts the power of incentives the principal can use, since too strong incentives will be interpreted by the agent as a lack of trust and will free him from guilt for a dishonest behavior. We show that if the risk sharing concern is not very important, the principal will choose a standard contract based on purely financial contract. On the other hand, as the importance of risk sharing increases, either due to higher risk aversion of the agent or increased noisiness of the environment, the principal will choose to invoke the social norm. Reliance on the social norm will result in positive effort and profits even if risk sharing concerns become infinitely important. The last conclusion is robust with respect to introduction of private information about the trustworthiness of the agent. I believe that study of such models can bring new interesting insights into ethical finance literature and business.

## 7.4 High-Performance Work Systems and Interaction-Based Approach to Socioeconomic Behavior

Recently, the attention of researchers was in human resource management was caught by so-called high-performance work systems (HPWS). HPWS are organizations that utilize a managing approach which differs radically from the traditional hierarchical one. The main features of this approach, as summarized in Pfeffer (1998), are the following: employment security; selective hiring of new personnel; self-managed teams and decentralization of decision-making as the basic principles of organizational design; comparatively high compensation contingent on organizational performance; extensive training; reduced status distinctions and barriers, including dress, language, office arrangements, and wage differentials across levels; extensive sharing of financial and performance information throughout the organization. Among the successful companies adopting this approach are, for example, Men's Wearhouse, Southwest Airlines, Procter and Gamble.

HPWS approach to managing human resources is fundamentally different to the traditional one. For a summary of the later see Lazear (1995). Some principles employed by HPWS are in direct contradiction with the traditional approach. For example, team self-management and compensation based on organizational performance is believed to create moral hazard in teams problem (Holmström 1982), reduced status distinctions reduce competition prizes and makes it harder to induce the first best based on relative performance evaluations (Lazear 1995).

Lawrence and Lorsch (1967) documented that the difference in the human resources management strategy depends on the size and type of organization. Small enterprises rely primarily on the financial incentives, big organization rely on financial incentive to some extent, but also put a value on a commitment of workers to the organizations, while civil services do not rely on financial incentives at all. Lawrence and Lorsch come to a conclusion that there is no uniformly optimal way to design an organization.

The best studied way to design organization is through a system of incentive contracts. The main idea of proponents of HPWS, on the other hand, is to create an organization based on employee involvement rather than on explicit financial incentives. However, the traditional approach offers few tools to model this idea formally. In this paper, I apply the interaction-based approach to socioeconomic behavior developed by Brock and Durlauf (2001) to explain the performance of HPWS. I will also study the dependence of performance of HPWS from the size through some numerical examples.

The main difference of the interaction-based approach from other types of economic modeling is its focus on direct interdependence between economic actors. In Brock and Durlauf (2001), this is achieved by postulating social preferences. From the point of view of the long-run outcome, postulating social preferences is equivalent to sticking with individual preferences, but assuming that agents are boundedly rational and adjust their choices gradually, where the adjustment reflects partially the gradient of the individual's utility and partially imitation of peers' choices (Basov 2007).

Before modeling performance of a HPWS, let us briefly review of a simple variant of the interaction-based model of socioeconomic behavior by Brock and Durlauf (2001). The model introduced below has been used to interpret out-of-wedlock births and high school dropout rates (Brock and Durlauf 2001).

Consider the population of I individuals. Suppose that each individual faces a binary choice problem. Let the elements of the choice set be labeled $-1$ and 1. Suppose that each individual's utility is quadratic in her actions and in the actions of others and each individual experiences a pair of stochastic shocks $\varepsilon_i(-1)$ and $\varepsilon_i(1)$ that influence the payoffs associated with the respective choices. Each individual is assumed to possess expectations which apply to the choices of the others in the population. Formally,

$$U(\omega_i) = h\omega_i - \frac{1}{2}E_i\sum_{j\neq i}J_{ij}(\omega_i - \omega_j)^2 + \varepsilon_i(\omega_i),$$

where $\omega_i \in \{-1, 1\}$ and $E_i(\omega_j)$ is the expectation the individual $i$ possess about the choice of individual $j$. Assume that all terms $J_{ij}$ are positive. They measure the disutility of nonconformity. Typically, one will assume that $J_{ij}$ is big if individuals i and j consider themselves to be peers and close to zero otherwise. This means that this term can be manipulated by changing the perception of individual $j$ by individual $i$.

Random terms are assumed to be independent and extreme value distributed, which implies

$$\Pr(\varepsilon_i(-1) - \varepsilon_{-i}(1) < \gamma) = \frac{1}{1 + \exp(-\beta\gamma)}, \beta > 0.$$

The probability of realization of the value $\omega_{-i}$ is now given by

$$\Pr(\omega_{-i}) = \frac{\exp(h\omega_i + \beta E_{-i}\sum_{j\neq i}J_{ij}\omega_i\omega_j)}{Z}$$

where $Z$ is a normalization factor. Assuming that the choices of individuals are independent conditional on $E_i(\omega_j)$ one can derive the joint distribution of choices in the population. To close the model one has to assume that expectations $E_i(\omega_j)$ are validated in the equilibrium.

Let us assume, following Brock and Durlauf (2001) that

$$J_{ij} = \frac{J}{I-1}$$

and let $E_i(\omega_j) = m$ for all values of $i$ and $j$. Then the equilibrium condition is

$$m = \tanh(\beta h + \beta Jm).$$

The hyperbolic tangent is defined by

$$\tanh(x) = \frac{\exp(x) - \exp(-x)}{\exp(x) + \exp(-x)}.$$

The number, the sign, and the stability of the solutions crucially depend on the value of the parameter $\beta J$.

The last insight is important as we apply the model to the problem of optimal organizational design. To develop this application, assume that an organization consists of two layers, a lower layer with $n_1$ workers and an upper layer with $n_2$

workers. Suppose workers of both layers have to choose whether to work hard or shirk. I will model it assuming that they are choosing an effort level $e \in \{e_L, e_H\}$ Suppose that the output of the worker is a random variable with expectation equal to the effort level chosen. Concentrate for a moment on creating proper incentives for the lower layer.[9] One way to do it is to stipulate two values of wage $w_H$ and $w_L$ for the workers of two levels and promote a worker from lower to the higher level based on her relative performance. In principle, this scheme allows to achieve the first best level of effort (Lazear and Rosen 1981). However, if $w_L$ is restricted to be nonnegative (limited liability constraint), as the size of the enterprise becomes larger and the variance of output conditional on effort increases the above-mentioned scheme becomes too costly to the owner. Intuitively, this happens because the probability of winning the tournament decreases as the number of workers increases, and, hence, higher prizes are needed to induce effort. If an explicit incentive contract for the lower layer entails large distortions due to poor observability of effort or strong risk aversion of the employees, the conventional organization is doomed to perform poorly.

An unexpected solution in this case is to give up the idea of creating explicit pecuniary incentives and to rely on social forces. This can create corporate culture capable of providing incentives to both layers.

Let us consider the consequences of the reduction of the wage differential between layers. This action makes little sense in a conventional model, at least as long as we abstract from the rent-seeking behavior. However, it can be justified in the interaction-based model of socioeconomic behavior. To proceed further, let us introduce following notations:

$$\omega_1 = e_H - \frac{e_H + e_L}{2}$$

$$\omega_2 = e_L - \frac{e_H + e_L}{2} = -\omega_1$$

and choose normalization $\omega_1 = -\omega_2 = 1$. Then the choice of effort is equivalent to choice of $\omega_i$. Let the utility individual i gets from choosing $\omega_i$ be

$$U(\omega_i) = h\omega_i - \frac{1}{2}E_{-i}\sum_{j \neq i} J_{ij}(\omega_i - \omega_j)^2 + \varepsilon_i(\omega_i),$$

where $h < 0$. Here, the first term is disutility of effort common to all individuals, the second term represents disutility of disconformity with one's peers, and the last term is an individual specific disutility of effort. Assume no promotion decisions are

[9]Wage of high layer employees should be understood as the certainty equivalent of the incentive scheme higher level workers face, which motivates them to take proper level of effort. Also, high layer employees can have their incentives stronger aligned with that of the organization even in the absence of explicit financial incentives via the career concern motive.

made and let $J_{ij} = 1$ if individuals i and j belong to the same layer, and $J_{ij} = \gamma$, for some $\gamma \in [0, 1]$ if individuals belong to different layers. Let $\gamma$ be a decreasing function of the wage difference $w_H - w_L$. The last assumption captures the idea the smaller the wage differential more similar are individuals to each other, and, hence, bigger the disutility of nonconformity. Decreasing differences in dress, language, and scope of responsibility has presumably similar effect. Assume that random terms are independent and extreme value distributed

$$E_i(\omega_j) = m_k$$

if individual $j$ belongs to layer $k$. Then the equilibrium of the model is determined from the following system:

$$\begin{cases} m_1 = \tanh(\beta h + \beta((n_1 - 1)m_1 + \gamma n_2 m_2)) \\ m_2 = \tanh(\beta h + \beta(\gamma n_1 m_1 + (n_2 - 1)m_2)) \end{cases} \tag{7.10}$$

It is straightforward to establish that system (7.10) possesses at least one solution. Indeed, it defines a continuous mapping of square $[-1, 1] \times [-1, 1]$ into itself. Since the square is convex and compact, existence of a solution is guaranteed by the Brower fixed point theorem. We will refer to the solutions of the above system as equilibrium organizational structures, or simply equilibria.

To study the properties of equilibria let us assume that

$$\beta n_i < 1, \beta\left(n^1 + n^2 - 1\right) > 1,$$

and $|h|$ is small enough in a sense which will be made precise later. Further, assume that $\gamma(\cdot)$ is a step function, i.e.,

$$\gamma = \begin{cases} 1, \text{ if } w_H - w_L \le w \\ 0, \text{ if } w_H - w_L > w \end{cases}.$$

If $w_H - w_L > w$ then equation for $m_1$ and $m_2$ decouple and system the reader can persuade herself by simple graphical analysis that it has the unique solution where both $m_1$ and $m_2$ are negative and increasing in absolute value in the size of the layer. Hence, workers on both layers on average shirk and shirking becomes more severe as the size of the layer increases.

The latter observation can explain why large organizations may find it too risky to rely on social forces. If the exact form of function $\gamma(\cdot)$, for example, the exact location of the jump, is unknown, than shirking at equilibrium will be more extreme is such organizations. Therefore, they may choose to rely on better understood conventional financial incentives.

On the other hand, if $w_H - w_L \leq w$ there exists $H(h) > 0$ such that system (7.10) has a symmetric positive solution which can be found from

$$m_1 = m_2 = m = \tanh(\beta(h + (n_1 + n_2 - 1)m)),$$

provided $|h| < H(h)$. Hence, a positive mean effort can be induced by decreasing the differences between layers, but this is exactly the practice of HPWS. Note, however, that the solution with negative $m$ still exists. Therefore, the principal will face the problem of equilibrium selection.

To get some filling of what levels of effort can be sustained in the equilibrium let us consider two numerical examples.

*Example 1* Let us assume that

$$n_1 = 96, n_2 = 97, \beta = 0.01$$

and

$$h \in \{0, -5, -10, -15, -20\}.$$

Then for each value of $h$ there are three symmetric equilibria.

$$m_1(h), m_2(h), m_3(h).$$

The efforts levels in these equilibria can be found numerically and are summarized and are given by

$$m_1(0) = -0.95, m_2(0) = 0, m_3(0) = 0.95$$

$$m_1(-5) = -0.96, m_2(-5) = 0.06, m_3(-5) = 0.95$$

$$m_1(-10) = -0.96, m_2(-10) = 0.11, m_3(-10) = 0.94$$

$$m_1(-15) = -0.97, m_2(-15) = 0.16, m_3(0) = 0.93$$

$$m_1(-20) = -0.97, m_2(0) = 0.21, m_3(0) = 0.92.$$

In this example, the size of each layer's population is close to the critical

$$\beta n_i \approx 1$$

and equilibrium with high average effort level exists. Let us next consider small layers

$$\beta n_i \approx 0.5.$$

*Example 2* Let us assume that

$$n_1 = n_2 = 51, \beta = 0.01$$

and

$$h \in \{0, -2.5, -5, -7.5, -10\}.$$

Then for $h = 0$ there are three equilibrium levels of effort

$$(-0.17, 0, 0.17),$$

while for each value of $h$, except for zero there exists there is only one equilibrium, $m(h)$ level of effort whose sign is the same as the sign of $h$. The values can be found numerically and are

$$m(-2.5) = -0.43, m(-5) = -0.52, m(-7.5) = -0.57, m(-10) = -0.62.$$

For absolute values of $h$ smaller than 0.0665 an equilibrium with a positive average effort will exist but the effort will be smaller than 0.17. For example, for

$$h \in \{-0.05, -0.06, -0.065\}$$

the highest equilibrium mean efforts are 0.137, 0.123, and 0.1, respectively.

These by numerical examples suggest that HPWS rules allow to sustain high average effort in equilibrium provided organization is big enough. The main advantage of this approach is that it is not necessary to pay information rent, the disadvantage is existence of a bad equilibrium with low average effort, which means that an organization has to solve coordination problem. The size of the organization will tend to exacerbate the latter problem. So, very bid organizations may find HPWS rules too risky.

As an organization gets smaller, the system of social incentives is no longer capable to generate equilibria, where majority of the workers work hard, but is able to somewhat mitigate moral hazard. However, its general performance is poor which is in rough agreement with stylized facts mentioned above.

It is also worth noting that, even though under some circumstances an HPWS is capable of sustaining sufficiently high average effort, it is always lower than $e_H$. Hence, explicit financial incentives are preferable unless the environment is too risky or workers are too risk averse. Since different organizations differ in observability of effort, size, and structure, the results of the paper can explain why no uniformly optimal way of organizational design exists.

## 7.5 Social Norms and Incentives: What Have We Learned?

In this chapter, I provided some examples where social norms interfered with purely financial forces to determine the optimal incentive structure. As we saw in Sect. 7.3, reliance on social norms can allow one achieve decent performance even in the environments, where reliance on standard financial contracts can fail. However, evoking social norms can also have its costs. Usually social norms are more complicated than just honesty or reciprocity, and may restrict behavior of the principal by mandating, for example, that she does not expose employees to too high risk or does not fire them during a recession. It may also prevent the decision-maker to invest in certain assets, prohibit short sales or charge of excessive interest,[10] and entail transaction costs to verify that the institution is indeed complaint with social norms it tries to exploit.

Another, more subtle, cost of relying on social norms is that the norms may be misunderstood by economic agents. For example, being offered above-market wage, an employee might simply assume that she is better than a replacement a firm can find on the market, rather than seeing it as a gift that needs to be reciprocated with hard work. She might even assume that if she is so good to deserve this wage, probably she can afford to shirk a bit. Therefore, other thinks been equal, relying on social norms can work best in small organizations with shared culture, rather than in multinational corporations with diverse labor force.

One can also ask a question: where do social norms come from in the first place? This question attacked by theorists in different fields. Common to all this attempts is practice of building of quantitative models of behavior. For example, game theory suggests individuals can calculate the cost or benefit behind possible behavioral outcomes. Under these theoretical frameworks, choosing to obey or violate norms becomes a more deliberate, quantifiable decision tackled by the literature on evolution of conventions.[11] An earlier psychological model that also assumes that the individuals are able to quantify effects of their decisions is the return potential model, developed by Jackson (1966).

A convention (a social norm) in these models is typically equilibrium in a coordination game and therefore following a social norm is individually rational. An exception is Basov (2007), who assumes that the agents are mobile and payoffs depend on location, and shows that stable stationary strategy profile will fail to be equilibrium at almost all locations. However, even if one takes point of view that conventions are equilibria of some game, it will only imply that the prescribed behaviors were optimal in the environment, where such behaviors evolved. The

[10]Provisions like this exist, for example, in the area of Islamic Finance. For a modern economic theory perspective on Islamic Finance, see Basov and Bhatti (2016).

[11]See, for example, Young (1993), Kandori et al. (1993), Hofbauer and Sandholm (2002), and Basov (2007).

crucial insight of evolutionary game theory is that behaviors change slowly, while environmental change can be quite rapid, therefore one can be justified to take social norms as given and not necessarily been optimal responses to the system of economic incentives, the point of view taken in this book.

## References


Akerlof, G. A. (1976). The economics of caste, the rat race, and the other woeful tales. *Quarterly Journal of Economics, 90*, 599–617.

Akerlof, G. A. (1982). Labor contracts as partial gift exchange. *Quarterly Journal of Economics, 97*, 543–569.

Axelrod, R. (1984). *The evolution of cooperation*. New York, NY, USA: Basic Books.

Baker, G., Gibbons, R., & Murphy, K. J. (2002). Relational contracts and theory of the firm. *Quarterly Journal of Economics, 117*, 39–84.

Barron, J. M., & Gjerde, K. P. (1997). Peer pressure in an agency relationship. *Journal of Labor Economics, 15*, 234–254.

Basov, S. (2007). *Partial differential equation in economics and finance*. New York: Nova Publishers.

Basov, S., & Bhatti, M. I. (2016). Islamic finance in light of modern economic theory. Palgrave-Macmillan: Basingstoke, UK.

Basov, S., & Bhatti, M. I. (2013). Optimal contracting model in a social environment and trust-related psychological costs. *The BE Journal in Theoretical Economics (Contributions), 13*, 1–14.

Basov, S., & Danilkina, S. (2010). Multitasking, multidimensional screening, and moral hazard with risk neutral agents. *The Economic Record, 86*(s1), 80–86.

Benabou, R., & Tirole, J. (2003). Intrinsic and extrinsic motivation. *The Review of Economic Studies, 70*, 489–520.

Bernheim, B. D. (1994). A theory of conformity. *Journal of Political Economy, 102*, 841–877.

Bohnet, I., Frey, B. S., & Huck, S. (2001). More order with less law: On contract enforcement, trust, and crowding. *The American Political Science Review, 95*, 131–144.

Brock, W. A., & Durlauf, S. N. (2001). Discrete choice with social interactions. *The Review of Economic Studies, 68*, 235–260.

Che, Y. K., & Yoo, S. W. (2001). Optimal incentives for teams. *American Economic Review, 91*, 525–541.

Fehr, E. (2000). Do incentive contracts crowd out voluntary cooperation?. Institute for Empirical Research in Economics of University of Zurich, Working Paper #34, http://www.iew.uzh.ch/wp/iewwp034.pdf

Fehr, E. E., & Gächter, S. (2000). Cooperation and punishment in public goods experiments. *American Economic Review, 90*, 980–994.

Fehr, E., & Schmidt, K. (1999). A theory of fairness, incentives, and contractual choices. *Quarterly Journal of Economics, 114*, 817–868.

Fehr, E., & Schmidt, K. M. (2002). Theories of fairness and reciprocity—evidence and economic applications. In M. Dewartripont, L. P. Hansen, S. Turnovsky (Eds.) *Advances in economic theory, eighth world congress of econometric society*. Cambridge, UK: Cambridge University Press 2000.

Festre, A. (2010). Incentives and social norms: A motivation-based economic analysis of social norms. *Journal of Economic Surveys, 24*, 511–538.

Fischer, P., & Huddart, S. (2008). Optimal contracting with endogenous social norms. *American Economic Review, 98*, 1459–1475.

Ghosh, P., & Ray, D. (1996). Cooperation in community interaction without information flows. *Review of Economic Studies, 63*, 491–519.

Gintis, H. (2000). Strong Reciprocity and Human Sociality. *Journal of Theoretical Biology, 205*, 1–11.

Hart, O. (2001). *Norms and the theory of the firm*. Harvard Institute of Economic Research, DP#1923. http://papers.ssrn.com/taf?abstract_id=269234

Hofbauer, J., & Sandholm, W. H. (2002). On the global convergence of stochastic fictitious play. *Econometrica, 70*, 2265–2294.

Holmström, B. (1982). Moral hazard in teams. *Bell Journal of Economics, 13*, 324–340.

Huck, S., & Rey-Biel, P. (2006). Endogenous leadership in teams. *Journal of Institutional and Theoretical Economics, 162*, 1–9.

Huck, S., Kübler, D., & Weibull, J. (2010) Social norms and economic incentives in firms, IZA Discussion Papers 5264.

Jackson, J. (1966). A conceptual and measurement model for norms and roles. *Pacific Sociological Review, 9*, 35–47.

Kandel, E., & Lazear, E. P. (1992). Peer pressure and partnerships. *Journal of Political Economy, 100*, 801–817.

Kandori, M. (1992). The Use of Information in Repeated Games with Imperfect Monitoring. *Review of Economic Studies*, *59*: 581–593.

Kandori, M., Mailath, G., & Rob, R. (1993). Learning, mutation and long run equilibria in games. *Econometrica, 61*, 29–56.

Kettell, B. (2010). *Islamic finance in a nutshell*. West Sussex, UK: John Wiley and Sons.

Khan, M. M., & Bhatti, M. I. (2008). *Developments in Islamic banking*, New York, NY, USA: Palgrave Macmillan.

Lawrence, P., & Lorsch, J. (1967). *Organization and environment*. Cambridge, MA, USA: Harvard University Press.

Lazear, E. P. (1995). Corporate culture and the diffusion of values. In H. Siebert (Ed.), *Trends in business organization: Do participation and cooperation increase competitiveness?*. Tubingen, Germany.

Lazear, E. P., & Rosen, S. (1981). Rank-order tournaments as optimum labor contracts. *Journal of Political Economy, 89*, 841–864.

Levine, J. (2003). Relational incentive contracts. *American Economic Review, 93*, 835–857.

Mace, R. (2000). Human behavior: Fair game. *Nature, 406*, 248–249.

Mussa, M., & Rosen, S. (1978). Monopoly and product quality. *Journal of Economic Theory, 18*, 301–317.

Pfeffer, J. (1998). *The human equation: Building profits by putting people first Boston*. Boston, MA, USA: Harvard Business School Press.

Sethi, R., & Somanathan, E. (2003). Understanding reciprocity. *Journal of Economic Behavior & Organization, 50*, 1–27.

Sliwka, D. (2007). Trust as a signal of social norm and the hidden costs of incentive schemes. *American Economic Review, 97*, 999–1012.

Young, P. (1993). The evolution of conventions. *Econometrica, 61*, 57–84.

# Chapter 8
# Miscellaneous Models

In this chapter I will deal with models, which are difficult to fit within any of the categories discussed above. In the first Section of this chapter, I discuss a model, where the market demand for a monopolist's good exhibits some viscosity. The model is motivated by an observation that in many markets, the aggregate demand adjusts slowly to a price change. Such a behavior can arise, for example, if each consumer adjusts her demand gradually. Another reason, which primarily applies in the case of a service, such as a subscription to a magazine or a long-distance company, is the attention budget. In this case, each consumer divides her attention between different choices she has to make and revisits each of her choices only from time to time. When revisiting a problem, the consumer makes a rational decision but only a small fraction of consumers is revisiting a particular choice problem at each moment of time. The last case was thoroughly discussed by Radner (2003). In his paper a consumer who has a willingness to pay for a service $v$ and faces price $p$ revisits her decision to subscribe for a service from time to time. The choice is binary, consumer can either subscribe to a service or unsubscribe. Since each consumer changes her decision rarely, the demand adjusts gradually to a price change. Viscous demand can also arise if the consumption good is addictive (see, Becker and Murphy 1988). Demand dynamics in that case is more complicated, however, since addictive behavior presupposes existence of a stock variable, consumption capital.

Applicability of the concept of limited attention in not limited to binary choice models. Marketing literature considered choice from arbitrary sets under assumption of limited attention and arrived at the notion of *consideration sets.* The idea is that given choice set $S$, the choice correspondence of a consumer is determined by

$$c(S) \subset \underset{x \in \Gamma(S)}{\operatorname{argmax}}\, U(x),$$

where function $U(\cdot)$ captures the consumer's preferences and $\Gamma(S) \subset S$ is the set of options considered by the consumer. One has to make some assumptions about



S. Basov, *Social Norms, Bounded Rationality and Optimal Contracts*,
Studies in Economic Theory 30, DOI 10.1007/978-981-10-1041-5_8

correspondence $\Gamma(\cdot)$ to be able to deduce some information about preferences from choices. The question was considered in Lleras et al. (2010), Richter (2011), Masatlioglu et al. (2012), who investigated revealed preference relationships induced by different axioms imposed on consideration sets. Note that in these type of the models consumers behave rationally within the consideration set, however, the choice of consideration set itself is not driven by any optimization procedure.[1]

In the first Section of this chapter I consider a more drastic deviation from the standard model. It is similar to dynamic bounded rationality models I considered in Chap. 6. As in those models, consumers face a repeated choice of a continuous quantity of a product produced by a monopolist. Their choices follow gradient dynamics; they are adjusted gradually in the direction of the increase of their utility. However, this model is different from the models considered in Chap. 6 in allowing customer turnover.

I remain agnostic about the source of such a behavior. One possible interpretation is that the boundedly rational consumers exercise a simple numerical algorithm directed at the maximization of their utility. Another interpretation is that the consumers are fully rational but face some psychological adjustment costs of changing consumption habits.[2]

The latter interpretation of the gradient dynamics is due to Friedman and Yellin (1997). I will also assume that some consumers are constantly leaving the market and are replaced by new consumers. The dynamic nature of the demand in the model allows drawing some parallels between this paper and the experience goods literature. The main difference of the experience good model from the model presented in this chapter is that in the former consumer is imperfectly informed about the product's characteristics, the change of demand in time occurs due to resolution of uncertainty with experience (see, for example, Ackerberg 2001 and references there in). In the model considered in this chapter, however, the information is perfect and demand changes for the reasons discussed above.

The second Section considers auctions where bidders high experts to advise them on the optimal bidding strategy. Experts are assumed to be fully rational, while the bidders are rationally-bounded, but if unsatisfied with the auction outcome can ask the experts to justify their advice. Experts will incur costs if they fail to justify their advice. One can interpret it either as a damage to their reputation or loss of job. Experts are fully aware of this possibility and take justifiability constraint into account, when deciding on their advice. Here I present a model, based on the paper by Basov and Danilkina (2007a) and use to argue that justifiability constraint will not affect equilibrium in the second price sealed-bid auction, but will affect it in the first price sealed-bid auction, breaking the revenue equivalence. The final Section considers a boundedly rational model of addiction.

---

[1]Except for the Richter (2011) paper, where this choice itself is driven by an independent preference relation.

[2]Numerous papers demonstrate that habits may play an important role in a variety of economic contexts. Examples can be drawn from fields as diverse as consumption and saving decisions (Faria 2001; McKenzie 2001) and brand choice decisions (Chintagunta et al. 2001).

## 8.1 Monopoly Pricing with Viscous Demand and Customer Turnover

Consider a monopolist operating in a market populated by consumers who behave as described above. At each moment in time the monopolist should trade-off the short-run incentives to charge a very high price (since the instantaneous demand does not depend on the price) with the long-run incentives to charge a static monopoly price. Hence, for such a market, the time path of the monopolist's prices acquires significance. In this respect this paper fits into the dynamic monopoly literature (see, for example, Dudey 1995, 1996 and references there in). There are two main differences in this paper from the traditional dynamic monopoly literature. First, is that the adjustments are made by consumers rather than by the monopolist. Second, the consumers make their choices myopically, not taking into account the consequences of their decisions on the monopolist's pricing policy.

In this Section I formulate the profits maximization problem for a monopoly and provide a complete solution in the case when a consumer's utility is quadratic in the monopolist's good and quasilinear in money. Hence, the monopolist is facing a box demand. I show that in this case there exists a unique price-quantity path that maximizes the monopolist's long-run profits. The optimal policy is to set the price equal to zero if the initial demand is below the optimal long-run level and at the maximal possible level if the initial demand is above the optimal long-run level, and keep it until the quantity reaches the optimal long-run level. Then the price is set to be equal to the optimal long-run price. Intuitively, if there is a fad, that is consumers purchase more than they optimally should, the monopolist fully exploits it. Note that fads die out quickly. The duration of a fad is of the order of magnitude of the inverse of the maximal possible price and converges to zero if the price cap goes to infinity. On the contrary, if the monopolist's product is stigmatized, i.e. the initial demand is lower than it rationally should be, the monopolist will set the price at zero until the target penetration level will be reached and will stabilize the price at the static monopoly level from that time on. Periods of stigma, unlike fads, can be rather prolonged.

An interesting question is how the monopoly's long-run profits depend on the rate of the customers' turnover. I show that if the average demand of the newcomers is high enough then the profits are always increasing with the rate of turnover. Otherwise, the monopoly's profits decrease in the rate of turnover up to a certain level and increase afterwards.

Suppose the monopolist can engage in activities that affect the turnover rate. Assume, for example, that the monopolist has a fixed budget, which it can either use to build relations with the existing customers or advertise and attract the new ones. Then building relations with the existing customers decreases the turnover rate, while advertising increases it. If the average demand of newcomers is large enough (they are already persuaded that the product is good) the monopoly will choose to advertise, while in the opposite case it may choose to develop relations with the existing customers instead.

Even though the literature on dynamic monopoly and experience goods abides, the literature that assumes gradual customers adjustment in response to the change in price is rather meager. The earliest theoretical paper in this vein is Selten (1965). In Selten's model finitely many firms repeatedly face the market. Time is discrete and the change of the demand for a firm between two consecutive periods equals the difference between the weighted average of the prices charged by all firms in the previous period and the price charged by the firm in the current period. Selten demonstrated existence of a subgame perfect equilibrium if the number of periods is fixed and known in advance.

Phelps and Winter (1970) studied a model in which there is a very big number of small firms. The evolution of the demand share of a firm is assumed to be determined by its own price and the customer weighted mean of the other prices.

Rosenthal (1982, 1986) and Chen and Rosenthal (1996) studied models of duopoly with "customer loyalties." In each of these models customers change their loyalties according to a "rule of thumb." These rules are different in each paper. The general idea is that customers tend to choose a provider who offers a lower price, but their behavior exhibits some inertia.

In all these papers customers behavior follows some "rule of thumb." Though these rules seem plausible, no attempt is made to justify them. Radner (2003) tries to justify the "viscosity" of demand assuming it has been caused by the limited "attention budget." He, however, does not provide an explicit derivation of the demand viscosity from a model of the optimal allocation of attention to tasks.

As I discussed above, the gradient dynamics, on the other hand, can be justified on various grounds. In fact, customers who survived long enough in the market will make near optimal choices. However, due to the customer's turnover, the price and quantity do not converge to the rational equilibrium even in the limit of an infinitely patient monopolist.

### 8.1.1 A Model of Viscous Demand

Consider a monopolist who faces a population of identical consumers. If a consumer purchases $x \in [0, a/b]$ units of the monopolist's product and holds $m$ units of money she derives utility:

$$v(x,m) = ax - ((bx^2)/2) + m.$$

The preferences for good $x$ exhibit satiation at level $a/b$ but are strongly monotonic for $x \in [0, a/b)$. If a consumer has wealth $w$ and purchases $x$ units of the monopolist's good at price $p$, she derives utility

$$u(x) = ax - \left(\frac{bx^2}{2}\right) - px.$$

Assume that the initial choice of a consumer is a random variable with a probability density function $f_0(\cdot)$. Each consumer adjusts her choices with time according to the rule:

$$\frac{\mathrm{d}x}{\mathrm{d}t} = u'(x) = a - bx - p. \tag{8.1}$$

Rule (8.1) is known as the gradient dynamics and was extensively studied by Arrow and Hurwicz (1960). At each moment $t$ some consumers leave the market and are replaced by the newcomers. The choice of a newcomer is a random variable with the same probability density function $f_0(\cdot)$ as the initial choice of a consumer. The turnover rate, that is the rate at which the existing consumers leave the market and are replaced by the new ones, is constant and denoted by $v$.

Let $f(x,t)$ be the population density of choices at time $t$. Then the time evolution of $f(x,t)$ is governed by:

$$\frac{\partial f}{\partial t} + \frac{\partial}{\partial x}((a - bx - p)f) = v(f_0 - f). \tag{8.2}$$

To see where Eq. (8.2) comes from, assume $\varphi(\cdot) : R_+ \to R_+$ is any continuously differentiable function of the choice variable. Then the expectation of its value evaluated at choices made at time $t + \Delta t$, i.e., $\varphi(x(t + \Delta t))$ can be calculated in two different ways. On the one hand:

$$E[\varphi(x(t + \Delta t))] = \int_0^{+\infty} \varphi(x)f(x, t + \Delta t)\mathrm{d}x.$$

On the other hand, one can write:

$$E[\varphi(x(t + \Delta t))] = (1 - v\Delta t) \int_0^{+\infty} \varphi(x(t + \Delta t)) + v\Delta t \int_0^{+\infty} \varphi(x)f_0(x)\mathrm{d}x + o(\Delta t),$$

where $x(\cdot)$ is the solution of (8.1) with initial condition $x(t) = x$. Equating the two expressions, expanding them in Taylor series up to $O(\Delta t)$ terms, and using (8.1) one obtains after simple transformations:

$$\int_0^{+\infty} \left(\frac{\partial f}{\partial t} + \frac{\partial}{\partial x}((a - bx - p)f) - v(f_0 - f)\right)\varphi(x)\mathrm{d}x = 0.$$

Since this equation should hold for any continuously differentiable function $\varphi(\cdot)$, one arrives at (8.2).

Let $\mu$ denote the average demand of the newcomers and $z(t)$ be the average market demand, i.e.

$$\mu = \int_0^{+\infty} xf_0(x)\mathrm{d}x,\; z(t) = \int_0^{+\infty} xf(x,t)\mathrm{d}x.$$

It is easy to see that (8.2) implies that the evolution of $z(t)$ is governed by the following ordinary differential equation:

$$\frac{\mathrm{d}z}{\mathrm{d}t} = a - bz - p + v(\mu - z). \tag{8.3}$$

The monopolist chooses price to solve:

$$\max_{p\in[0,m]} \int_0^{+\infty} e^{-\rho t}(p(t) - c)z(t)\mathrm{d}t$$

subject to (8.3), where $\rho > 0$ is the discount factor, $c$ a constant marginal cost of production $(c<a)$ and $m$ is the price ceiling, which is introduced for purely technical reasons and should be thought of as being arbitrary large. Let us also make the following assumption about the parameters of the model:

$$\frac{m-c}{b+\rho+v} > \frac{a}{b} > z(0),\; m > \frac{a+\mu v}{b+v},\; \mu < \frac{a}{b}.$$

The monopolist faces a standard optimal control problem. To arrive at the solution, form the present value Hamiltonian:

$$H = (p-c)z + \lambda(a - bz - p + v\mu - vz).$$

Assume that the average demand at time zero is $z_0$. Then applying the maximum principle, one concludes that at the optimal path the following conditions should hold:

$$\frac{\mathrm{d}\lambda}{\mathrm{d}t} = c - p + \lambda(b + v + \rho)$$
$$\frac{\mathrm{d}z}{\mathrm{d}t} = a - bz - p + v(\mu - z)$$
$$z(0) = z_0,\; \lim_{t\to+\infty} \lambda(t)e^{-\rho t} = 0$$

$$p(t) \in \operatorname*{argmax}_{p\in[0,m]} H.$$

Performing the maximization, one obtains:

$$p(t) \in \begin{cases} \{0\}, & \text{if } z(t) < \lambda(t) \\ [0, m], & \text{if } z(t) = \lambda(t) \\ \{m\}, & \text{if } z(t) > \lambda(t) \end{cases}.$$

Using these equations and the parametric restrictions introduced above, one can conclude that the optimal solution would entail charging either zero or the maximal possible price for a finite period of time and settling for a constant intermediate price after that. More precisely, let us define

$$z^* = \frac{a + \mu v - c}{b + 2v + 2\rho},\ p^* = \frac{(a + \mu v)(b + v + \rho) + c(b + v)}{b + 2v + 2\rho}$$

Then if $z_0 < z^*$ the monopolist should start by charging zero until the demand reaches level $z^*$ and charge $p^*$ from that moment on. On the other hand, if $z_0 > z^*$ the monopolist should start by charging $m$ until the demand reaches level $z^*$ and charge $p^*$ from that moment on.

The solution described above is known is bang-bang solution. Intuitively, if there is a fad, that is consumers purchase more than they optimally should, the monopolist fully exploits it. Note that since the time derivative of demand depends upon the negative of the price, the fads die out quickly. The duration of a fad is of the order of magnitude of the price cap and converges to zero if the price cap goes to infinity. On the contrary, if the monopolist's product is stigmatized, i.e. the initial demand is lower than it rationally should be, the monopolist will set price at zero until the target penetration level will be achieved and stabilize price at a static monopoly level from then on. Periods of stigma, unlike fads, can be rather prolonged.

It is interesting to observe that, despite the fact that for any given price surviving consumers will eventually make the optimal choice, for any $\rho > 0$ the long-run price is above and the long-run quantity below the price the monopolist would have charged and the quantity she would have produced had the customers been rational even if there is no customer turnover. Intuitively, this happens because in the short-run the demand is not responsive to the price. Hence, the monopolist's short-run incentives dictate her to set the price as high as possible. Hence, if the monopolist discounts future, price will be above the optimal price on the market with the rational consumers. From now on I am going to assume that the monopolist is infinitely patient, i.e.

$$\rho = 0+.$$

Note that in this case the long-run price is always greater than it would have been had the consumers been rational. As long as

$$\mu < \frac{a - c}{b}$$

(the average demand of newcomers is less than a rational consumer would buy from a competitive firm), the quantity produced by the monopolist is smaller than it would have been had the consumers been rational.

### 8.1.2 *The Customer Turnover Rate and the Monopolist's Profits*

Our next objective is to study how the rate of the population turnover affects the profits of an infinitely patient monopolist. Using the optimal pricing strategy described above one can see that the monopolist's long-run profits are[3]:

$$\Pi(v) = \frac{(a + v\mu - c)^2}{4(b + v)}. \tag{8.4}$$

Define $z_m$, the optimal level of monopolist's production if the consumers were rational, by:

$$z_m = \frac{a - c}{2b}.$$

If there had been no turnover the optimal long-run production would have converged to this level. Differentiating (8.4) with respect to $v$ one obtains:

$$\Pi'(v) = \frac{(a + v\mu - c)(\mu(1 + (\frac{v}{2b})) - z_m)b}{2(b + v)^2}.$$

Therefore, if $\mu > z_m$, the monopolist's profits always increase in the turnover rate, while if $\mu < z_m$ the monopolist's profits are U-shaped.

Now let us assume that the monopolist can engage in activities that can slightly affect the turnover rate. More precisely, let $v \in [v_n - \delta, v_n + \delta]$ where $v_n$ is the natural turnover rate and $\delta$ sets the limits within which the monopolist can manipulate it. For example, assume that a monopolist has some resources[4] she could spend either on advertising the product to new customers or building relations with the existing ones. Let us assume that if the resources are split equally then the inflow of new customers equals the outflow of the old ones. Also assume that additional $1 spend on the advertising increases the inflow of the new customers by the same amount as taking $1 away from building the relations increases the

---

[3]In the limit of the infinitely patient monopolist the value of the initial demand and the price ceiling are irrelevant, since the long-term price, $p^*$, does not depend on them.

[4]The total amount of resources should itself be a solution to an optimization problem. I do not model this choice explicitly here.

outflow of the old customers. Then the size of the population of customers remains constant and monopolist is effectively choosing the turnover rate. Advertising will increase the turnover while building the relations with the existing customers will decrease it. Our previous discussion suggests that if newcomers are sufficiently optimistic about the monopolist's product ($\mu > z_m$), the monopolist should spend all her resources on advertising, while if newcomers are pessimistic and $\delta$ is small enough all resources should be spent on the building of relations with the existing customers.

To summarize, the optimal policy for the monopolist depends on the initial demand. If it is law, the monopolist should initially charge zero price and keep it at that level till target penetration level is reached and then charge the stable long-run price. If the initial demand is high, the monopolist should start charging the maximal possible price to drive the demand to its long-run level and then charge the constant long-run price. The long-run price would be higher than it would have been had the customers been rational. The long-run quantity will be lower than in a market with rational customers, unless the newcomers are overly optimistic. If the monopolist has a limited control over the turnover rate she will try to push it up, for example by advertising, when the newcomers are optimistic and push it down, for example by building relations with the existing customers, when the newcomers are pessimistic.

## 8.2 Auctions with Opportunistic Experts

This Section is based on Basov and Danilkina (2007a). In this model the decision makers themselves are fully rational but are concerned that they may be forced to justify their decisions to a principal who is not fully rational and cannot grasp complex concepts, such as Bayes-Nash equilibrium. Basov and Danilkina start with the following example. Suppose you are called upon to advise a client who has to participate in a sealed bid first price auction. There are two bidders and their values come from a uniform distribution on $[0, 1]$. Assume that the realized value of your client is 0.8. What bid would you recommend her to submit? If you believe that your client's opponent will play the unique equilibrium strategy, your advice should be 0.4. Now suppose that your client's opponent submitted a bid of 0.45 and your client lost the auction. In this case you may be forced to justify your advice. Your client might ask why you shaded your bid by so much. After all, had you submitted a bid of 0.5, for example, your client would have won and enjoyed a considerable surplus of 0.3. She may have little patience for formal arguments, in which case you will be fired.

Basov and Danilkina (2007a) developed the framework that will allow incorporating the justifiability concern into the expert's objective function in the auction-theoretic context. Note, however, that similar considerations are relevant in a wide variety of context. Economic advisors for a government, experts giving investment advice to a pension fund, personal financial planners, and military advisors, among other specialists may all take similar considerations into account, which may lead to a choice of suboptimal options. When devising our institutions, care should be taken to minimize such concerns. In auction theoretic framework, Basov and Danilkina have shown that such constraint can be avoided altogether using the second price seal-bid auctions.

The concept of the justifiability of a strategy in a game was first introduced by Spiegler (2002). He assumes that a strategy in an extensive form game is justifiable if a player is armed with "smashing" counter-arguments against ex-post critiques. Having a smashing counter-argument means that faced with a critique of his action the player will accept the critic's logic and show that her ex-post recommendation would have exposed the player to the same critique in the opposite direction. The concept is, however, specialized for extensive form games and cannot be used in our context.

Basov and Danilkina (2007a), on the other hand, assumed that the client feels disappointed if she did not win the auction, but could have won it by submitting a bid below her valuation. In this case she asks the expert to justify her strategy. The client does not understand complex arguments; therefore the expert is unable to explain that the strategy she recommended was in fact ex-ante optimal. Instead, she can invoke recommendations of other experts and say: "look, what I have recommended is not that different from what they did." Here I assume that the probability that the expert fails to justify her bid is proportional to the difference between her bid and the opponent's bid.

If the expert fails to justify her recommendation, she incurs some cost, $c$. For example, in the case when the expert is fired if she fails to justify her decision, the cost is the difference in the values of being employed and unemployed. These values can be calculated, for example, in a job search model. Basov and Danilkina (2007a), allow for more general justification technologies, but this does not affect the essence of the results. The logic is that the words of the expert carry more weight if the other expert behaved similarly.

Below, I consider two auction formats: the first price sealed-bid auction and the second price sealed bid auction without a reserve price. We will see that in the first price auction the justifiability consideration increases the optimal bid, while in the second price auction bidding one's true value remains the weakly dominant strategy. Hence, the first price auction raises more revenue and will be preferred by the seller. This happens because the justifiability concern makes a risk-neutral expert effectively risk-averse. Both auctions remain efficient.

Note, however, that the last conclusion depends on full symmetry of the model. For example, if one client punishes the expert more severely if she is disappointed than the other,[5] then her expert will always advice more aggressive bid conditional on valuation in the first price sealed-bid auction, which can lead to inefficiency. This will not happen in the second price sealed-bid auction.

[5]Think of a dictator who shoots the expert if he did not win, but the price was below her valuation.

### 8.2.1 The Model

Assume there are two buyers who want to buy one unit of a good. The seller possesses only one unit and sells is through a sealed bid auction. Assume that the buyers' valuations are independent and come from the same distribution $F(\cdot)$. Normalize the support of this distribution to be the unit interval and assume it is absolutely continuous with respect to the Lebesgue measure with the Radon-Nikodym derivative $f(\cdot)$. Assume also that

$$f(v) > 0 \text{ for any } v \in [0, 1].$$

We assume that the buyers cannot themselves come up with optimal bidding strategies and therefore each buyer hires an expert to bid in the auction. The expert observes the buyer's value and is paid fraction $\beta > 0$ of her surplus.

If the buyers had complete faith in the experts, this model would have been equivalent to the model were the buyers bid directly, apart from the fact that they would have shared their payoffs with the experts. However, we assume that the buyers always have doubts in the expert's expertise. To model these doubts, I assume that if the buyer is not satisfied with the result of the auction, she will ask the expert to justify her choice. If the expert fails to do so she will incur cost $c \geq 0$. This cost can be interpreted as the psychological cost of her failure to persuade the buyer of the viability of the strategy. Another interpretation is that the expert is fired and $c$ represents the difference in values of being employed and unemployed. We assume that the buyer is not satisfied with the result of the auction and feels regret if and only if she had not won the auction and there existed a bid below her valuation that would have allowed her to win. In this case the buyer will ask the expert to justify her strategy. The probability that the expert will fail to justify the chosen strategy is proportional to the difference between her bid and the winning bid. Let $b(v)$ denote the bid of the expert when her client's valuation is $v$.

The first observation made by Basov and Danilkina (2007a) is that in a second price sealed-bid auction justifiability concern does not matter and as in the standard case each expert has a weakly dominating strategy

$$b(v) = v.$$

Indeed, since given this bidding strategy, a buyer never feels regret (because, if the auction is lost the winning bid was above the buyer's valuation) the result follows from the standard result for the second price auction (Vickery 1961).

The situation is different in the first price sealed-bid auction, since due to the shading of the bid the client will sometimes feel regret. Therefore, the characterization of equilibrium is more complicated. To arrive at it, let us assume that both experts bid according to the same strictly increasing differentiable function $b(\cdot)$. If the client's valuation is $v$ and the expert bids $b(v')$ her payoff is:

$$\Pi(v, v') = \beta(v - b(v'))F(v') - \gamma c \int_{v'}^{b^{-1}(v)} \left(b(x) - b\left(v'\right)\right) f(x) \mathrm{d}x. \tag{8.5}$$

The first term on the right hand side is the expected monetary payoff to the expert, where $\beta$ is the proportion of the buyer's surplus paid to the expert. The second term is the expected cost that arises from the failure of the expert to justify her bidding decision ex-post, where the integral is the expected difference between the expert's and the winning bid provided that the expert's bid is below the client's valuation, and $\gamma \geq 0$ is the proportionality coefficient. The case $\gamma = 0$ corresponds to the standard first price auction where the interests of the client and the expert are aligned perfectly. At equilibrium the expert should find it optimal to bid in accordance with the client's true value. Therefore, one can use the first order condition for the expert optimization evaluated at $v' = v$ to arrive at the following functional-differential equation for the bid function:

$$(v - b(v))f(v) + \alpha(F(b^{-1}(v)) - F(v))b'(v) = b'(v)F(v), \tag{8.6}$$

where parameter

$$\alpha = \frac{\gamma c}{\beta} > 0$$

measures the relative strength of justifiability concern.

It is easy to see that the optimal bid is an increasing function of $\alpha$. One has simply to express the objective function (8.5) of the expert as function of $(v', \alpha)$ and note that it satisfies increasing difference in incremental return in this pair of variables. Therefore, $v'$ is increasing in $\alpha$ and the assertion follows from the observation that the optimal bid increases in the value of the client.

Let us consider the special case, when the values come from a uniform distribution on $[0, 1]$, i.e.

$$F(v) = v.$$

It is straightforward to verify that in that case solution of Eq. (8.6) is given by:

$$b(v) = \frac{1 + \alpha}{2 + \alpha} v.$$

It is easy to see that the bid is increasing in $\alpha$. For $\alpha = 0$ it equals to half of the value as it should be in the first price auction without justifiability concern, while as $\alpha \to +\infty$ the expert's bid converges to the client's valuation.

Basov and Danilkina (2007a) considered more general justification technologies and valuation distributions and had demonstrated that qualitatively the results stay the same. To summarize: an important observation is that justifiability concern has no effect on the equilibrium bid in the second price sealed-bid auction but affects the bidding in the first price sealed-bid auction. Therefore, the first price auction will tend to generate higher expected revenues for the seller than the second price auction, i.e. the introduction of the justifiability concern violates the Revenue Equivalence Theorem.

In the simple symmetric model, the efficiency of allocation under both auction formats is preserved. However, since the expected costs for the experts arising from the failure to justify their strategy are zero in the second price auction and positive in the first price auction, the second price auction is more efficient. Moreover, as I argued above, the choice of the format is likely to affect the efficiency of the allocation if one abandons the symmetry assumption. An important lesson taken from this observation is that justifiability concern can have important impact when devising social institutions. Protecting experts from the need to justify their advice may increase social welfare. For example, one might argue that advice to the government should be provided by tenured academics that cannot be fired from their jobs by the government.

## 8.3 A Model of Boundedly Rational Addiction

The theory of rational addiction developed by Becker and Murphy (1988) stretches the credibility of rational choice models to their limit. Indeed, a typical alcoholic or a drug addict is hardly ever an image that comes to mind when one tries to imagine a rational, optimizing consumer. On the other hand, Becker and Murphy felt that "…much behavior would be excluded from the rational choice framework if addictions have to be explained in another way." Such an explanation will, indeed, be unsatisfactory if the rational choice framework is assumed to be the main explanatory framework for microeconomic behavior.

The point of view that the rational choice explanation is the only proper explanation for the economic phenomena, which was dominant at the time Becker and Murphy wrote their paper, came lately under attack. In the previous chapters of this book I presented numerous models that challenged the utility maximization paradigm. Once one accepts that non-rational explanations of economic phenomena are possible a question arises: How likely is that the addictions are explainable by a rational model? There are at least three reasons to doubt such an explanation. First, a model of rational addiction requires an ability to forecast future price movements, which an individual is unlikely to possess. Second, most drug addictions occur at early age (around 14), when the cortex (part of the brain responsible for forward thinking) is not fully formed yet. Third, the addictive drugs severely impair the ability to think rationally.

It is often argued that the rational addiction model is supported by the data (see, for example, Becker et al. 1991), and therefore no other explanation of addiction phenomena is necessary. We will argue that though the data allow us to reject the joint hypothesis that consumers maximize their instantaneous utility and the good is non-addictive, not much more can be said. Any model that makes the consumer to react to prices and produces a continuous consumption path is consistent with the data.

Basov and Danilkina (2007b) developed a model of addiction, assuming the consumers to be boundedly rational. Bounded rationality is modelled using the dynamic approach, similar to the approach taken in Chap. 6 of this book, so consumers are assumed to adjust the consumption of the addictive good gradually, with the rate of adjustment proportional to the marginal utility of consumption. Such behavior is in agreement with the commonsense view that addiction reflects myopic behavior.

Here I review the paper by Basov and Danilkina and show that depending on the values of the parameters of the model, two scenarios are possible. Under the first scenario the level of consumption of the addictive good converges to a stable steady state and the comparative statics is similar to those of Becker and Murphy (1988). In particular, the long-run level of consumption of the addictive good is sensitive to its price. Under the second scenario the consumption of addictive good runs away to infinity and a price policy is ineffective.

### 8.3.1 The Model

Following Becker and Murphy (1988), let us assume that the utility of a consumer depends on the level of consumption of the addictive good, $c$, and the stock of the consumption capital, $S$. In particular, it is given by $v(\cdot,\cdot)$, where

$$v(c,S) = u(c,S) - \mu p_c c,$$

where function $u(\cdot,\cdot)$ is twice continuously differentiable, weakly increasing in the first argument, concave, and satisfies

$$u_{Sc} > 0.$$

Parameter $\mu > 0$ is the marginal utility of money, and $p_c$ is the price of the addictive good. The evolution of the consumption capital is given by:

$$\frac{\mathrm{d}S}{\mathrm{d}t} = c - \delta S,$$

so the consumption capital depreciates at rate $\delta$, but can be increased by consumption. So far, the setting is the same as in Becker and Murphy (1988). The crucial difference is that the dynamics of the consumption variable is not governed by the rational choice model. Instead, here I assume that its evolution follows[6]:

$$\frac{dc}{dt} = v(u_c(c, S) - \mu p_c),$$

for some $v > 0$, i.e. the rate of change of the consumption of addictive good is proportional to its marginal utility.[7]

Therefore, the consumption path and the evolution of consumption capital can be found as a solution to a system of the first order differential equations. A similar description can be obtained using optimal control theory and assuming that the consumer maximizes the present value of utility as in Becker and Murphy (1988). Of course, the differential equation for $c$ in their approach differs from the one above.

A more crucial difference, however, is that in the above description the dynamics has two independent degrees of freedom, i.e. both the initial value of $S$ and the initial value of $c$ can be set independently, while in Becker and Murphy approach once the initial degree of addiction, $S(0)$, is set, the initial value of $c$ is determined by the Pontryagin Maximum Principle. This observation implies that different concepts of stability should be applied in these cases.

To summarize, in our case the consumption of the addictive good and the consumption capital are given by a solution of the following Cauchy problem:

$$\begin{cases} \frac{ds}{dt} = c - \delta S \\ \frac{dc}{dt} = v(u_c(c, S) - \mu p_c) \cdot \\ S(0) = S_0, c(0) = c_0 \end{cases} \tag{8.7}$$

Let us start the analysis of system (8.7) by studying the properties of its steady states. The steady states are determined by:

$$\begin{cases} c = \delta S \\ u_c(c, S) = \mu p_c \end{cases}$$

Note that the steady state level of consumption in this model is higher than in Becker and Murphy, since the individual neglects the effect of current consumption on the future utility. Let us investigate two possible scenarios: one in which the unique asymptotically stable steady state exists and the other in which the consumption of the addictive good runs away to infinity.

---

[6]In Basov and Danilkina (2007a) a consumer behaves according to the rational addiction model as long as consumption capital, $S$, is below a certain threshold, and behave in boundedly rational way once the threshold is passed. The consumer, however, cannot foresee the change in her behavior.

[7]A subscript accompanying a function, as usually, denotes a derivative with respect to the corresponding variable.

### 8.3.2 Unique Asymptotically Stable Steady State

Assume that in addition to the properties assumed above the consumer's utility satisfies:

$$\lim_{S\to+0} u_c(\delta S, S) = +\infty, \lim_{S\to+\infty} u_c(\delta S, S) = 0,$$
$$\delta u_{cc}(\delta S, S) + u_{Sc}(\delta S, S) < 0.$$

Under the above assumptions, the system possesses a unique asymptotically stable steady state. Indeed, the last of these conditions imply that function $u_c(\delta S, S)$ is strictly decreasing in $S$, while the first two conditions guarantee that it takes all non-negative value. Therefore, it takes value $\mu p_c$ exactly once.

Therefore, we argued that there exists a unique steady state. Checking its asymptotic stability by linearizing system (8.7) and establishing negative definiteness of the matrix of linearized system is straightforward.

It is also straightforward to observe by totally differentiating the system describing the steady state that steady state consumption of the addictive drug depends negatively on its price and on the marginal utility of income. These results are similar to those in Becker and Murphy (1988). This implies that it is difficult to differentiate empirically between the model presented here and that of Becker and Murphy, at least if one observes data only on population level.

The crucial difference, however, that the path by which the steady state is reached is not unique. It is determined by the initial conditions. In particular, the short-run level of consumption is an exogenous independent variable, which can be determined by the social conditions, while in the Becker and Murphy's model it is determined by the initial level of the consumption capital.

### 8.3.3 The Run-Away Regime

Now, let us assume that

$$\delta u_{cc}(\delta S, S) + u_{Sc}(\delta S, S) > 0$$

and that there exists $S$ such that

$$u_c(0,0) < \mu p_c < u_c(\delta S, S).$$

The first condition implies that the cross-partial derivative $u_{Sc}$ is large and positive, so the good is strongly addictive. The second condition guarantees that in this case there exists a unique unstable steady state of a saddle type. Therefore, depending on the initial capital stock and consumption level the consumption can either fall to zero or run-away to the infinity.

Note a crucial difference with Becker and Murphy model (1988). Their model has only one degree of freedom, i.e. the initial stock of the addictive capital, which fully determines the dynamics. Consumption in each moment of time uniquely determined given the individuals degree of addiction by optimization of the Hamiltonian, which takes in the account the instantaneous utility and the effect on the future tastes. To the contrary, in the model presented here, the initial level of consumption is an additional independent variable. I will return later to economic implications of allowing for an extra degree of freedom.

### *8.3.4 Multiple Steady States*

So far I have discussed two regimes: the Becker and Murphy regime, corresponding to the case when the good is not too addictive and the run-away regime, corresponding to case, when the good is strongly addictive. If neither of these possibilities is realized over the entire range of the degrees of addiction one can have multiple steady states. The simplest functional form of $\varphi(S) = u(_c S, \delta S)$ that allows for the multiple steady states is a cubic polynomial. Assume:

$$\varphi(S) = -a_0 S^3 + a_1 S^2 + a_2 S + a_3,$$

where $a_0 > 0$ and let parameters of the model be such that equation

$$\varphi(S) = \mu p_c$$

has three distinct positive solutions: $S^0 < S^* < S^1$. Then system ( 8.7) possesses three steady states: two of them $(S^0, \delta S^0)$ and $(S^1, \delta S^1)$ are asymptotically stable, while $(S^*, \delta S^*)$ is asymptotically unstable. The $(S, c)$—plane can be separated into two basins of attraction for two asymptotically stable steady states. The line separating them (the separatrix) can be found as the unique solution of the following Cauchy problem:

$$S'(c) = \frac{c - \delta S}{v(u_c(S, c) - \mu p_c)}, S(c^*) = S^*,$$

where $c^* = \delta S^*$.

### *8.3.5 Discussion of Empirical Evidence*

Here I presented a model of rationally-bounded addiction and found that many conclusions are similar to that of the paper of Becker and Murphy (1988), making empirical selection between them difficult. In particular, empirical support for the BM model is usually derived from running a regression (see, Becker et al. 1991)

$$c_t = \alpha + \beta_0 c_{t-1} + \beta_1 p_t + \beta_2 c_{t+1} + \varepsilon_t$$

and claiming that $\beta_0 > 0$ is an evidence for addiction, $\beta_1 < 0$ supports utility maximization, while $\beta_2 > 0$ can be taken as an evidence for forward looking behavior. One can argue, however, that if the consumption is a smooth function of time (as it is in our model) and one knows the values of consumption at two time periods one can use them to interpolate for the consumption value in the intermediate time period. For example, if $c_t = t^2$ then it is easy to check that:

$$c_t = -1 + \frac{c_{t-1} + c_{t+1}}{2}.$$

Therefore, though positive values of $\beta_0$ and $\beta_2$ allow us to reject the model of a consumer who maximizes the instantaneous utility derived from the consumption of a non-addictive good, it does not allow us to say more than that. A more sophisticated version of regression that includes $p_{t-1}$ used, for example, by Olekalns and Bardsley (1996) allows one to exclude a fully myopically rational model of addiction in a spirit of Orphanides and Zervos (1998). On the other hand, experimental results reported by Fehr and Zych (1998) support the hypothesis that the behavior of addicts is, at least to some degree, myopic. The model of Basov and Danilkina that postulates myopic boundedly rational consumers is consistent with both: empirical findings of Olekalns and Bardsley (1996) and the experimental results of Fehr and Zych (1998). The negative value of coefficient $\beta_1$, on the other hand, simply implies that the consumers respond to price, which they do in the current model. Therefore, this fact cannot be taken to support the idea of fully rational behavior.

### *8.3.6 Switching Regimes and Policy Applications*

Assume that all individuals start as rational consumers described by the model of Becker and Murphy (1988). However, becoming addicts clouds their ability for rational deliberation. In particular, as their addiction stock, $S$, exceeds some critical level, $S_{cr}$ their behavior switches from the rational forward looking behavior towards myopic boundedly rational behavior discussed above. For a detailed development of a model along this lines, see Basov and Danilkina (2007b). Here we want to discuss two possible policy interventions: tax and prohibition. Taxing the addictive good will effectively increase its price and decrease the steady state level of consumption and addictive capital stock, decreasing or fully eliminating the incidence of myopic boundedly rational behavior. Prohibition, however, does not have any effect on price. This effect was documented by Basov et al. (2001) and further investigated by Caulking et al. (2006). The only users who comply with prohibition are recreational users who used to consume small quantities of the drugs (Basov et al. 2001), i.e. the users with high $\mu$, who are unlikely to become strongly addicted. Therefore, prohibition leads to Pareto inferior outcome: hard users are not affected and recreational rational users suffer utility loss from not being able to consume the substance.

In summary, a crucial conceptual difference of the model presented here from the model of rational addiction suggested by Becker and Murphy (1988) is that dynamics of our model is determined by two independent variables: the initial stock of the addictive capital (the degree of addiction) and the initial consumption, while the first of these variables suffice to fully determine the rational addiction dynamics of Becker and Murphy. One can interpret the degree of addiction as a genetic predisposition, while initial consumption as a variable related to social conditions. Under this interpretation, our model allows one to disentangle effects of genetics from the effects of social environment. It is worth noting that at the limit of fast adjustment ($\nu \to \infty$) the additional degree of freedom is lost and our model converges to the model of myopically rational consumers (Orphanides and Zervos 1998).

The above mentioned difference allows one to test our model against the Becker and Murphy model. Consider a government policy that can affect directly consumption of a drug but not the degree of addiction. Suppose the government has resources only for a short-term policy (lasting for time $\tau << 1/\delta$). Such a policy will not be efficient in Becker and Murphy model, in a sense that once it is lifted the consumers will resume their previous consumption patterns. It will, however, have some effects in our model. In particular, assume that the parameters are such that the model has two asymptotically stable steady states: a dirty state corresponding to a high level of consumption of the addictive good and a clean steady state corresponding to a low level of its consumption. Consider individuals whose current consumption/degree of addiction puts them just above the separatrix. Before the policy was introduced they were headed to the dirty steady. The policy, however, will make them move below the separatrix and move to the clean steady state. Note, that the effect of the policy will be exacerbated with the passage of time, rather than cease once the policy is lifted. This observation can be used to test the model and has potentially interesting policy implications.

The model presented here can be also naturally extended to incorporate peer effects. Importance of peer effects is well-documented. Their role increased recently due to the invention of social media. For example, the survey performed by The National Center on Addiction and Substance Abuse at Columbia University shows how "digital peer pressure" is having more of an effect on kids than ever before. It found that 45 % of respondents said they've seen pictures on Facebook or other sites of their peers drinking or using drugs. Of the adolescents who have seen images of substance use among their peers, 75 % say it makes them feel encouraged to do the same, and 47 % said the people pictured look like they're having fun.

The most natural way to incorporate such effects into the model is to add a social learning component (for example, imitation of peers or preferences for conformity) to the equation, governing the evolution of consumption. For a discussion of gradient dynamics in a population of agents who also engage in imitation, see Basov (2007).

## References


Ackerberg, D. A. (2001). Empirically distinguishing informative and prestige effects of advertising. *RAND Journal of Economics*, *32*, 361–333.

Arrow, K. J., & Hurwicz, L. (1960). Stability of gradient process in n-person games. *Journal of Society of Industrial and Applied Mathematics, 8*, 280–294.

Basov, S. (2007). *Partial differential equation in economics and finance*. New York: Nova Publishers.

Basov, S., & Danilkina, S. (2007a). Auctions with opportunistic experts. *The BE Journal in Theoretical Economics (Topics), 7*, 1–11.

Basov, S., & Danilkina, S. (2007b). Bounded rationality, taxation, and prohibition. In: Proceedings of the Econometric Society Australasian Meeting. https://editorialexpress.com/cgi-bin/conference/download.cgi?db_name=ESAM07&paper_id=159

Basov, S., Jacobson, M., & Miron, J. (2001). Prohibition and the market for illegal drugs. *World Economics, 2*, 133–158.

Becker, G., & Murphy, K. (1988). A theory of rational addiction. *Journal of Political Economy, 96*, 675–700.

Becker, G., Grossman, S., & Murphy, K. M. (1991). Rational addiction and the effect of price on consumption. *American Economic Review: Papers and Proceedings, 81*, 237–241.

Chen, Y., & Rosenthal, R. W. (1996). Dynamic duopoly with slowly changing customer loyalties. *International Journal of the Industrial Organization, 14*, 269–296.

Chintagunta, P. K., Kyriazidou, E., & Perktold, J. (2001). A panel data analysis of household brand choices. *Journal of Econometrics, 103*, 111–153.

Dudey, M. (1995). On the foundations of dynamic monopoly theory. *Journal of Political Economy, 103*, 893–902.

Dudey, M. (1996). Dynamic monopoly with nondurable goods. *Journal of Economic Theory, 70*, 470–488.

Faria, J. R. (2001). Habit formation in a monetary growth model. *Economics Letters, 73*, 51–55.

Fehr, E., & Zych, P. K. (1998). Do Addicts Behave Rationally?. *Scandinavian Journal of Economics, 100*, 643–662.

Friedman, D., & Yellin, J. (1997). *Evolving landscapes for population games*. University of California Santa Cruz, Mimeo.

Lleras, J., Masatlioglu, Y., & Nakajima, D., Ozbay, E. (2010). When more is less: limited consideration. University of Michigan Working Paper. http://econweb.umd.edu/~ozbay/clc.pdf

Masatlioglu, Y., Nakajima, D., & Ozbay, E. (2012). Revealed attention. *The American Economic Review, 102*, 2183–2205.

McKenzie, D. (2001). *Consumption growth in a booming economy: Taiwan 1976-96.* Economic Growth Center, Yale University, Discussion Paper #823.

Olekalns, N., & Bardsley, P. (1996). Rational addiction to caffeine: an analysis of coffee consumption. *Journal of Political Economy, 104*, 1100–1104.

Orphanides, A., & Zervos, D. (1998). Myopia and addictive behaviour. *The Economic Journal, 108*, 75–91.

Phelps, E. S., & Winter, S. G. (1970). Optimal price policy under atomistic competition. In E. S. Phelps (Ed.), *Microeconomic foundations of employment and inflation theory.* W. W. Norton: New York, NY, USA.

Radner, R. (2003). Viscous demand. *Journal of Economic Theory, 112*, 189–231.
Richter, M. (2011). Choice theory with equivalence. Mimeo. https://sites.google.com/site/richtereconomics
Rosenthal, R. W. (1982). A dynamic model of duopoly with customer loyalties. *Journal of Economic Theory, 27*, 69–76.
Rosenthal, R. W. (1986). Dynamic duopoly with incomplete customer loyalties. *International Economic Review, 27*, 339–406.
Selten, R. (1965). Speiltheoretische Behandlung eines Oligopolmodells mit Nachfragetragheit. *Zeitschrift fur die Gesamte Staatwissenschaft, 121*, 301–324.
Spiegler, R. (2002). Equilibrium in justifiable strategies: A model of reason-based choice in extensive-form games. *Review of Economic Studies*, *69*, 691–706.
Vickery, W. (1961). Counterspeculation, auctions and competitive sealed tenders. *Journal of Finance*, *16*, 8–37.

# Chapter 9
# Conclusions and Directions for Further Research

Evidence collected during the past three decades establishes beyond reasonable doubt that one has to go beyond standard subjective expected utility maximization paradigm to explain many commonly observed economic phenomena. This realization gave rise to the development of plethora of different models that deviate to greater or lesser extent from the standard model.

Models of ambiguity aversion, other regarding preferences, and many behavioral models[1] deviate from the standard model in the minimal possible way, since they continue to impose assumption of maximizing behavior. Bounded rationality models, on the other hand, constitute a more drastic deviation, since behavior of agents is no longer at outcome of maximizing some criterion. The review of these models in the book was intended to convince the reader that such models shed important light on many interesting questions. Is it possible to mitigate the trade-off between incentive compatibility and efficiency? Why many real life contracts are incomplete? What is the incidence of bounded rationality and what are the conditions that will make a principal (monopolist) choose to educate/obfuscate employees (customers)? How does provision of optimal incentives modify when the principal has an option to harness power of social norms? These and many other questions are illuminated by these new approaches.

In the introduction I set of the agenda for this book. Here I will reflect on how this agenda was fulfilled and what challenges lie ahead. I started in Chap. 2 with a discussion of models of ambiguity. Models of ambiguity aversion together with model of rank dependent utility, and some behavioral modes, such as theory of hyperbolic discounting, prospect theory, model of loss-averse preferences, to name just the most famous models, falls into category of model of nonstandard preferences. Such models found wide applications ranging from the theory of general equilibrium to foundations of incomplete contracts, and robustness of optimal contracts. Such

[1]Behavioral models were not subject of this book. This reflects the research interests of the author and does not imply that the author believes they are less important than the models considered here.



S. Basov, *Social Norms, Bounded Rationality and Optimal Contracts*,
Studies in Economic Theory 30, DOI 10.1007/978-981-10-1041-5_9

nonstandard preferences may mitigate some of most ubiquitous trade-offs, for example, between incentive compatibility and efficiency, but also may create new inefficiencies, such as excessive simplicity (linearity) and incompleteness of real life contacts[2] and prevalence of fiat money. It is important to realize how nonstandard preferences affect real life outcomes and what the proper response is in institutional design and contracts offered to economic actors. In this book I provided a review of theory that underlines some of nonstandard preferences. A good review of importance of nonstandard preferences for economic outcomes based on the evidence from the field is Della Vigna (2007), who draws attention to an extensive literature in behavioral Industrial Organization, indicating significant importance of nonstandard features for the market outcomes. For example, Della Vigna comments on the paper by Lee and Malmendier (2011), who provide an example of overbidding in eBay auctions.[3] Focusing on items that are always available at a stable posted price, they end up showing that 42 % of auctions end at a price above the posted price. Della Vigna also distinguishes between nonstandard preferences, nonstandard believes, and nonstandard decision making. In this book the first two categories are merged, while the third is referred to as boundedly rational decision making.

In Chap. 3 I discussed evolutionary roots that are likely to underlie the most common deviations from the rational behavior. I also suggested that different features of preferences, both standard and nonstandard, as well as decision rules and social norms may coevolve and proposed some directions for developing a model of coevolution of preferences and decision rules. For example, I noted that ambiguity aversion may also evolve to counterbalance the preferences for excessive risk taking that in turn may evolve, according to Dekel and Scotchmer (1999), in winner-take-all environments.

Chapter 4 discussed issues of complexity and their relevance for the development of optimal contracts. An important insight from this chapter is that complexity of the environment can be an important part of explanation of reliance of heuristics in decision making, persistent mistakes, and structure of optimal contracts. However, the remaining challenges are how one should model complexity and how are effects of complexity affected by nonstandard preferences, such as ambiguity aversion, loss aversion, etc., and by social norms. Also, as I pointed out in the book, the very concept of complexity has different meanings in different areas of science. Therefore, another challenge is which of these concepts should be adopted.

In Chap. 5, I discussed mechanism design problem when the choice of the agents is governed by a static probabilistic model and argued that a particularly interesting applications of this approach arize in screening. As I pointed out in the text, technically, this happens because the choice correspondence is usually not lower-semi-continuous at the zero value of the irrationality parameter, when set of utility maximizers contains more than one element. As a result, infinitesimally small

[2]The latter is widely recognized as a source of hold up problems.

[3]Lee and Malmendier define a case of overbidding when the final auction price is higher than a posted price for the same good available on eBay itself.

degree of irrationality can have significant effect on the nature of optimal contracts. A model of bounded rationality presented by Laffont and Martimort (2002) takes special care to avoid such a discontinuity. They consider a model of monopolistic screening, where consumers may make a mistake when choosing an option from a menu, but are fully aware of this possibility a priori. Under such assumptions the Revelation Principle still holds and the effect of the mistake is effectively to increase proportion of low types. Basov (2009), on the contrary, takes a view that such a discontinuity is the central feature that makes the study of screening under bounded rationality interesting from a theoretical point of view and important from a practical one. Therefore, Basov considers a more drastic deviation from rational model in the context of monopolistic screening with finite types, assuming that consumers' choice probabilities are driven by Luce model. In that case, Revelation Principle no longer holds and the number of the different items on the monopolist's optimal menu will differ from the cardinality of types. In particular, higher quality goods will tend to come in more flavors. The latter conclusion is borne out by empirical studies by Basov et al. (2011).

Basov and Mirrlees (2009) dealt with boundedly rational model with continuous set of types by introducing bounded rationality in Mussa and Rosen (1978) model. The model is well suited for discussing the incidence of cost of boundedly rational behavior. Of a particular importance is the observation that, since the consumers in this model earn information rents, the monopolist may benefit from bounded rationality of the consumers even if the latter reduces social surplus. This means that the monopolist will have an incentive to obfuscate consumers. This incentive is discussed in a different framework by Basov and Danilkina (2015), who considered a Bertrand oligopoly with boundedly rational consumers and allowed the firms to manipulate the degree of rationality at a cost. Note that in this paper the active players, the oligopolists, are fully rational. They are shown to have incentives to obfuscate consumers, but this incentive decreases as the number of the firms increases. Whether the competition will decrease incentives to obfuscate in Basov and Mirrlees model is a question for further research. I also have drawn attention to the possibility that mistakes may be unavoidable, since having completely cool head necessary to avoid them will also make the decision maker care less about the consequences of the decisions. Finally, I drew attention to a trailblazing paper by Anderson et al. (1998), the only paper in Chap. 5, which discusses a game (all-pay auction) between boundedly rational agents.

Chapter 6 considers design of optimal contracts in an environment where agents gradually adjust their choices due to learning. In such models contract design plays dual role: it affects steady state distribution of choices, but it also affects the rate at which learning occurs. One interesting conclusion that emerged from the model studies in that chapter is that even if the agents in the long-run converge to the static optimal decision the optimal contract need not converge to the optimal static contract. In the context of hidden-action principal agent model, where the agent follows gradient dynamics, based on Basov (2003), I have shown that the optimal incentives are lower powered than they would have being under full rationality.

Chapter 7 considers interaction of social norms with financial incentives. Some interesting conclusions are reached in this literature. For example, Basov and Bhatti (2013), argue that under social norm of trust two distinct cultures emerge: a bureaucratic culture characterized by low power incentives and reliance on social norms and corporate culture characterized by high power incentives with no reliance on social norms. The medium powered incentives largely disappear. Social norms can also reinforce the idea that contractual incompleteness can be caused by the decrease of the value of the optimal complete contract. If the value of the optimal complete contract is eroded to a high degree by uncertainty of the environment, which can be due to both technological and market uncertainty in translating the unobservable effort into observable output, and mistakes made by the agents in selecting the optimal level of effort in response to the contract offered, the parties can choose to rely on a social norm, for example, reciprocity, giving rise to an efficiency wage contract. I also discussed parallels between this model and the models developed by Hart and Moore and Segal and discussed in Chap. 4. Some other applications, such as discussion of models of high performing working systems and practice of hiring decisions of multinational corporations operating in the developing countries, show the scope of usefulness of this approach.

Chapter 8 deals with miscellaneous models that do not easily fall under a particular heading. It deals with issues as broad as a monopoly facing viscous demand with customers' turnover, incorporating justifiability constraint into auction theory, and boundedly rational model of addiction. In the context of latter model, I argue for relative merits of different government policies, such as taxation and prohibition.

I started this book by arguing that ample empirical evidence does not easily fit into conventional subjective expected utility maximization paradigm with standard preferences and proposed that two broadly classified ways to deal with this discrepancy is to assume either nonstandard preferences or bounded rationality. The latter approach is characterized by driving a wedge between choices and preferences, violating the revealed preferences doctrine. Important questions are how to incorporate such deviations in the economic theory and how they should affect economic decision-making in general and mechanism design in particular. In this book, I provided plenty of examples dealing with these issues.

Another area were deviations from rational behavior are important is area of behavioral finance. I did not touch the area in the book but will comment on some recent trends and possible developments in the conclusion.

Recently there have been significant achievements in developing models of financial processes and phenomena from a behavioral perspective in the finance literature. Of a particular interest is the effect of behavioral biases on the dividend policy. This type of models fall in the category of models with nonstandard preferences and are similar in spirit to the loss-aversion model, I briefly touched in the book.

With the development of information economics it was hypothesized that the payment of dividends can increase the value of the firm if this provides signals in regard to the financial health of the firm. DeAngelo et al. (1996) examine the signaling content of dividend decisions made by managers of companies whose annual earnings decline after nine or more consecutive years of growth and find that almost 70 % of the managers of such companies increase dividends in the year that their firm's long-standing record of consecutive earnings increases is broken. They conclude that the dividend decisions are broadly consistent with the view that the sample firms' dividend increases are not informative signals because managers suffer from a behavioral bias, overoptimism. It leads them to overestimate future earnings when growth prospects fade. DeAngelo et al. (2008) present a synthesis of academic research on corporate payout policy and conclude that managerial signaling motives, clientele demands, tax deferral benefits, investors' behavioral heuristics, and investor sentiment have at best minor influences on payout policy, but that behavioral biases at the managerial level and the idiosyncratic preferences of controlling stockholders plausibly have a first-order impact upon the dividend decision.

Extensive research has focused on managerial overconfidence and optimistic behavior in the corporate finance literature. Heaton (2002) demonstrates that optimistic managers believe capital markets undervalue their firm's risky securities and may pass up positive net present value projects that must be financed externally whereas optimistic managers overvalue their own corporate projects and may wish to invest in negative net present value projects even when they are loyal to shareholders. Malmendier and Tate (2005) show overconfident CEOs overestimating the returns of investment projects, and investing more when internal funds are sufficient, whereas if internal funds are not sufficient, they will not issue new equity to increase investment in projects because overconfident CEOs believe their firm shares are undervalued by the market. Furthermore, Malmendier and Tate (2008) show that overconfident CEOs overestimate their ability to generate returns and as a result, they overpay for target companies and undertake value-destroying mergers. Ferris et al. (2013) find that overconfidence influences the number of offers made by a CEO, the frequency of diversifying acquisitions made, and the choice of deal financing. More specifically, they find that overconfidence is an important factor in explaining the number of offers made by a CEO.

However, there is a scarcity of research on the impact of managerial overconfidence on dividend policy. One of the few papers that address the issue is Ben-David et al. (2007), who do not find any significant relation between the short-term overconfidence measure based on the decile ranking of individual volatility of short-term forecasts of the S&P 500 and the propensity to pay dividends. They do find some support for a negative relation between the decile ranking of the individual volatility of a long-term overconfidence measure based on the ten-year forecasts of the S&P 500 and the propensity to pay dividends. Moreover, their study does not examine the determinants of the dividend level or dividend payout ratio. They rather examine whether the firm pays dividends in the current year or not. Deshmukh et al. (2013), henceforth DGH, develop a model of the dynamic interaction between CEO overconfidence and dividend policy. Their model predicts that (a) an overconfident CEO pays a lower level of dividends relative to a rational CEO, (b) the difference in the dividend payout between higher- and lower-growth firms is smaller in firms managed by overconfident CEOs; and (c) the stock price response to announcements of dividend changes is an increasing function of the uncertainty about CEO overconfidence. Consistent with their prediction, they empirically find that the level of dividend payout is lower in firms managed by overconfident CEOs, and the difference in the dividend payout between higher-growth and lower-growth firms is smaller for firms with overconfident CEOs. Furthermore, they document that the positive relation between dividend payout and cash flow is stronger in firms with overconfident CEOs. They also find that the magnitude of the positive stock price response to announcements of dividend increases is higher in firms in which there is greater uncertainty about the level of CEO's overconfidence. They assert that this finding is consistent with their hypothesis that dividends provide information about CEO overconfidence.

Recently, Basov et al. (2013) developed a model in which managers are overconfident over two dimensions: pride and egotism. In the case of pure pride the model reduces to that of DGH. In this version of the model overconfident managers pay lower dividends. This feature is also shared by the model of Heaton (2002) who showed that in this case managers will have incentives to keep cash flows inside the firm and pay lower dividends. The mechanism behind their result is, however, very different.

Basov et al. also considered the opposite case of pure egotism and argued that in that case overconfident managers pay higher dividends. In the general model, the way overconfidence affects dividends is determined by the interaction between pride and egotism. The different components of overconfidence may have different effects on the dividend policy. If one assumes that pride and egotism are uncorrelated, then the estimate obtained by DGH of overconfidence on the dividends level can be interpreted in our model as an unbiased estimate of pride on dividends. If, on the other hand, pride and egotism are positively correlated, then DGH underestimate the negative effect of pride on dividends.

A critique may complain that new approaches to economic modeling presented in this book explain a bit too much. After all, isn't it possible to explain any behavior by invoking a social norm or a boundedly rational decision making procedure? This critique deserves to be addressed. First, one may argue that even the standard model can explain too much if one does not make any particular assumptions about preferences. One example of this is Sonnenschein–Mantel–Debreu theorem (see, for example, Mas-Colell et al. 1995). Therefore, one still needs some model of preference formation to bring discipline to the field. Of course, the task is made more complex by the need to have a model for formation of preferences, social norms, and decision rules. However, as hinted in Chap. 3, the problem is not intractable. Indeed, the study of social norms, bounded rationality, and other deviations from the standard model is still in its infancy and the lack of modelling discipline is a temporarily phenomenon. It is interesting to compare current situation in economics with the situation that prevailed in physics in the first 30 years of the twentieth century. At that point classical physics was capable of explaining most of the phenomena physicists dealt with, expect for few such as black-body radiation, structure of the atom, and photoelectric effect that were not easily explained within the classical paradigm. Ad hoc hypotheses, all of them involving quanta in one way or another, were suggested to address these issues.

Situation resembled the one we currently have in economics, if one identifies standard economic model with classical paradigm, and all deviations with ad hoc quantum hypotheses. In physics the situation was eventually resolved with creation of quantum mechanics and clarification of the limits of the classical paradigm. I hope similar resolution will be possible in economics. Evolutionary point of view, briefly outlined in Chap. 3, may help to start to bring discipline to these new approaches to explaining economic behavior.

## References

Anderson, S. P., Goeree, J. K., & Holt, C. A. (1998). Rent seeking with bounded rationality: An analysis of all-pay auction. *Journal of Political Economy, 106*, 828–853.

Basov, S. (2003). Incentives for boundedly rational agents, 2003. *The BE Journal in Theoretical Economics (Topics), 3*, 1–14.

Basov, S. (2009). Monopolistic screening with boundedly rational consumers. *The Economic Record, 85*, S29–S33.

Basov, S., & Bhatti, M. I. (2013). Optimal contracting model in a social environment and trust-related psychological costs. *The BE Journal in Theoretical Economics (Contributions), 13*, 1–14.

Basov, S., & Danilkina, S. (2015). Bertrand oligopoly with boundedly rational consumers. *The BE Journal for Theoretical Economics (Topics), 15*, 107–123.

Basov, S., & Mirrlees, J. A. (2009). Nonlinear pricing under bounded rationality. *SSRN Electronic Journal.* http://papers.ssrn.com/sol3/papers.cfm?abstract_id=1399924

Basov, S., Danilkina, S., & Prentice, D. (2011). When does variety increase with quality? *SSRN Electronic Journal.* http://papers.ssrn.com/sol3/papers.cfm?abstract_id=1242662

Basov, S., Balachandran, B., & Theobald, M. (2013). Dividends and managerial overconfidence, (with Balasingham Balachandran and Michael Theobald). *SSRN Electronic Journal.* http://papers.ssrn.com/sol3/papers.cfm?abstract_id=2228612

Ben-David, I., Graham, J., & Harvey, C. (2007). *Managerial overconfidence and corporate policies*. NBER Working Paper No. 13711.

DeAngelo, H., DeAngelo, L., & Skinner, D. J. (1996). Reversal of fortune: dividend signaling and the disappearance of sustained earnings growth. *Journal of Financial Economics, 40*, 341–371.

DeAngelo, H., DeAngelo, L., & Skinner, D. J. (2008). Corporate payout policy. *Foundations and Trends in Finance, 3*, 95–287.

Dekel, E., & Scotchmer, S. (1999). On the evolution of attitudes towards risk in winner-take-all games. *Journal of Economic Theory, 87*, 125–143.

Della Vigna, S. (2007). *Psychology and economics: Evidence from the field*. NBER Working Paper No. 13420.

Deshmukh, S., Goel, A. M., & Howe, K. M. (2013). CEO overconfidence and dividend policy. *Journal of Financial Intermediation, 22*, 440–463.

Ferris, S. P., Jayaraman, N., & Sabherwal, S. (2013). CEO overconfidence and international merger and acquisition activity. *Journal of Financial and Quantitative Analysis, 48*, 137–164.

Heaton, J. (2002). Managerial optimism and corporate finance. *Financial Management, 31*, 33–45.

Laffont, J. J., & Martimort, D. (2002). *The theory of incentives*. Princeton, NJ, USA: Princeton University Press.

Lee, Y. H., & Malmendier, U. (2011). The bidder's curse. *American Economic Review, 101*, 749–787.

Malmendier, U., & Tate, G. (2005). CEO overconfidence and corporate investment. *Journal of Finance, 55*, 2661–2700.

Malmendier, U., & Tate, G. (2008). Who makes acquisitions: CEO overconfidence and the market's reaction. *Journal of Financial Economics, 89*, 20–43.

Mas-Colell, A., Whinston, M. D., & Green, J. R. (1995). *Microeconomic theory*. Oxford: Oxford University Press.

Mussa, M., & Rosen, S. (1978). Monopoly and product quality. *Journal of Economic Theory, 18*, 301–317.

The manufacturer's authorised representative in the EU is Springer Nature Customer Service Centre GmbH, Europaplatz 3, 69115 Heidelberg, Germany. If you have any concerns regarding our products, please contact ProductSafety@springernature.com

Printed and bound by CPI Group (UK) Ltd, Croydon, CR0 4YY
30/09/2026
02225444-0019